D1479180

DEATH IN THE CONGO

DEATH IN THE CONGO

Murdering Patrice Lumumba

Emmanuel Gerard

Bruce Kuklick

Harvard University Press

Cambridge, Massachusetts

London, England

2015

Library of Congress Cataloging-in-Publication Data

Gerard, E. (Emmanuel)
Death in the Congo : murdering Patrice Lumumba / Emmanuel Gerard, Bruce Kuklick.
pages cm.
Includes bibliographical references and index.
ISBN 978-0-674-72527-0 (alk. paper)
1. Lumumba, Patrice, 1925–1961—Assassination.   2. Congo (Democratic Republic)—
History—Civil War, 1960–1965.   3. Belgium—Foreign relations—Congo
(Democratic Republic)   4. Congo (Democratic Republic)—Foreign
relations—Belgium.   5. United Nations—Congo (Democratic Republic)
6. Hammarskjöld, Dag, 1905–1961.   7. Congo (Democratic Republic)—Foreign
relations—United States.   8. United States—Foreign relations—Congo
(Democratic Republic)   9. Congo (Democratic Republic)—Politics and
government—1960–1997.   I. Kuklick, Bruce, 1941–   II. Title.
DT658.22.L85G47 2015
967.5103'1—dc23   2014015902

For Greet and Tizzy

Contents

Illustrations and Maps

MAPS

People and Places, 1960

Justin BOMBOKO, minister of foreign affairs and later chair of the College of Commissioners

Antoine GIZENGA, deputy prime minister and later leader of the Stanleyville regime

Joseph ILEO, president of the senate and designated prime minister in September

Albert KALONJI, president of the secessionist state of southern Kasai

Joseph KASA-VUBU, president of the republic and leader of the Alliance des Bakongo (ABAKO)

Patrice LUMUMBA, prime minister and leader of the Mouvement National Congolais (MNC)

Joseph MOBUTU, colonel, chief of staff of the Armée Nationale Congolaise (ANC)

Godefroid MUNONGO, minister of the interior of the secessionist state of Katanga

Victor NENDAKA, director of the Sûreté from September

Jason SENDWE, leader of the Balubakat, opposed to the Conakat

Moïse TSHOMBE, president of the secessionist state of Katanga and leader of the Conakat

BELGIUM

Count Harold d'ASPREMONT LYNDEN, deputy chief of staff to
Eyskens; head of Belgian technical mission to Katanga, July–August;
minister of African affairs from September, Christian Democrat

BAUDOUIN, king of the Belgians

Marcel DUPRET, consul general and then ambassador to Congo
(Brazzaville)

Gaston EYSKENS, prime minister, Christian Democrat

André LAHAYE, principal agent of the Belgian Sûreté de l'État in the
Congo and adviser to the Congo's commissioner of the interior

Louis MARLIÈRE, colonel, chief of staff of the Force Publique; adviser
to Mobutu and to the commissioner of defense

Robert ROTHSCHILD, deputy ambassador to the Congo, July; deputy head
of Belgian technical mission to Katanga, August; head, September; director
of Congo desk in foreign affairs ministry in Brussels, from October

Paul-Henri SPAAK, secretary-general of NATO, Socialist

Guy WEBER, major of the Belgian army, military adviser to Tshombe

Pierre WIGNY, minister of foreign affairs, Christian Democrat

THE UNITED STATES OF AMERICA

William BURDEN, ambassador to Belgium

Larry DEVLIN, CIA chief of station in the Congo

C. Douglas DILLON, under secretary of state

Allen DULLES, director of the CIA

Dwight David EISENHOWER, president, Republican

Christian HERTER, secretary of state

John KENNEDY, senator from Massachusetts, running for the presidency,
Democrat

Henry Cabot LODGE, ambassador to the UN, resigned in September to
run for the vice presidency, Republican

Richard NIXON, vice president, running for the presidency, Republican

Clare TIMBERLAKE, ambassador to the Congo

THE UNITED NATIONS

Ralph BUNCHE, under-secretary-general, special representative of the secretary-general in the Congo, July–August

Andrew CORDIER, under-secretary-general, special representative of the secretary-general in the Congo, end of August to September 8

Rajeshwar DAYAL, special representative of the secretary-general in the Congo from September 8

Dag HAMMARSKJÖLD, secretary-general

Ben Hammou KETTANI, Moroccan general seconded for service to the UN in the Congo

OTHERS

Fidel CASTRO, leader of Cuba

Nikita KHRUSHCHEV, first secretary of the Communist Party and premier of the Soviet Union

Kwame NKRUMAH, president of Ghana, former British colony

Fulbert YOULOU, president and premier of Congo (Brazzaville), former French colony

NOTE ON PLACE NAMES

We have used Congo place names as they were in 1960. Bakwanga is now Mbuji-Mayi; Elisabethville, Lubumbashi; Jadotville, Likasi; Leopoldville, Kinshasa; Luluabourg, Kananga; Port Francqui, Ilebo; Stanleyville, Kisangani; Thysville, Mbanza-Ngungu. Also: Ruanda-Urundi, Rwanda and Burundi.

To see a world in a grain of sand . . .
And eternity in an hour.

WILLIAM BLAKE

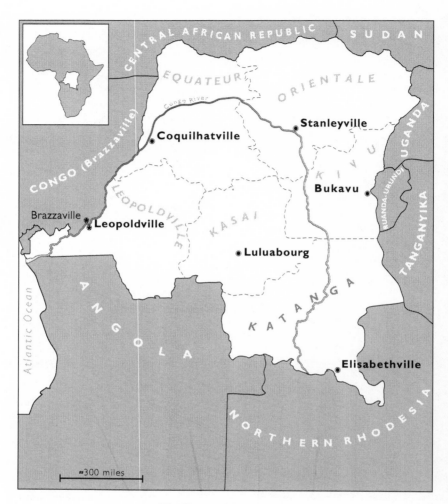

The Congo, June 30, 1960

Introduction

A T THE END OF JUNE 1960 Belgium hurriedly relinquished its vast
colony of the Congo to the country's first democratically elected government. Prime Minister Patrice Lumumba, a talented and unrestrained
African nationalist, led the new republic. A charismatic leader, Lumumba had high hopes for directing his new state into an honored place
on the continent and into the world political community. Yet stability in
the just-born nation immediately broke down. A mutinous Congolese
army spread havoc, and Belgium dispatched its military to protect Belgian citizens. In the distant southeast of the Congo the province of Katanga seceded. By midsummer the United Nations had intervened with
peacekeeping troops from various countries. The communists of the
Soviet Union and more assertive African rulers saw an opportunity to
move the continent away from the domination of the former European
empires. Apprehensive of the spread of communism, the United States
maneuvered behind the scenes.

In January 1961, six months after independence, Lumumba was murdered in Katanga. On February 13, officials in Katanga announced his
death, but with a story so fishy that almost no one believed it. Furious
protests took place around the world. In a blistering denunciation the
Soviet Union blamed the imperial powers and asked that the United

Nations leave the Congo. The Soviets demanded the resignation of the Swedish secretary-general of the UN, Dag Hammarskjöld, whom they saw as the chief henchman of the colonialists. Predictably, people marched in Moscow, but the largest crowd, of over one hundred thousand, assembled in Beijing, China. Perhaps predictably too, demonstrators grabbed headlines in Africa and Asia: Casablanca in Morocco; Khartoum in Sudan; Accra in Ghana; Bombay and New Delhi in India; Karachi in Pakistan; and Colombo in Sri Lanka. Incensed mobs particularly excoriated Belgium, and assaulted many of its citizens. In Cairo, Egyptians burned the Belgian embassy. Angry groups, however, also turned out in Western European capitals—London, Dublin, Bonn, Paris, and Rome—and in Washington, D.C., and Chicago in the United States.

In New York City, pickets took to the streets in Harlem and outside the headquarters of the United Nations. Inside, on February 15, 1961, Hammarskjöld blasted those "for whom truth [was] a function of party convenience." He expressed his "deep regret" at the "revolting crime." The new American ambassador to the United Nations, Adlai Stevenson— twice candidate for president of the United States and a renowned and revered liberal—gave his maiden speech, and stood up for the UN. He defended Hammarskjöld, a few feet away, and pleaded for the UN to stay in the Congo. Its people must have the "free and untrammeled exercise" of their rights "to independence and to democracy." Stevenson "deplore[d]" Lumumba's "unhappy and despicable fate" and "condemn[ed] those responsible for it, no matter who they may be." Then Stevenson had to stop. Some sixty protesters burst into the auditorium. They yelled about the connivance of Hammarskjöld and the United States in Lumumba's death, and about Belgian subversion of democracy in the Congo. Men and women threw punches and fought with surprised and unprepared guards. Diplomats looked on with shock and distress until attendants subdued the invaders. The rabble-rousers had only dim beliefs about the transgressions and lies of the international politicians. The statesmen, however, more clearly understood their own responsibility. Yet these men could not comprehend that their dissembling could provoke such a response.[1]

For over fifty years the circumstances of the assassination have absorbed scholars and fascinated the general public. Something about Lumumba's trajectory and the manner of his death offended global opinion, and has continued to attract attention—at the United Nations, in Belgium and the United States, and in the Congo itself. Many people—white and black—had plotted his downfall. Nonetheless, their autobiographies, memoirs, and first-person narratives distanced the authors from anything that had to do with the murder. But the contemporary evidence contradicts these recollections, and shows their self-serving nature.

Within a year of the murder, the United Nations conducted an inquiry that was incomplete but not inaccurate in some of its conclusions. In 1975, in the aftermath of the Watergate scandals and the offenses of President Richard Nixon, the United States Senate explored various compromised activities of American presidents in the 1960s and early 1970s. Among many other things, the Senate discovered plans by the Central Intelligence Agency to assassinate Lumumba. After Lumumba's death, the United States had propped up Joseph Mobutu, who would rule the Congo for thirty years. When the end of the Cold War weakened Mobutu, the Congo held a "Sovereign National Conference" in 1991. This body investigated the Lumumba murder as one of the most prominent violations of human rights in Africa. In 2000, Belgians reacted to widespread concern about their nation's complicity, and organized a serious examination. Four historians went over the evidence, and a parliamentary report of 2001 implicated Belgium. The country officially apologized to the Congo.

Our international history of the Congo's politics in 1960 integrates the perspectives of four competitors—the Congo's inexperienced politicians; a righteous but flawed United Nations; an arrogant and destructive United States; and an entrenched Belgian bureaucracy determined to maintain imperial prerogatives. The arresting and complex tale has intersecting narrative lines and an intercontinental array of characters. Different political styles and conventions require explanation and consideration; the reward is an understanding of a momentous event.

The Congo in 1960 shows the roots of empire, and also the exercise of power without mercy. The ruin of Lumumba displays in purest form the vicious character of society without sovereignty, and illustrates the deepest problems of political ethics. While primordial questions of life and death make for a compelling story, the murder of a nation's foremost official does not resemble a killing in a barroom brawl. Assassination is an unnerving event that threatens our safety and undermines our assumptions about how politics yields peace and protection.

CHAPTER ONE

The Congo of the Belgians

I T IS JANUARY 17, 1961, in the bush of Katanga, almost 10 P.M. Frans Verscheure, the thirty-five-year-old Belgian inspector of police, counsels the local force. In giving orders to muscle Patrice Lumumba's body into a shallow trench, he has just made himself an accessory to the murder of the prime minister of the Congo. Through force of habit, this trained law enforcement officer glances at his watch to record the moment of the shooting, 9:43 P.M. Then, briefly, the headlights from the automobiles that have lit up the gruesome scene blink out. In the utter darkness, Verscheure hears the wilderness breathing. He feels himself shivering. He is drenched with sweat, and suddenly afraid. His hands are wet and sticky, and although he cannot see, he knows that it is blood. The idea grips him that he is not in his own country. How did he end up with the blood of the Congo's leading politician on his hands?

Leopold's Congo

In the last quarter of the nineteenth century, England, France, Germany, Italy, and Portugal divided up much of Africa, but could not figure out how to parcel out the great landmass in the middle of the continent. To prevent significant squabbles, the Europeans awarded the Congo to

5

Leopold II, king of the Belgians, in his own person as head of "the Congo Free State." It was eventually divided into six immense provinces— Leopoldville on the west coast; Équateur to the north and Orientale to the northeast; Kivu to the east; Kasai in the middle of the country; and Katanga, with a more complex administration, in the far southeast.

Leopold thought that this magnificent land might increase Belgium's leverage and his prestige. Through this colony, he would unite his tiny nation, divided between Catholics and secularists, haves and have-nots, and speakers of French and of Flemish, a language virtually identical to Dutch. In contrast to a Belgian elite that wanted common ground on the edge of northwest Europe, the Belgian people had little interest in empire, and oversight of this private kingdom—a little less than one-third the size of the present-day United States and almost eighty times larger than Belgium—cost even more than Leopold possessed. The king signed agreements with private shareholders and corporations outside of Belgium, with other Western nations, with wealthy entrepreneurs in Belgium, and with the Belgian government. The Congo was not a domain where rulers somehow linked up with the ruled. Leopold discounted the interests of the Africans and ran the immense area to generate revenue for investors.

The Europeans made the Congo, as they made other African countries, with little regard for prior social or governmental boundaries. The Great Powers swaggered around the continent with no idea of its history or natural features. They ignored ethnic and linguistic frontiers, as well as previous political conditions. In part, attempts to secure advantage over other Europeans, or to conciliate them, determined the new lands. An immense Congo Free State came into being but did not exhibit nationhood as conceived by Europeans and Americans—a single people, a communal sense, a public history, geographical homogeneity, a common culture, shared customs, one language, or unifying military expeditions. It would be wrong to argue that the Congo had an image of its past that Leopold erased in order to dominate. Colonialism instead invented the Belgian Congo, and Leopold discovered the "Congolese" for the benefit of Europeans primarily located in the Belgian capital of Brussels.

Two examples of a lack of cohesion deserve mention. On the Atlantic shore of Africa, the territory known as the Bas-Congo formed a fragment of the old Kongo kingdom. The Europeans partitioned this ancient coastal empire among the French Congo to the north, Leopold's Congo, and Portuguese Angola to the south. The Congo's capital city of Leopold-ville would grow up here in the 1920s, as well as the province of the same name. But the people in this region often saw their future in a restored Kongo state, and not in the larger but different sort of entity of the whites. From the Congo River on the coast, Leopoldville gave Europe access to the interior. If the Belgians thought of nation building, however, they would not have chosen this headquarters, which lay distant from the heart of Africa.

A different sort of anti-centralism existed in the southeast. There, in Katanga, around what would be the mining center of Elisabethville, Leopold fought off the English. British Rhodesia abutted this portion of the Congo. The English and Belgians scuffled over its mineral wealth. Leopold won a narrow victory in Katanga but yielded a substantial say in the businesses to English interests. Katanga was allocated to the Congo but had a large measure of autonomy and a different status from other areas of Belgian-run Africa. Katanga generated most of the Congo's profits, and its influential companies—among them the huge mining enterprise Union Minière du Haut Katanga—made their owners rich. These men often looked to nearby English power in the south; they also wanted a direct line to Brussels, not an administration from Leopoldville. As one Belgian diplomat put it, Leopoldville and Elisabethville were as far apart as Paris and Istanbul.[1]

Over the past century Leopold II has been condemned for twenty years of abominable rule in his "outpost of progress."[2] A series of scandals, an international investigation of atrocities, and growing opposition of the Belgian establishment to the king's policies concluded in 1908 when he relinquished his fiefdom to the Belgian government. Reformers and politicians reasoned that a colonial government might still engage the populace and assist in lifting it up.

The Belgian Congo

When Belgium took over, the pact between the state and the capitalists persisted, though Brussels made the improvements of an honest

shopkeeper. The Europeans had undermined traditional rural existence, although Africans who lived in villages or the inland likely identified only with their ethnic group, and still paid homage to indigenous
chiefs. Blacks by the thousands, however, disappeared from the homes
of their families, either because of Belgium's economic demands or because of the attraction of a wider sphere of life. Africans streamed to the
cities that were the creation of Europeans—Leopoldville and Elisabethville, at either end of the country; Coquilhatville, Stanleyville, and Luluabourg in the interior; and other municipalities of any size. Workers
received living quarters, medical attention, and a social environment
conducive, the Belgians thought, to African life. The Europeans built
elementary schools to guide the locals to their place in a colony and to
low-level jobs. A peculiar protective rule flowered in the middle of the
continent, though Belgium ignored political rights and higher education.[3] It did not, moreover, encourage European immigration. Although
particularly in Katanga and Kivu a few white settlers, *colons,* called the
Congo home, both the official and unofficial masters usually stayed only
a number of years, and returned to Belgium for long vacations before a
permanent departure.[4] Later on, when civic interest glimmered among
the Africans, everyone thought of a black polity. In any event, Belgium
treated neither blacks nor whites as citizens, if citizenship has anything
to do with claims individuals can make on a regime, or with participation in it, or obligations they might owe it. In this sense, the Congo still
had no government, only a form of supervision.

Nonetheless, by the early twentieth century, pride in the Congo helped
overcome differences in Belgium itself, where the cultural divide had
enlarged between a Francophone Walloon south and a mainly Dutch-
speaking Flanders in the north. French, an international language, easily
predominated in Belgium, but by the first decades of the twentieth century Dutch gained more credibility through a Flemish national movement. The imperialists all had fluent French, the official language in the
Congo, although the majority of the Belgians there had spoken Flemish
at birth. Yet those whose mother tongue was Flemish rarely had the
better jobs and sometimes projected their own feelings of a sort of inferiority onto the locals. The Africans, however, helped to make for a cultural
peace among the colonialists. The tensions between the Flemish and the

Walloons in the Congo diminished because, as whites (and French speaking), they occupied a different moral space from that of the blacks.[5]

Social Change

Colonies had evoked distrust from the end of World War I in 1918, but after 1945 the democratic struggle of World War II put the European empires on the ropes, and corroded the Belgian order that had developed from 1910 to 1940. Africans continued to move to the cities, where they lived in ghettos known as *cités*. These town dwellers felt every day the differences between the lives of the colonizer and colonized, and the intrinsic discrimination of color. The Africans may have traveled from place to place, so they knew about the similar features of cities, and about the large world beyond the villages. In the *cités* men had conversations about who ran things, although their discussions did not extend beyond municipal boundaries. Certainly Leopoldville's intrigues and gossip would not tell us much about the rest of the Congo.

In urban areas a new class grew up, the *évolués*. Education is one key to understanding them. The Roman Catholic Church was one of the few unifying institutions, and delivered widespread primary lessons, as did Protestant missions. The Africans rarely went beyond such classes because colonial authorities structured education to prevent the birth of a privileged group. In theory all the native inhabitants would prosper together; in practice the Europeans afforded only basic tuition, concentrating on the rote observance of rules. The schools trained pupils for bottom-level participation in the workforce, and transmitted values of subservience. The Africans were supposed to acknowledge the guardianship of Belgium and unquestionably accept inferiority. The imperialists discouraged studies that did not fit into their economic needs, and argued that the Africans had no capacity for higher learning.[6]

In the second quarter of the twentieth century, missions began to offer secondary education. Teachers in the early grades gave more substantial lessons to promising scholars, who gained stature after the war. The Africans spoke many languages, and had some commercial lingua francas, including Kituba, Lingala, Swahili, and Tshiluba. Spoken French inevitably signaled one's status as an *évolué,* and ambitious Africans learned the language. They picked up Franco-Belgian culture and made fun of Flemish. The worst thing to call a Belgian in the Congo was *Flamand,* the French for Fleming. Commentators believed, truly or not, that disaffected Africans would only attack native Flemish-speakers among the whites.[7] For more educated blacks, Flemish equated with a secondary language like Lingala. *Évolués* compared black status in the Congo to Flemish inferiority in Belgium. They also saw the differences between themselves and Africans unschooled in Western ideas as akin to those between French and Flemish speakers in Belgium.

Only exceptional Africans graduated from high school, and only a pitiful few went beyond. In the 1950s a tiny number made it to Belgian universities. Leopoldville and Elisabethville set up their own universities, but they had no rank and hardly any native students. Some Africans, however, had the opportunity for advanced study in religious institutions, and many Africans also had medical training, although the profession of physician was naturally denied them. Yet those who learned French in the upper grades, or spoke French because of religious or technical study, could move in different spheres; so too could those Africans who received just basic lessons but gained expertise in French.

Some Belgians encouraged this new class to believe that if it, for example, gave up polygamy and adopted Western mores, Belgium would grant concessions that would eventuate in equality. This "immatriculation" exemplified the ambiguity of the experience of the *évolués,* living between two worlds. At home, with knives and forks, they sometimes ate apart from their wives, who sat on the floor using their fingers in a communal bowl. At formal dinners with whites, African men appeared with only one woman, although they might have had multiple wives. Because the women usually did not speak French, they did not understand the denigrating remarks the Belgians made about Africa to their husbands. As a white female put it, the wives lagged "hundreds of years behind . . . [their husbands] in evolution."[8]

In this curious world, where they were both native and foreign, the husbands somehow associated with the oppressor, although they hoped for a time of their own autonomy. They were not entirely comfortable in their own skins. Only the *évolués* among the Africans had an intellectual understanding of colonialism. They also accepted the supremacy and preeminent worth of Europe. The wealth; the technological ascendancy; the civility; and the globe-spanning bureaucracies convinced these French-speaking natives of the superiority of the West. Perhaps most important, they believed in their status. These Frenchified Africans conceived that they had come up from an inferior way of life. In comparison to Belgium, the Congo lay far down a scale of existence; the *évolués* must elevate the Congo to the Belgian level. Their conventionality has struck all academics, who have made this kind of analysis standard in appraisals of native elites in colonies.[9] Its validity in the Congo needs to be underscored.

Because these Africans also hated the injustice apparent in their lives, they did not just want a country fashioned in a Western model. They must drill the ordinary future citizen into civilization. Critics have called the *évolués* "bourgeois." After independence these Africans wanted to replicate the social structure of the Belgian Congo, but with a more generous commitment to a nonsegregated society that they instead of Belgians would administer.

African Nationalism

In the 1950s, the French faced revolutions against their rule in Indochina and Algeria; the English had to deal with the embarrassing apartheid of Rhodesia and a rebellion in Kenya. Soon Britain and France were giving up their colonies, and by the late 1950s Belgium suddenly reckoned with its own loss. From 1958 to 1960, Brussels, in disarray, made concession after concession to the Africans in the Congo. The European view that Africans might take over but would look to the old colonial powers for money and governance had a certain plausibility. The Belgian administration would remain intact, as would political and economic affairs. Brussels hoped more than planned for this outcome. The province of Katanga had for a time just such an agenda: the Africans there obliged Brussels. Such leaky bargains floundered because once independence filled the air, loathing of the Europeans could immediately well up. Moreover, the Europeans panicked about their safety as soon as Belgium admitted the possibility of independence. For everyone, empire lost its legitimacy and Europe its unassailability.

While Belgium's conception of independence had an unreal aspect, the expectations of the Congo's youthful politicians had a touch of fantasy. They had not had to fight for their liberty. Political leaders in Brussels barely contested the issue, and seemed simply to throw up their hands in surrender. The Africans perhaps would have had a better chance if they had waged and won a bitter ten-year war. Then they would have forged bonds that prompted cooperation, run an army, outlined political structures, and trained lieutenants in administration.[10] Instead, prominent men from various regions of the Congo first met one another in Brussels in 1958, when they traveled to the World's Fair.

As Africa clamored for an end to empire, the seeds of misfortune were planted. Westerners held up their democracies as the only worthwhile model for civilization, although their practices in the colonies failed to live up to that model. The imperialists had destroyed older political affiliations, or had used them not to foster representative government, but to set groups at one another's throats. Now the Africans would receive large pieces of territory with which to fabricate European sorts of countries.[11]

Politically active Africans under Belgian rule were all labeled nationalists, although this label disguised great differences over the degree of centralization they envisioned. In the late 1950s, the *évolués* talked about independence apart from a Congo nation. They intensely debated the sort of country or countries they would run—unitary, national, federal, confederated—but never *how*. Books of the era were filled with analyses of the possibilities of formal organization, but never of administration. African "political parties" barely functioned as coalitions, and even then they focused on local and ethnic self-rule, alternatives to the European Congo, but not governance itself.

Joseph Kasa-Vubu, head of ABAKO—the Alliance des Bakongo—led the struggle for independence.[12] A mono-ethnic party, ABAKO worked at first to reconstitute a Kongo state on the west coast of Africa at the mouth of the Congo River. The deliberate Kasa-Vubu, a former clerk and Catholic seminarian, persisted through the 1950s in pushing for self-rule for the Kongo people. Such a principled stand won Kasa-Vubu few friends among the whites, and Belgium jailed him in 1959 after the famous January riot in Leopoldville. An honest man, he still lacked the fire to build his ethnic party into something more. ABAKO differed from the other notable provincial party, the Conakat—the Confédération des Associations Tribales du Katanga—which arose from the original ethnic groups in Katanga. ABAKO was an ethnic grouping. The Conakat, on the contrary, was regional and drew its strength from the southern part of the semiautonomous province. In the late 1950s, Conakat's head, Moïse Tshombe, a businessman, wanted a state in the east, as Kasa-Vubu did in the west. In Katanga, however, white settlers, mining concerns, and the lure of southern Africa induced Europeans to bargain with responsive Africans. Perhaps the multiethnic Conakat would govern but allow the whites special license and the lion's share of profit from their businesses. Tshombe had credentials in Katanga but could never escape being seen as an accomplice to empire.

Patrice Lumumba's Mouvement National Congolais (MNC) contrasted with these parties. The MNC was splintered itself, and the strength of nationalism was often associated with the personal appeal of the extraordinary Lumumba. Both Catholic and Protestant missions educated him intermittently for ten years in Kasai Province. He also studied and read on his own, driving himself to fluency in French. From the Batetela, a minor ethnic group, Lumumba soon went north to the large town of Stanleyville. The post office employed him. He devoted himself to self-improvement and politics, and worked for *évolué* magazines. A youthful book he wrote on the colonial politics and culture of the Congo, *Congo: My Country,* was published after his death. Although the movement for independence pushed him to more militant positions, Lumumba's cultural conservatism was noticeable. He did not like imperialism, but believed that Brussels had uplifted the Congo. Nationalism was his watchword; anti-Belgium rhetoric came only second. A splendid intellect flashed through the experience others had of him.

Lumumba's career took a detour when he went to prison in 1956–1957 in Stanleyville for embezzling funds from the mail service. Thereafter he moved to Leopoldville but did not give up on politics. He frequented the bars of the *cité* as a successful representative of Polar beer and as a coming politician. He got results by nonstop frenetic activity in a culture in which other men moved patiently. A tireless organizer, he was a mesmerizing speaker of both French and African languages; he also wrote stirring French.

Tall, slim, and handsome, Lumumba had a dazzling smile, and piercing eyes that glittered through a signature pair of spectacles. Critics disliked his obvious attraction to women, and their interest in him. He was a dapper dresser and supple dancer, with a physical intensity that was obvious. Critics also charged that the Congo's equivalent of marijuana fueled his political and sexual exertions through the nights. Following one conventional practice among the *évolués,* Lumumba forswore polygamy but discarded, in turn, two earlier wives while making his way as a "civilized" black man wishing for an equally *évolué* women. He had three wives in six years, between 1945 and 1951. This practice mixed African custom with Western legalities. Lumumba's third wedding was traditionally arranged—she was fourteen, he was twenty-five—and his bride had no claims to *évolué* status. After this final marriage, Lumumba continued the liaisons that characterized his adult life. His most enduring sexual relationship was with an independent woman from Leopoldville. He developed his most intense intellectual connection with a woman who became his secretary in 1960; a child they conceived was born after his murder. His third wife gave birth while he was living in the prime minister's residence. Children from more than one relationship lived in his homes.[13] Western diplomats used his way of life to discredit him but were fundamentally frightened by his open flouting of their conventions.

When he founded the MNC in 1958, Lumumba was in his early thirties, the average age of the Congo's politicians stepping onto a grand stage. In December of that year many of the continent's politicians noted his appearance at the All-African Peoples' Conference in Ghana. Lumumba's speeches and tactics—words and deeds—enticed many among the fifteen million whom he—like the Belgian colonialists—called the Congolese. *Évolués* who came to political eminence credited his brilliance and his way with language, and accepted him as their leader. He could, however, understand and articulate the demands of a wider public, and certainly had an impact on city dwellers and even villagers. Lumumba's enthusiasm and sincerity aroused in his listeners the profound emotional and intellectual allure of a native land. Nationalist ideas were more than an atmosphere that he created. For him, as for his mentor Kwame Nkrumah of Ghana, federalism or confederalism in contrast to African nationalism amounted to ethnic separatism. Western exploitation of "tribal divisions" would accompany "the suicide of Africa."[14]

At the same time Lumumba could also infuriate; he was volatile, flamboyant, and impulsive. While he had a strong core of adherents among the *évolués,* others worried that they could not compete with him, and would never prosper in public life if Lumumba thrived. The most important of his opponents did not believe in the "Congolese" nation, and wanted something different. Detractors found him a destabilizing presence and rightly agonized that he would make the blood of the whites boil. Europeans—and later Americans—did react negatively to Lumumba. His nationalism was too assertive, his tactical movements too unpredictable, and his regard for Western prerogatives too constrained.

A potent figure in Africa in the eighteen months before independence, Lumumba towered over that world in the first months of the Congo's independence. Although he was center stage, his slender and impassioned figure, always in motion, is seen as if from the corner of the eye. What he did and the meaning of what he said were never just reported but always construed by others. Lumumba became the incarnation of the hopes and fears of common folks in the Congo, and of the African politicians in Leopoldville and elsewhere with whom he battled or cooperated. He entered the dreams and nightmares of Western leaders; of the *colons;* of the international left; and of the heads of emerging nations. It is almost impossible to get a feeling for his inner life.

Lumumba's writings and speeches still carry an emotional punch. How credible were his aspirations? As prime minister, he presided over territory that did not have Western administrative resources, and Lumumba took the West's nationalism as a model. He and his associates had neither the apparatus nor the experience to run a country. Moreover, Belgium's unusual governance first supplied patterns for the Congo. Lumumba favored the French language but also wanted his Congolese to pursue mutual benefits, as the Flemish and Walloons did in Belgium. When some Flemish speakers suggested that an independent Congo might have two official languages, as Belgium did, Congolese nationalists countered by arguing that if Flemish became official, so should all the common languages in the Congo. Such a foolish idea refuted itself.[15] None of these discussions attended to whether Africans on their own might make one or two or many governmental units work. Yet Belgium, the United States, and the United Nations all paid more than lip service to a unified Congo, the goal of the MNC. The Belgians did not turn over their spacious colony just to see it vanish.

The Belgians Yield

Toward the end of 1958 Brussels initiated a study that would generate reforms and perhaps some kind of foreseeable sovereignty for the Congo. Then on January 4, 1959, before Belgium announced the findings, Leopoldville rioted. Africans demanded immediate changes, and turmoil continued throughout the year. Brussels promised independence and then stalled. The government disagreed on the timing, faced opposition at home to any military intervention, and lost control of the situation. In early 1960, Belgium gave way. Both sides joined a roundtable conference in Brussels, where the deliberations took a radical turn. The Africans were adamant about instituting immediate independence. The excitement peaked when Brussels, under duress, declared that Lumumba would attend the meeting. He had returned to Stanleyville in October 1959 to mobilize its *cité*. Arrested for inciting riots, he was sentenced to jail for a second time on January 21, 1960, and taken from Stanleyville to Katanga's Jadotville, which had a proper prison away from the center of Lumumba's popularity. A few days later, on January 25, officials in Belgium ordered the MNC leader freed and flew him to the roundtable. Lumumba was too influential a leader not to participate. He made a dramatic appearance in Brussels on January 26, the marks of his prison manacles still on him. When a wary Kasa-Vubu boycotted the proceedings, a magnetic Lumumba took over the meetings and became a hero.[16]

The roundtable agreed on June 30, 1960, as independence day, and then set a date for elections in the Congo. Africans were to work in tandem with Belgian officials to get on-the-job training in administration. In April a second roundtable negotiated economic relations. Preoccupied with the coming vote, the Congo's politicians minimally participated in these consultations. Belgium also approved a provisional constitution. This *loi fondamentale* determined the structure of the Congo's government, which would function similarly to Belgium's. The electorate in the Congo would choose a house of representatives. In a complex procedure the six provinces would select a senate. The house and senate together formed the parliament. Although the head of state (the president) would have the formal right to appoint the prime minister and the other members of the cabinet, the parliament would have to endorse the government. The *loi fondamentale,* however, gave the Belgian king, Baudouin, the job of anointing the first prime minister and his cabinet, though the king delegated this task to Walter Ganshof van der Meersch, a minister with ad hoc responsibilities in the Congo. A vote of the Congo's parliament would pick the president, after it had decided on a prime minister.

Elections took place from May 11 to May 25, 1960. Political parties gained legislative seats according to the share of the vote they obtained. Distinct from a winner-take-all system, such a system, copied after Belgium's, encouraged the proliferation of parties in a land where sectional and ethnic affiliations multiplied minor political groupings. At the end of May the results at once fixed the house of representatives. Newly chosen legislatures in the six provinces decided on their members for the Congo's national senate. Lumumba's party, the MNC, easily had the greatest number, although it had won far less than a majority. With thirty-six seats out of 137, only the MNC had backing across the country. In early June Lumumba presumed that he would lead. In Leopoldville, however, Ganshof van der Meersch stalled. The Belgians did not want the capricious Lumumba as prime minister, and on June 17 Ganshof van der Meersch pushed Lumumba aside and asked Kasa-Vubu to form a government.

Although Kasa-Vubu had a monopoly in the Bas-Congo and a stronghold in the capital, he had few endorsements elsewhere. A vote on June 21 by the parliament exposed Kasa-Vubu's weakness as an all-Congo leader. Ganshof van der Meersch conceded and settled on Lumumba, who named an inclusive government on June 23. In selecting his ministers, Lumumba did leave out a few critical politicians who were recognized as uncompromisingly antagonistic to the prime minister, most notably any significant follower of Katanga's Tshombe, leader of the Conakat. Also absent: Albert Kalonji from Kasai, a former big wheel in the MNC, who had broken with Lumumba and become a personal enemy; and Jean Bolikango, a chief member of the opposition to Lumumba in Équateur Province. The next day Lumumba engineered the election of Kasa-Vubu as president. The government of most major groups and parties, and the vote for Kasa-Vubu to the presidency, steered the prime minister to cooperation.

On June 29 the newborn Congolese government approved a Treaty of Friendship with Belgium, the other important document, in addition to the *loi fondamentale,* that fashioned the road map for independence. According to the treaty, the Belgian civil service—some ten thousand people—and the one thousand white officers commanding the black soldiers in the Force Publique would remain; Brussels would pay the salaries of these men. Belgium would also maintain its metropolitan military forces in three bases. Lumumba signed because his government had no options. It could not itself run an administration or an army. Through ingenious legal constructions Belgium also tried to keep the "Congo portfolio," the stock-holding interests of the former colony, out of the hands of the new state.[17]

The formal transfer of power was set for June 30. Few insiders bet on the new regime to perform independently, or even to operate effectively with assistance. The partnership between Kasa-Vubu and Lumumba, they whispered, would not survive. Divided itself, Belgium could not inculcate unifying ideas. The struggle for independence had nurtured nationalism; zeal for it declined as colonial authority caved in. More cynical onlookers wondered how Brussels would stay in control.[18]

CHAPTER TWO

Independence

BAUDOUIN, KING OF THE BELGIANS, had a lofty sense of his obligations to his people and to his imperial nation, divided but Roman Catholic. Although a man of substance, he lacked humor and took himself very seriously. The European powers had selected the first Leopold from suitable nobility to reign in Belgium when they had accepted the new state in 1830 to buffer quarrels nearer home than Africa. Baudouin's great-great-uncle, the famous second Leopold, had been a shrewd and capable monarch. The great-grand-nephew sympathized with what he learned of his memorable relative's abolition of the slave trade in the Congo and his promotion of the heathen and backward blacks to Christianity. From his boyhood, Baudouin had saccharine and invincibly ignorant beliefs about his family and Belgium in Africa, and early determined to have the Congo live up to his storybook notions.

World War II had posed impossible choices about the loyalties and duty of public figures. Belgian ministers had escaped to England, but Leopold III, Baudouin's father, had not followed. During the war, even though people admitted his courage in not leaving his country, Leopold III had an awkward patriotic but pro-fascist position in Nazi-run Europe. Then the defeat of Germany had defiled Leopold III as a collaborator, and after a long dispute—the Royal Question—Belgium's politicians had forced him to abdicate.[1] The son grew up with a plain knowledge of how the nation thought his father had failed. In 1950 Baudouin ascended to the throne at age twenty. "The sad king" wanted to serve Belgium, restore the legacy of his father, and carry on the ancestral vocation in the Congo. Baudouin made a jubilant visit there in 1955, and another more fleeting one in 1959 when the future of the colony was in question.

Like many Belgians in the 1950s, Baudouin could not conceive that his country might give up the Congo. He shared the special foot-dragging of Belgians in respect to the political development of their colonies. Some in Brussels urged that emancipation would come about over generations. In the mid-1950s talk of a thirty-year emancipation stunned the Belgian public. Then, in August 1958, Charles de Gaulle proposed to end France's empire in Africa and spoke of a French Union. De Gaulle addressed France's Africa from Brazzaville in the French Congo, just across the Congo River from Leopoldville. The Belgians often took their signals from France, and de Gaulle's views disturbed Baudouin. Brussels could not see a way to go it alone.

In a radio speech in Belgium after the Leopoldville riot of January 1959, the king looked to gradual independence and a continued close association. Baudouin had reveries about a smooth transition and something more. His fancies burnished the idea of a Congo-Belgium community, two equal and conjoined peoples in a royal commonwealth. Clearer thinkers supposed that Belgium might continue as the power behind the façade of a black government that would permit white good sense to prevail and leave economic relations unaltered. Deep fears also preyed on Baudouin's mind: independence might nourish the primitive roots of the Congo and choke the seeds of Catholic civilization, sown for seventy-five years. The king had met Lumumba on his first trip to the Congo—the Stanleyville évolués had criticized Lumumba for the "hand gestures" and "flood of words" with which he addressed the king. On Baudouin's briefer visit to the Congo in late 1959, another demonstration had occurred in Stanleyville, where Lumumba was in jail when Baudouin passed through the city. The monarch would try to work with the black man, but feared Lumumba was an extremist. He might pilot the king's Congolese away from a friendly union. Baudouin unenthusiastically flew to Leopoldville for independence day, June 30, yet still expected to give a lesson to the Congo republic and inculcate into it sorely needed discipline.

Other cares competed for Baudouin's attention. The king kept an "Intimate Diary" that described his religious longings and his personal creed. Churchmen advised him, particularly Bishop Leo Suenens, who became spiritual head of the Roman Catholics in Belgium in 1961. With an imperfect intellect, the young king struggled to combine private fulfillment and sovereign duty in an errant world. Belgians knew his father as a womanizer and as a man with firm ideas. Baudouin had firm ideas but no women. The father had established a Boy Scout troop in the palace to bring in friends for the lonely child, and now in 1960 at age twenty-nine Baudouin was looking for a wife. Early that year, in Switzerland, he was introduced to Fabiola Fernanda, a Spanish noblewoman two years older than he. In the spring Baudouin asked Monsignor Suenens for help with matchmaking. Suenens relied on a sixty-year-old Irish Catholic sister, Veronika O'Brien, who had a fastidious reputation for spiritual insight. After a visitation from the Virgin Mary, O'Brien orchestrated some discreet private time for Baudouin and Fabiola.[2]

On July 5, 1960, just a few days after the independence ceremonies, Baudouin would journey incognito to the Catholic shrine of Lourdes in France. He went on his own pious pilgrimage but also to see Fabiola. They prayed and talked earnestly as they walked around Lourdes. Baudouin came home smitten; at last he had an attachment, and the dynasty would continue. In September the couple announced their engagement; they would marry in December. For the first six months of the Congo's independence, both romance and high politics occupied Baudouin. He focused entirely on his kingly job, which made the most worldly demands on someone who was most certainly not a man of the world.

June 30

Just before 11 A.M. on June 30, 1960, a motorcade took King Baudouin and his entourage to the newly designated parliament building in Leopoldville. There, Baudouin would address the recently elected legislators, Belgian public figures, international dignitaries, and the hierarchy of the churches in the Congo. President Kasa-Vubu would answer; the prime ministers from each country would sign a proclamation of independence; the notables would adjourn to lunch.

Dressed in a regal white uniform adorned with medals, Baudouin directed his words to "his" Congolese. Like Lumumba, the king also wore spectacles, but he peered through thick glasses. He told the assembled Africans that independence "crowned the work that the genius of Leopold, a champion of civilization," had initiated. The Belgian pioneers who followed and who built the country also deserved "our admiration and your thanks." Despite the greatest difficulties, they had succored the Congo, and now the Africans "must prove that we have been right to trust you." The natives owed Belgium a debt of gratitude, and Baudouin told them that "independence is not realized by the immediate satisfaction of facile enjoyment, but by work, respect for the freedom of others and the rights of minorities, by tolerance and the order without which no democratic regime can subsist." The king implied that the Congolese were ill-equipped to deal with independence, and ought indeed to pray for their country. His language dripped with imperial condescension made worse because Baudouin did not seem aware of his arrogant attitude. A number of contemporaries saw the problem, although the Western press thought the speech adequate if uninspired. He received some conventional applause.

Joseph Kasa-Vubu, the Congo's president and Baudouin's ceremonial equal, properly replied. At the roundtable discussions in January, Kasa-Vubu, who had every claim to be the *primus inter pares* among the Congo's participants, had disappeared in a fit of complaint. He had given Lumumba his opportunity, and now Kasa-Vubu had gotten the number-two job. The president knew that the Africans were proud of Lumumba because the Belgians did not intimidate him. The prime minister took the language of empire and used it to cow the master. He couldn't be all bad if every white hated him. At the same time Lumumba was worrisome. Although he might dominate an argument, he might anger *les Flamands* beyond their tolerance and sail the Congo into uncharted territory. Only Kasa-Vubu could restrain Lumumba. Nonetheless, it also occurred to Kasa-Vubu that he might be ill-suited for his consolation prize of a job. An unimpressive and indolent orator, he was always ready for a meal followed by a nap. Kasa-Vubu spoke without character but said what was appropriate. "Belgium had the wisdom not to oppose the

Lumumba enters parliament, a triumphant prime minister
on independence day. (© *BelgaImage*)

current of history, and—a deed without precedent in the story of peaceful decolonization—she let our country pass directly from foreign domination to full independence." He circuitously passed judgment on Belgium. Yet Kasa-Vubu perceived the slap in the face the king had just given to the Africans. Struck by Baudouin's hauteur, the president cut the last part of his text that was to genuflect to the king's solicitude for the Congo. Again the guests clapped courteously.

Lumumba's Speech

Various stories have interpreted the circumstances surrounding the speech that Lumumba decided more or less at the last minute to give. The prime minister inserted himself into the program when he learned about Baudouin's proposed condescending lecture. In Lumumba's view, from the 1880s into the first decade of the twentieth century, Leopold II and his agents had barely taken the blacks for human beings but instead for expendable commodities. The Africans carried out the wishes of stockholders in mining enterprises. Even Marxist analyses of capitalism held more subtlety than what had gone on. Europeans had forced the Congo into slave labor. When the blacks did not die but failed to measure up in various ways, they might have their hands cut off, or their wives and children shot, or receive deadly beatings with an especially nasty whip, the *chicote*. So Lumumba thought.

He believed too that when the Belgian state had taken over in 1908, the situation had hardly progressed. The colonizers looked at the Congo as a rare resource, necessary to Belgian revenues. Although the Africans did learn how administration in the Congo worked at its lower levels, and how the master race lived, the Belgians limited the Africans to menial positions and meager salaries. The authorities hired people like Lumumba as salesmen. White-owned companies, Lumumba knew, had *évolué* personnel; they sold to other Africans merchandise whose profits went to Europeans.

The French language had clarified all this to Lumumba. One journalist wrote in 1958 that Lumumba was "a good schoolchild"—"one can easily see he has been trained by the Flemings [in French]."[3] Lumumba had also said "we have our national Flemish" languages, referring to Kituba, Lingala, Swahili, and Tshiluba, and wanted every person of merit in the new Congo to master French. The nascent political parties stipulated the ability to debate in French as necessary for any public man. As one urged, "the language of Voltaire, and it alone, must become our national language."[4] French opened to Lumumba another world. He was informed about the bright lights of Europe, and the darkness of Africa, and he located himself in a pecking order of refinement where, he could see with his own eyes, Africa resided at the bottom. Yet while Lumumba mimicked the whites, French simultaneously allowed him to articulate the oppression of imperialism. The prime minister knew of the talk of an African and European commonwealth, which would rest on a supposed mutual respect. Again Lumumba could see that even such a commonwealth would have a "color bar." No Belgian could think around a segregated society and its intolerance. Two-faced white rhetoric only made people like Lumumba more aware of their debased position.

Finally, he had in mind how the Belgians had tried to invest Kasa-Vubu as prime minister instead of him. They had publicly disregarded Lumumba. Brussels hoped to use the opposition to him and the uncertainties that even the parties closest in orientation to the MNC might feel. Nonetheless, Belgian antipathy to the one soaring native figure—Patrice Lumumba—had energized the Africans. While Belgium had yielded, Lumumba had hardly forgotten the disrespect. Alert to his own power—and now under his own government—he would enlighten them. Lumumba wrote a rejoinder to Baudouin beforehand, although the prime-minister-in-waiting also altered it while the king and the president had the stage. Lumumba's talk immediately attracted worldwide attention. Even today, more than fifty years later, his words arouse thought.

Seated next to Belgium's prime minister, Gaston Eyskens, Lumumba wore the maroon sash that designated the Great Ribbon of the Order of the Crown. The night before the king had awarded it to Lumumba, as he did to Kasa-Vubu. Tense and intense, the prime minister went to the lectern with an electrifying self-assurance. "Congolese men and Congolese women, victorious fighters for independence, today victorious," he began, "I greet you in the name of the Congolese government." "All of you, my friends, who have fought tirelessly at our sides, I ask you to make this June 30, 1960, an illustrious date that you will keep indelibly engraved in your hearts, a date of significance that you will teach your children, so that they will make known to their sons and to their grandsons the glorious history of our fight for liberty." This rhetoric ignored that the Belgians had thrown in their hand without taking a trick.

Rhetoric of a different sort followed:

> We are proud of this struggle of tears, of fire, and of blood that . . . put an end to the humiliating slavery that force imposed upon us. This was our fate for eighty years of a colonial regime; our wounds are still too fresh and painful for us to drive them from our memory. We have known harassing work, exacted in exchange for salaries that did not permit us to eat enough to drive away hunger, or to clothe ourselves, or to house ourselves decently, or to raise our children as creatures dear to us.

We have known ironies, insults, blows that we endured morning, noon and evening, just because we were the negroes. Who will forget that to a black, one said "tu," certainly not as to a friend, but because the more honorable "vous" was reserved for whites alone? . . . We have seen that in the towns there were magnificent dwellings for the whites and crumbling shanties for the blacks; that a black was not admitted in the motion-picture theaters, in the restaurants, in the stores of the Europeans; that [on boats] a black traveled in the hold, at the feet of the whites in their luxury cabins. . . . All that, my brothers, we have endured. . . .

Together . . . we are going to show the world what the black man can do when he works in freedom, and we are going to make the Congo the center of the sun's radiance for all of Africa. . . . We are going to end the suppression of free thought and see to it that all our citizens enjoy to the full the fundamental liberties foreseen in the Declaration of the Rights of Man. . . . We are going to rule not by the peace of guns and bayonets but by a peace of the heart and the will.

So that we will reach this aim without delay, I ask all of you, legislators and citizens, to help me with all your strength. I ask all of you to forget your tribal quarrels. They exhaust us. They risk making us despised abroad. I ask the parliamentary minority to help my government through a constructive opposition and to limit themselves strictly to legal and democratic channels. I ask all of you not to shrink before any sacrifice in order to achieve the success of our huge undertaking. . . . Your Majesty, excellencies, ladies, gentlemen, my dear fellow countrymen, my brothers of race, my brothers of struggle—this is what I wanted to tell you in the name of the government on this magnificent day of our complete independence. . . . Long live independence and African unity! Long live the independent and sovereign Congo![5]

In this consummate performance Lumumba said what most of his compatriots felt. Several times applause interrupted him, until at the end the Africans stood in an ovation. Baudouin grimaced in his seat, the veins in his neck taut. Later, friends and foes alike would report that Lumumba had said: We are your monkeys no longer. He did not, but many got that message. The Belgians believed that Lumumba had insulted them in front of the world. He had pointed out the wickedness of colonialism when the West was trying to convince itself and anyone who would listen of the system's benevolence and necessity.

In his oration the prime minister had only mentioned that Belgium had accepted "the flow of history." While the Congo would "stay vigilant," it would respect its obligations, "given freely" in the Treaty of Friendship. Later that day, after both countries had signed the proclamation of independence, Belgian politicians forced Lumumba to make amends at the luncheon. He stood up at the head table: "I would not want my thoughts misinterpreted." He briefly praised Belgian efforts, and anticipated that the two countries would join hands in the future.

He had done damage, nonetheless, and done it well. No one misinterpreted him. He solidified Belgian hostility, and exhibited a mercurial militancy. The UN and US reports were consistent in telling of Baudouin's paternalism, Lumumba's passionate and erratic nationalism, Belgian irritation, and ambiguous prospects for the future.[6] Lumumba's speech was unstoppable, like an arrow shot from a bow.

The independence day talks laid out two futures for Africa. Baudouin advised the Africans, at the bottom of a single scale of progress, to continue tutelage. It would eventually take them to a better place but through a long interim in which they would remain less than full citizens. Lumumba dismissed the colonial heritage. He proposed that Africa seek a civilization on a par with that of Europe, and would have the Congo a self-determining power at the hub of the continent. When Baudouin returned to Belgium the next day, and soon drove from Brussels to Lourdes to greet his wife-to-be, his humiliation before an international audience gave him much to think about in addition to his peculiar courtship. The Martinique poet Aimé Césaire asked if the sky would fall in "because a nigger has dared, in the world's face, to curse out a king?"[7]

Things Fall Apart

June 30 fell on a Thursday, and in the long first weekend of July the Congo's Force Publique maintained order during many festivities and staffed honor guards for a great many self-important politicians. With their new high salaries, many of the legislators went out to buy late-model American cars that, escorted by soldiers, they loved to drive themselves.

Leopold II had organized the Force Publique as an army in 1885–1886. With efficient European officers and African soldiers from all over the

Congo, the Force Publique did not back up any foreign policy but patrolled other Africans. The Belgians had taught the enlisted men that their more primitive fellow inhabitants needed heavy-handed oversight. The Belgian general Émile Janssens commanded the Force Publique. He had lobbied for an Independent Congo State, which Baudouin would lead, as Leopold II had so many years before.[8] Now Janssens had to accept the leadership of a black politician. In the aftermath of independence, servicemen anticipated immediate improvements in their wages and prestige. The army—some twenty-four thousand men—did not differ from civilians who thought that independence meant wealth, automobiles, and good housing—everything that the Europeans had previously monopolized. The troops resented their new rulers, who already had some of these items, and with independence came open antipathy to the Belgians-only officer corps. On Monday morning, July 4, ordinary soldiers in Leopoldville refused to take orders. Agitators suggested that the military should get privileges like the politicians and did not have to obey Europeans. The next morning General Janssens laid down the law to the African personnel at headquarters: after independence the army would not change.

Critics have unanimously condemned Janssens for shattering the Force Publique. He certainly shared the racial views of other Belgians, but his July 5 announcement—blunt and foolish though not uncommon—simply called for the army to go on as before. At the same time, soldiers loyal to African politicians not included in Lumumba's government took advantage of Belgian insensitivity. Ethnic divisions undermined the Force Publique. That night troops at Camp Hardy in Thysville, some eighty miles to the south of Leopoldville, declined to restore order in the capital and would not be able to be counted on in the future. The prime minister acted at once to end the trouble. On July 6, Lumumba promoted all soldiers by one grade and when the situation got worse dismissed Janssens. Two days later he exchanged all the Belgian officers with Africans, although the great majority of the Europeans remained, with the consent of the enlisted men, as advisers. In most instances the soldiers would elect their leaders. On July 9, the government decided on the new command for the Force Publique, renamed the Armée Nationale Congolaise (ANC). The cabinet selected Victor Lundula, an African veteran of World War II, as the first black general to succeed Janssens, although Lundula was stuck in Elisabethville and would only take up his place at the end of the month. A confidant of Lumumba, Joseph Mobutu was promoted to colonel. Just twenty-nine, Mobutu had a position in the Lumumba cabinet and had been a sergeant in the headquarters of the Force Publique for seven years. Displaying leadership by calming the soldiers, Mobutu became chief of staff. These measures came too late. The mutiny spread around Leopoldville and to other parts of the Congo. The army wanted more from independence than Lumumba could give, and troops in the Bas-Congo turned their anger against Europeans—seizing money, property, and in some cases women.

After the first week in July, the ANC no longer existed as a national force. Rather, squads of soldiers terrified everyone. Some enlisted men accepted no discipline; others gave their loyalty to certain political functionaries, or to their region or ethnic peers. Various bands intimidated one another. Because of its irregular pay, the army often threatened action to get salaries, or rampaged for food and supplies. Belgian civilians lost their nerve as the ANC dissolved. A shocking scenario was coming true. Around Leopoldville Europeans hastened to "the Beach," the waterfront, where a ferry would take them across the Congo River to Brazzaville in the former French Congo. They fled the country and left the public administration and the economy disorganized.

Kasa-Vubu and Lumumba sensed their precarious situation and their need of the whites. The two feared a gory uprising by their countrymen, and its possibility mortified the president and prime minister. On July 9 the two men embarked on a Congo-wide plane trip to get the new *armée* in hand and to restore normal life. Nonetheless, Belgian troops intervened on July 10 to rescue harassed Europeans, first in Elisabethville and soon in other parts of the new republic. As Brussels sent in more soldiers, they clashed with the ANC, and the Congo's military dismissed the Belgian officers serving as advisers. The army was now decapitated.[9]

A crucial event occurred on July 11, when Moïse Tshombe in Katanga declared his province's independence. Supporters of Tshombe had long disliked the idea of a unified Congo, especially one led by Lumumba. In southern Katanga, around the capital of Elisabethville, Tshombe had a committed following. Katanga and its mines, Belgium's prize in Africa,

generated wealth for the West. Between Tshombe and the Europeans in
Elisabethville an accord existed, not always amiable but mostly effective. Tshombe wanted out from under the Lumumba nationalists, and
the Europeans needed a foothold in a Congo falling to pieces. They had
to have Tshombe as much as he had to have them, and Belgian military
officials lent him a hand. On July 12, backed by the Belgian troops,
Tshombe and his government in Katanga prevented Kasa-Vubu and Lumumba from landing their plane in Elisabethville. Furious at their own
weakness and angry at Belgium, the president and the prime minister
flew elsewhere. Lumumba especially lost any commitment to come to
terms with Brussels, although Kasa-Vubu did not lag far behind.

A series of confused moves manifested the wretched naïveté of the lo-
cal politicians. They first asked for American intervention but then, on
July 13, applied to the USSR to monitor events. On July 12 and 13 Kasa-
Vubu and Lumumba appealed to the United Nations to stop Belgian ag-
gression, oust the Belgian military, and end the secession. In the early
morning of July 14, in New York, in a first resolution on the Congo, the
Security Council of the United Nations asked for the withdrawal of the
Belgian troops and authorized its secretary-general, Dag Hammarskjöld,
to mount an international force for the Congo. That same day, Kasa-
Vubu and Lumumba broke relations with Brussels.

The Africans had little knowledge of the UN, did not comprehend its
American origins, and had no sense of the dismal weakness of the organization when it tried to act without the say-so of the powerful. Kasa-
Vubu and Lumumba expected immediate results: the Belgians would
exit forthwith, and the secession would collapse; the UN would oversee
domestic life, shape up the Armée Nationale Congolaise, and restore it to
working order; the UN would then say good-bye. Lumumba did not see
the makeshift nature of his administration, or his own at-risk position.
On the other hand, an elaborate and universally approved political process had occupied the world's attention for the first six months of 1960.
At the end of this process Lumumba had a critical and unassailable
status—the first democratically elected leader of the Congo.

The United Nations Is Inserted

Before the end of June 1960, Ralph Bunche, under-secretary-general of the UN, had arrived in Leopoldville as head of a mission that would give the Congo the organization's imprimatur and for a few weeks contribute to the transition. Now, Secretary-General Hammarskjöld put Bunche in a new and unexpected role as administrator of a huge operation in the Congo, named ONUC (Opération des Nations Unies au Congo). As perhaps the most famous African American of the middle of the twentieth century, Bunche, as no other, was thought to be the best man for the job.

With the aid of the American air force, soldiers from a number of African and nonaligned nations at once got their boots on the ground. The peacekeeping force would grow to almost twenty thousand from over twenty states. Soldiers from various countries came and went. The international army had different allegiances to the UN and to different factions of the Congo's government. The men from Kwame Nkrumah's Ghana, for example, had the reputation of acting only for Lumumba, and in part deserved that reputation. However, British officers commanded its soldiers. At times Ghana did not do what it could to uphold Lumumba but complied with UN instructions to do otherwise.[10] Overall, UN goals did not unify the soldiers from different lands, subject as much to home governments as to the ideal of global reconciliation.[11] UN functionaries finally demonstrated a sort of pacifism—they did not want to use their military except as a last resort; in truth, they feared to use the military at all, and more routinely resorted to bluff.

Still, by mid- to late July an international army in the Congo placated world opinion. The blue helmets, as they were called, offered an illusion of order, and at UN headquarters in New York City diplomats could work out solutions to this first great postcolonial dilemma.

CHAPTER THREE

The Empire Strikes Back

T HE BELGIANS FACED a whirlwind. In a few weeks' time they had gone from proud colonists to international pariahs. On June 30 the Congo gained independence "in total agreement and friendship with Belgium." Two weeks later, both countries found themselves almost at war, and the Congo severed relations. The UN harshly judged Brussels's resort to the military, and the Security Council urged the Belgian troops to decamp. The UN resolution of July 14 avoided the word *aggression,* which the Soviet Union wanted to use, but world opinion had accepted Lumumba's accusations against the former rulers. For decades Brussels had jealously protected its African empire, which also included Ruanda-Urundi, from the outside world, and had fiercely resisted the United Nations in devising a strategy for emancipation. Now the Belgians looked on as "their own Congo" came under UN guardianship.[1]

Belgium was unprepared. The rush to independence had taken up much of the government's energy over the past six months. Ministers blew hot and cold about the future, but did not expect the Congo's rapid collapse. Brussels was neither practically nor mentally ready for the army's effort, the secession of Katanga, or the repatriation of tens of thousands of Belgian nationals. As affairs grew to a full-blown emergency, Belgium had its pride hurt, misunderstood by the world and by its allies.

Ordinary citizens felt betrayed. Disapproving news outlets unsettled the politicians, who were floundering over a course of action.

The King and the Politicians

Belgian politics were as divided as the country itself. Socialists of a diluted sort had strength in the French-speaking south, while more conservative Catholic Christian Democrats attracted votes in the Flemish-speaking north. A small group of Liberals, interested in economic opportunity in a secular world, often held the balance of power. From the period before World War II until the 1950s, the Socialist Paul-Henri Spaak emerged as Belgium's stellar public figure. Quick and engaging, Spaak had a gift with words in both French and English. While he served three times as prime minister and acted, with interruptions, as Belgian foreign minister from 1936 to 1957, he also chaired the first General Assembly of the UN and showed talent in the various pan-European organizations working to construct a European union. At the time of the upheaval in the Congo, Spaak headed the civilian affairs of the North Atlantic Treaty Organization, NATO. As secretary-general of the Western security alliance, he was easily the most influential Belgian public figure, but nonetheless had a shrunken home base in an era of democratization and private entrepreneurship. He had social welfare concerns with an authoritarian tinge, and found enthusiasts in monarchical circles.[2] There, spokesmen for Baudouin's father, Leopold III, had been under siege since World War II.

This Royal Question—what to do with Leopold III—had dominated the nation until 1950, when Leopold stepped down and Baudouin took over. Throughout the 1950s, nevertheless, commentators spoke of the "kingship with two heads" because Baudouin lived with his father. Furious with the progressive tendencies of postwar Europe, reactionaries coalesced around the two royals. Leopold III and Baudouin hated "the politicians," who had damaged the nation when they had humbled the crown in the late 1940s and early 1950s.

From 1958 on, at home, Prime Minister Gaston Eyskens led these politicians with a government of Christian Democrats and Liberals. The only son of a middle-class family, Eyskens taught economics at the Catholic

University of Louvain. With the support of the Christian labor movement, he had found his way to the forefront of Belgian Christian Democracy as prime minister in the late 1940s. His attitude toward the Royal
Question—he had favored Leopold III's abdication—collided with that
of his own party and forced him to the sidelines for a few years. In 1958
he made a comeback and again became prime minister. With a great
sense of self-sufficiency, Eyskens played his cards close to his chest, con-
fident if not arrogant, not only in respect to the king but also his own
party's leaders. By 1960, however, his coalition had run out of steam.
This tough and capable man spoke for a group of declining vigor, and
often found his own ministers faltering and at odds.

The Congo hung like a millstone around the neck of the Eyskens government. A fellow of the Belgian-American Educational Foundation,
Eyskens had a master's degree from Columbia University in New York
City, but little experience in international politics except for a modest
job as vice president of the Social and Economic Committee of the UN.
He did not know much of the Congo, nor had he traveled there. Hoping
to postpone decolonization but deficient in the courage to do so openly,
his administration had yielded to the African politicians time after time.[3]
From outside Belgian politics proper, NATO leader Spaak criticized the
vacillating stance of the Eyskens regime and implied that Belgium ought
to pursue more forceful options in Africa.

In a cabinet of twenty men, no fewer than five made decisions about
the Congo. Minister of African Affairs August De Schryver fought with
Minister of Foreign Affairs Pierre Wigny. The division of responsibility
between the two departments lacked clarity and made for a wobbling
policy. Belgian and American sources described both ministers as equiv-
ocating.[4] De Schryver had two deputies. Raymond Scheyven looked
after the Congo's economic affairs. Walter Ganshof van der Meersch had
custody of other African matters; we have already encountered him negotiating with Kasa-Vubu and Lumumba over the formation of the Congo's cabinet, when his efforts to marginalize Lumumba damaged the trust
between Belgium and the African government. Four men more or less set
policy. When the troubles erupted, however, a fifth politician held all the
trump cards: Minister of Defense Arthur Gilson.

Reimposing Colonial Rule?

Belgium had three well-equipped military bases in the Congo: Kamina in Katanga; Kitona on the west coast near Leopoldville; and a naval headquarters at the mouth of the Congo River. The metropolitan forces—separate from the Force Publique—had steadily expanded. Kamina and Kitona each had five hundred paratroopers, and one thousand soldiers were ready in neighboring Ruanda-Urundi. The government had sent an additional four hundred men in May of 1960 to mollify the nervous whites. At that time Lumumba protested against this "occupation measure" and demanded the immediate pullout of the soldiers.[5] When the Treaty of Friendship with Belgium was on the table for signature a month later on the eve of independence, Lumumba—now prime minister and minister of defense—required a last amendment: Belgium would keep its bases, but the soldiers in them could act only with the explicit approval of the Congo's minister of defense.

At first, Brussels had not worried about the signs of mutiny. But the news got worse. Alarmed in the early morning of July 8 by the panic in Leopoldville and the exodus of the Europeans, Brussels sent reinforcements to the bases without notifying the Congo's government and against the advice of the Belgian ambassador in Leopoldville. In the early morning of July 10, after two days of hesitation and with upsetting reports from Elisabethville, where five people were killed, the Eyskens government set the troops in motion. On the evening of July 9, Eyskens had sent De Schryver and Ganshof van der Meersch to the Congo to obtain the permission that the treaty necessitated. Kasa-Vubu and Lumumba were making a circuit of the country by plane and could not be reached, and the ministers would be recalled on July 12 without having accomplished their purpose. In any event, the Belgian soldiers were deployed without Lumumba's approval. As a result of mutual suspicion, Brussels and Leopoldville could not cooperate. The last personal contact of a Belgian representative with Lumumba had come in a colloquy with the Belgian ambassador on the night of July 7. Lumumba had abruptly cut off that discussion when he received word of the arrest of four Belgians accused of intending to murder him.[6]

The Kamina troops reached the Luano airport in Elisabethville around 6 A.M. on July 10 to evacuate Belgians. Although the army initially kept a tight rein on its actions, its involvement spread rapidly. After Elisabeth-ville came Luluabourg, Matadi, Leopoldville, and other places. The policy shift resulted from the impulsiveness of Gilson, who overrode Foreign Minister Wigny, once Belgium had overcome the psychological hurdle and put matters in the hands of soldiers. On July 12, spurred on by the ministry of defense, the government switched to "a politics of military occupation." The troops took all important installations and guarded vital communication centers, weapons depots, and airports. Gil-son ordered that the forces should grow to ten thousand—some seventy-five hundred more would come from Belgium.[7] Because of the extent of the operation, he sent General Charles "Charley" Cumont, chief of staff of the Belgian army, to supersede the general previously giving orders. Consultation with the Congo's government was not in the cards, and the general ignored the Belgian ambassador in Leopoldville. From the mo-ment that Cumont arrived on July 13, the troops proceeded under his au-thority. They seized the Leopoldville airport the same day. The next day, July 14, neither the UN resolution asking for a withdrawal of the Belgian troops nor the cessation of diplomatic relations affected the intervention. Through July 25 no fewer than thirty "rescue operations" occurred.

The safety of its citizens legitimately concerned Belgium. The reports from the Congo and the influx of refugees at the Brussels national air-port inflamed public opinion. Belgium justified the military exploits as a humanitarian "sacred duty." Nonetheless, the initiatives went further. Brussels told the army not only to safeguard life and property but also to maintain order. Was not the maintenance of order Lumumba's sovereign prerogative? And how could Belgium justify the actions in Katanga? The Belgian military consolidated Tshombe's rule and disbanded the Force Publique. The Belgian government never exactly defined the pur-pose of the offensive strategy or the outcome it had in mind. If Brussels had feared running the Congo through force before June 30, it could not recapture the country with weapons now. Belgium repudiated the impli-cation that it wished to recolonize the Congo. Yet one of Eyskens's staff suggested a military protectorate under the UN.[8] Eyskens himself ar-gued that the Congo's government did not exist, and hence that he had carte blanche to bring a different regime to the ex-colony. Members of the Brussels administration, behind closed doors, as well as the press, prayed that Lumumba would fall and a more respectable Congo materialize. On July 13 Brussels sent a diplomat to Justin Bomboko, the Congo's minister of foreign affairs, who was at best lukewarm toward Lumumba. Could Bomboko bring about a coup? A day later, a member of the Belgian security agency, the Sûreté, left for Leopoldville to instigate plots to topple Lumumba. Eyskens thought about seizing the Leopoldville radio station to silence anti-Belgian propaganda, and rejected such a move only because UN soldiers were flying in. Brussels did not know just what it wanted to do with the ex-colony, but whatever it was, the natives would have no voice. Kasa-Vubu said it matter-of-factly: "Belgium disregarded us before independence, and continues to do so."[9]

General Cumont exhibited this colonial mentality. In the early afternoon of July 14, Kasa-Vubu and Lumumba suspended diplomacy. A few hours later, Cumont mortified the president and prime minister in an incident in Leopoldville, when he detoured the aircraft of the two men on its way to Stanleyville. The plane flew back to Leopoldville, circled the city, and landed only when Cumont could get to the airport himself and attempt to impose an understanding on the two Africans. They exchanged words with him but refused a conversation—in front of shouting European evacuees. The general, who despised politicians, nonetheless held clear ideas about the political course of action. He went home for brief deliberations. "Lumumba's position [is] still very strong," he told the American ambassador in Brussels. "Other Congolese . . . [are] afraid of him, and as soon as he returns to Leopoldville they cease their opposition. Only course seems to be to get rid of him."[10] After Cumont had bolstered Belgium's position, Defense Minister Gilson recalled the general: "Giving way to his warrior's disposition, Cumont tried to reconquer the Congo, and his behavior was too risky."[11] The impotent Belgian ambassador to the Congo called Gilson's policy "criminal," and General Cumont "a catastrophe."[12] The general did not throw in the towel, though. About a month later he ordered the military to kidnap Lumumba, without any reflection on the political consequences of such a measure. Soldiers were trained for the kidnapping, but in the end did not carry it out.[13]

The Dilemma of Katanga

On July 12, the day after he broadcast the separation of Katanga, Tshombe banned the landing of Kasa-Vubu's and Lumumba's plane at Luano airport

General Cumont with Kasa-Vubu and Lumumba. Cumont's desire to negotiate
was rebuffed on July 14. (*Royal Museum for Central Africa, Tervuren, Belgium*)

in Elisabethville. Both men were convinced that Belgium brought about
this traitorous act. The headstrong performance of the Belgian troops in
Katanga undoubtedly pushed Tshombe to the divorce. Another colorful
Belgian officer, Major Guy Weber, took center stage. He had commanded
the paratroopers that landed at Luano in the early morning of July 10.

A royalist patriot like Cumont, Weber did not respect elected officials in his own country, much less the African leaders. His assignment—given during a night of chaotic communications from home—was never precisely delimited, and Weber would bring his own interpretation to his directives. After he put down the mutiny of Katanga's Force Publique in Elisabethville, he reported to Tshombe, who without hesitation appointed Weber "extraordinary commissioner for the maintenance of order." Instead of evacuating the Belgians, Weber contacted the executives of the European businesses to find out under what conditions economic activity could resume. When Cumont arrived in Elisabethville on July 13, he confirmed Weber's appointment as Tshombe's military attaché.

The Belgian military aside, Tshombe got help from European companies, foremost the Union Minière du Haut Katanga, the third-greatest copper producer in the world, and the largest mining establishment in the Congo. An offspring of the Société Générale de Belgique, the primary financial and manufacturing group in Belgium, Union Minière employed more than fifteen hundred white executives and about twenty thousand black miners and servants. Through numerous related enterprises it managed vital sectors of Katanga's economy; it ran schools and hospitals and was considered a state within a state.[14] The company had long had questions about Lumumba. In March 1960, Union Minière had shuddered at his rising preeminence and that of his associates: "No doubt by July 1," wrote Union Minière's CEO, "these men will open all the big doors of the Congo to their friends in the East."[15] Union Minière had surely been sounded out before the secession occurred. The industrialist Jean-Pierre Paulus, manager of the company and Baudouin's former deputy chief of staff, said that he had encouraged a break, and cited the 1900 convention between the Congo Free State and Belgian industry about Katanga's territory to rationalize Katanga's autonomy.[16] Before noon on July 12 Union Minière in Elisabethville informed its head office in Brussels of Tshombe's declaration of independence, and recommended Belgian recognition of Katanga. The company would no longer pay taxes to the central government but to Katanga, and would make other funds available with loans. Minutes after having received this telex, Paul Gillet, the chairman of the board of Société Générale, unceremoniously telephoned Baudouin and assumed full Belgian cooperation with the breakaway regime.[17] Many Belgians were acting with a regal pretense of absolute power over the Congo.

With massive interests at stake, the secession of Katanga posed a dilemma for the government in Brussels. How could Belgium underwrite Elisabethville without immediately jeopardizing the rest of Congo and without permanently destroying its connection to Leopoldville? Brussels had resisted a split before June 30 for good reason. The Congo could barely survive minus Katanga, and an isolated Katanga could attract foreign interference.

Once again the irresolute Eyskens government found itself at loggerheads. During three crucial days, from July 12 until July 14, the ministers dithered over Katanga. Foreign Minister Wigny, aware of Belgium's international obligations, opposed secession. Defense Minister Gilson supported it, while Belgian soldiers in Elisabethville ensured a fait accompli. When Kasa-Vubu and Lumumba canceled relations with Brussels on July 14, they removed—unfortunately for themselves—a basic impediment to Belgian support for an independent Katanga. If the government of the Congo refused a connection to Brussels, why shouldn't Belgium encourage Elisabethville? Eyskens had little to lose. The UN resolution of July 14 did not prevent Brussels from going ahead. For the Eyskens government there was no need for UN troops in Katanga, where order had been restored. During the week that followed, the Katanga lobby in Brussels had its plea granted. On July 21—the Belgian National Day—Baudouin addressed his country on the radio. "Entire tribes led by honest and worthy people," the king said, "stayed friends with us, and they beseech us to help them build their independence in the middle of the chaos that was the Belgian Congo. Our duty requires us to honor every loyal request for cooperation."[18] That same day, Harold d'Aspremont Lynden was appointed by the cabinet as head of the *Mission technique belge,* the Belgian aid to Katanga. He left the next day for Elisabethville. Katanga's state-building now had become a priority of Brussels.

Count d'Aspremont and the Belgian Technical Mission

Prime Minister Eyskens employed d'Aspremont as deputy chief of staff. This Catholic aristocrat had his seat at the castle of Moufrin near the

French-speaking Ardennes, and came from an impressive political family with an old and noble lineage. His uncle Gobert, as grand marshal of the court, was part of Baudouin's inner circle. Attached to the royal family, young d'Aspremont had convictions rooted in the right-wing movements of the 1930s. Faithful to Leopold III during the German occupation and a member of the armed resistance, d'Aspremont found virtue in extreme Belgian nationalism and anticommunism. He also had connections in the financial world, and in 1961 would become manager of the Bank of Brussels. As Eyskens's deputy chief of staff, d'Aspremont had closely tracked the Congo events.

The roundtable of January–February 1960 had elevated Lumumba, and Brussels had come to worry that this unreliable man might take over the Congo. It was only after that conference that he was portrayed as pro-communist. D'Aspremont advised "political action": "The man to get rid of is Lumumba. Insist as much as possible on his contacts with foreign powers," he advised Eyskens.[19] Convincing himself of communist intrigues, d'Aspremont commissioned a Sûreté report in March of 1960 on Lumumba's ideology. For some Belgians during this period of the Cold War, communism occupied the same sort of malevolent place as it did for American public officials. For d'Aspremont the mutiny of the Force Publique and the subsequent turmoil in the Congo was due to a communist conspiracy. "The problem at hand is not just a Belgian problem," wrote d'Aspremont after a fact-finding visit to Katanga in mid-July; "it belongs to the entire Western world. If not resolved, the Congo will be communist in two months. In two years all of black Africa will be under the influence of the East."[20]

D'Aspremont dreamed of a scenario in which Katanga and other provinces in the Congo would free themselves from Leopoldville, and consequently undermine Lumumba. Then Belgium could rebuild the Congo as a federation or confederation without Lumumba. "It would be vain, and even childish, to imagine that we could ever get what we want from a Congo overseen by Lumumba and his gang. We would forfeit billions and risk the loss of lives of good men. Thus, there is only one hope: play the Katanga card and reconstruct a United States of the Congo as a confederated system."[21] According to d'Aspremont, Brussels had not just to smile on the departure of Katanga, but also to celebrate it in Kasai,

Kivu, and Équateur. In other words, Belgium would torpedo Lumumba by befriending Tshombe, as well as other anti-Lumumba regional politicians. Secession had a limited importance in itself, but multiple Katangas would destroy Lumumba and his soviet nationalism. After his mid-July trip to Elisabethville, d'Aspremont urged the Belgian cabinet to uphold Tshombe, who would accept a confederation, a loose form of an all-Congo government. Such a confederation would make it possible for Belgium to support Katanga and to keep up appearances to the outside world.

D'Aspremont was back in Elisabethville on July 23 as head of the new technical mission. That same day he met with the highest European officials to restructure the Tshombe regime. The Belgians would sort out the constitution, mint, court, and police. Over the next few days d'Aspremont urged Brussels to fly in competent people. "Our current goal," d'Aspremont told his colleagues at his arrival, "is not to obtain legal recognition. It is most important for the other provinces or regions to have the opportunity to join Katanga."[22]

Foreign Minister Wigny had been ignored in d'Aspremont's appointment. In New York deflecting the criticism of Belgium at the United Nations, he thought Eyskens incautious if not provocative. Wigny meant to supervise policy and sent to Katanga a diplomat from his own department, Ambassador Robert Rothschild. Soon, however, Rothschild himself accepted d'Aspremont's perspective. The Eyskens ministry was effectively going a long way to agreeing to an independent Katanga without consideration of international obligations or agreements with the authorities in Leopoldville. The Belgian parliament had granted sovereignty to the Congo as defined in the *loi fondamentale*. That document stated: "The Congo forms, in its actual borders, an indivisible and democratic state." Although formal Belgian diplomatic recognition of Katanga never occurred, the close informal connections made for a disturbing ongoing project.

Eyskens Resists the UN

Brussels had been indignant over the UN resolution of July 14, which would simply push Belgium out of the colony. Eyskens had not expected the demand to corral the troops, and took the position that they would remain spread over the Congo until the peacekeepers could guarantee the safety of whites. Furthermore, the Belgians did not see any reason for UN involvement in Katanga, which had established order. The eye-opener followed on July 22, when—after an ultimatum from Lumumba and strong language from the Soviet Union—a second UN resolution demanded a "speedy" withdrawal of Belgian soldiers from the Congo's territory; retiring to the bases of Kamina and Kitona would not suffice. In other words, the military presence of Belgium in the Congo that Lumumba had reluctantly accepted in the Treaty of Friendship would end. In these circumstances whites would not stay. Tension among the ministers in Brussels grew. The weak were willing to go along with the UN; Eyskens, among others, did not want to budge, and in any case wanted to stay in Katanga.[23]

Matters reached a fever pitch after a disappointing visit by Dag Hammarskjöld to Brussels on July 27. The secretary-general was in transit to the Congo, where he would negotiate with the local politicians about how to carry out the UN resolutions. Hammarskjöld anticipated that Belgium would be forthcoming and announce the retreat of its men, even from Katanga. At the same time, Hammarskjöld would not intrude into the Congo's domestic affairs. Tshombe might at least in the near future go his own way, and the UN might parley with Elisabethville before international troops would enter Katanga. The secretary-general realized that the UN forces would not get a grip on Katanga if the twenty thousand Europeans there were to leave. The next day, July 28, prodded by the UN and the Americans, Belgium did announce the recall of fifteen hundred soldiers. It was a token number, but made an important concession to Hammarskjöld and the United States. However, Eyskens did not relent on Katanga. He believed that UN troops in Elisabethville would empower Lumumba and thus ultimately end the Belgian presence. Censured at home as a coward, the Belgian prime minister also knew that powerful financial interests were at stake in Katanga and struggled to find a way to resist the pressures on Belgium. When Hammarskjöld flew a ranking assistant to Brussels for more talks, the government refused, at least publicly, to consider a deal over Katanga. But the Eyskens administration was on the brink of cracking.

Hammarskjöld and Wigny in Brussels. The secretary-general greets the Belgian foreign minister on July 27 before an unprofitable dialogue. (© *BelgaImage*)

On the evening of August 2, to the surprise of Eyskens, Hammar-skjöld declared in Leopoldville that UN troops would enter Katanga on August 6 with the consent of Brussels. Eyskens had given no such consent, but the secretary-general wanted to counter Lumumba's accusation that the UN was acting for the imperialists and to undercut the radicals in the Congo's government. When Tshombe threatened that Katanga would fight back, Hammarskjöld postponed the UN entrée into Elisabethville. Instead, on August 5, he appealed to the Security Council for a new endorsement in a meeting called for August 8. That made little difference for Belgium. The clock had started ticking. Eyskens received frightening messages from d'Aspremont that the UN soldiers would cause the whites to decamp and lead to anarchy. For d'Aspremont it was only a matter of time before not only Katanga, but also Kasai, Kivu, and even other provinces would force a confederated government on Lumumba. The Congo was on the brink of falling apart. Brussels should hold. In this crucial hour, Baudouin intervened. On August 5, the king called for Eyskens and insisted on the resignation of the cabinet. Within forty-eight hours he wanted a new group of ministers who would pursue more vigorous imperial formulas.

To Reinvent the Constitution

How do kings and queens carry on in a constitutional monarchy, governments like Great Britain, Sweden, or the Netherlands, and also Belgium? Americans find these European countries acceptable but perhaps in the twenty-first century quaint in their commitment to royalty. The typical view holds that these nations started off with a ruler all-powerful because of divine right. But slowly, over the centuries, the crown gave up its political fiat as democratically elected legislatures became more important. Today, a king wields only symbols; he receives worthy visitors, opens public gatherings, and speaks at solemn occasions. Whereas politicians are obsequious to the king in front of cameras, behind the public politeness, the figurehead follows those who are elected. In the United States, the president has both procedural and executive authority. In constitutional monarchies the king presides over ceremonies, while an elected politician, upheld by a majority of the parliamentary legislature, runs the government as prime minister. The politicians convey their programs to the king and receive his blessing, but blessing he has to give.

Reality differed in Belgium. The Europeans gave the Congo to Leopold II as an individual. Later, Leopold single-handedly bequeathed the Congo as a colony to Belgium, and in 1940 Leopold III, on his own, surrendered the Belgian army to the Germans. However, the monarchy acceded to limits. In the late 1940s the legislators forced Baudouin's father out. The abdication had left a bad taste in the mouths of those around the throne. The bad taste did not mean, however, that the royals would give up. The constitution said that the king "appoints and dismisses his ministers," and so, according to his entourage, he did not need the approval of parliamentarians. Nonetheless, a *government* could not carry on without the trust of the members of parliament, and so the sovereign, from the second half of the nineteenth century on, had to accept the ruling bodies forged by politicians. Governments had become governments of parliament and of political parties, not governments of the king. The king's men would contest this essential premise of constitutional democracy in the twentieth century.

Baudouin and the Eyskens government had a poor relationship. When the parliament had cast aside the old king in 1950, the monarch's misgivings about the politicians had reached a crescendo. Leopold III's continued presence in the palace kept the Royal Question alive, and by the late 1950s the Congo exacerbated the cleavage between democratic and antidemocratic impulses in Belgium. The colony fueled mistrust on both sides, and primordial domestic hatreds exposed themselves in competing Congo policies. Would the politicians who forced the abdication of Leopold III and who still held power in 1960—Eyskens, Wigny, De Schryver—now squander the Congo, the inheritance of the dynasty? That thought was unbearable to Baudouin and his courtiers. The Lumumba regime had been transformed into a Rorschach test about the nature of Belgium and its democratic dogmas.

The roundtable of January–February 1960 had rocked Baudouin, who since his trip to the Congo in 1955 had conceived an almost romantic connection to the colony. To salvage what he could, he had convened a "Crown Council" on February 18, 1960. Such a council traditionally gathered acting ministers and other members of the political elite—designated "ministers of state." While it did not have any constitutional authority, such a meeting of elders gave Baudouin a forum to express criticism of the current anemic politicians, and to pose critical questions about the future. In February, however, the king had found no rapport with his audience, which had accepted the Congo's speedy and unconditional independence as unavoidable.[24]

The ceremony in Leopoldville on June 30 had next affronted Baudouin. His adviser and his father's, Jacques Pirenne, had written the speech that extolled the genius of Leopold II and urged the Africans to learn respect for democracy. On July 9, urgently recalled from Lourdes as the Congo crisis unfolded, Baudouin secretly sat down with Pirenne before an appointment with Eyskens. The young king was bullheaded enough not to accept the need for circumspect advice even were it offered, but Pirenne, who appeared still to believe in the divine right of monarchs, did not counsel prudence. Pirenne dictated a letter that Baudouin gave to the prime minister that evening. Disregarding respect for parliamentary government, Baudouin prodded Eyskens to form a partnership of national union with the three major parties. According to Pirenne, such a partnership would fortify the king.[25] Eyskens did not immediately say no, but the next day the government turned Baudouin down: he did not create governments, the political parties did. This did not intimidate the king. He recommended instead the appointment of the Socialist opposition leader as a minister of state and called for a new Crown Council. The government refused to concur. After the UN resolution of July 14, Baudouin wanted to speak to the Security Council in New York, and the Belgian government yet again declined the king's wish.

On the National Day of July 21, however, Baudouin addressed the nation on the radio, again inspired by Pirenne. This was the speech that implicitly condemned Lumumba and praised Tshombe. Katanga now had Baudouin's undivided attention. On July 27 he had a private interview, very much against the will of Foreign Minister Wigny, with UN Secretary-General Hammarskjöld, then in Brussels. Baudouin followed up and wrote the secretary-general, defending the presence of Belgian troops in Congo and lobbying about Katanga.[26] A week later Baudouin's involvement reached a climax. On August 4 he saw Katanga officials and their military adviser, Major Weber. The party leader of the Christian Democrats, alerted by this meeting, formally warned the king not to precipitate another Royal Question. Still, the UN was poised to enter Katanga and force the Belgians out. The next day—August 5—an immovable Baudouin made his daring move and told Eyskens to leave office.[27]

The fierce and persistent criticism that the government had endured— the press was also demanding that Eyskens quit—gave Baudouin traction; he additionally insinuated that the ministers exuded incompetence. For some Belgians, too, the king held special power over the struggling political parties and could save the nation from degradation.[28] Public protest singled out not only parliament, but also the UN and the United States, which had deserted Belgium. Pirenne advised Baudouin to do nothing to indicate solidarity with the governing politicians. A vigorous Eyskens depended on a limp group of ministers, and confronted a monarchical interest incompletely committed to the constitution. The US embassy reported the tense situation and even noticed a threat to future relations among the Western allies. The Belgian ambassador at NATO, André De Staercke, told the Americans that "the failure of this [antidemocratic] movement to gain momentum up to now [the last week in July] can probably be attributed . . . to the happy circumstance that no able demagogue has so far appeared on the scene to take advantage of it. The principal hope in this situation is probably for an eventual return of [NATO head Paul-Henri] Spaak, but if resentment against the regime becomes too closely associated with NATO and with the policy of the western solidarity, even Spaak's oratorical talents may not be sufficient to channel things in a better direction."[29]

In February 1950, on the eve of the events that would deny the throne to Baudouin's father, Eyskens—then prime minister for the first time— had confided in the American ambassador: "In the long run it didn't make a difference . . . who exactly was king, because his job was to do as he was told by the prime minister if not playing golf or climbing mountains."[30] Now, on August 5, 1960, some ten years later, the young king pressed Eyskens to depart. In forty-eight hours, according to Baudouin, a new government had to be in place. The king allowed that he was negotiating with Spaak and Paul Van Zeeland, another celebrity of Belgian politics and an ally of the crown. Van Zeeland had been a successful prime minister in the 1930s and, for several years after the war, minister of foreign affairs.

Only two ministers of state, Spaak and Van Zeeland, had upheld the king during the Crown Council of February. In August Baudouin found them his last hope to turn the tide against spineless legislators and their policies of appeasement. Although a Christian Democrat, Van Zeeland had early on promoted Spaak. Each had challenged his own party, and each held the other in high esteem. Baudouin envisaged a new kind of non-parliamentary rule of "strong and wise men," a "cabinet of affairs." Baudouin and his rightist advisers meant to regenerate the monarchical privileges of the constitution of one hundred years earlier.

Negotiations between Spaak and Van Zeeland proceeded with difficulty. Katanga divided them. Van Zeeland wanted to recognize it, Spaak hesitated. While Van Zeeland had ambitions to become minister of foreign affairs once more, Spaak pointed out Van Zeeland's connection with financial groups in the Congo, which would weaken his position. Deliberations continued into the second week of August and lost momentum. The plans leaked and opponents stirred. Eyskens, who initially had accepted the inevitable fact of a new cabinet and who had not contradicted Baudouin on August 5, found his backbone. At an August 9 press conference he ushered in a new set of programs. Among other things he would cut the ground from under those antagonistic to government spending by reducing Belgium's contribution to NATO. This move away from the Western alliance would moreover allow him to set a new course in the Congo.[31]

On August 10, Eyskens offered to step down as prime minister. Baudouin was not satisfied and stipulated that the entire cabinet quit. In the afternoon the ministers decided to go along on one condition: Baudouin must charge Eyskens with the formation of a new government. They wanted to prevent the formation of a cabinet of affairs and the dissolution of parliament. When the king refused to accept any conditions, the ministers decided not to resign. The Eyskens government would thwart the king. Spaak, who had arrived the night of August 10 from NATO headquarters in Paris to negotiate with the monarch, soon had to conclude that Baudouin's initiative had failed. "The royal coup did not succeed," the American embassy later commented, although the disputes over Lumumba had nearly torn down Belgian democracy.[32]

Sovereign Victories

On August 17, Eyskens appeared before the Belgian parliament and asked for a vote of confidence. He acted to provoke the "strong men" behind the curtains who had come close to pulling him under. The Eyskens government had the votes, but was still so feeble that the prime minister began a give-and-take of his own to rearrange his cabinet. He did not have it easy. Trust between the two government parties—the Liberals and Christian Democrats—had evaporated. The prime minister did not have a new team until September 3. Ganshof van der Meersch had already left, contemptuous about the acquiescence over the Congo. Eyskens fired De Schryver and Scheyven, and Harold d'Aspremont Lynden took over with sole authority as minister of African affairs.

Foreign Minister Wigny was the real loser. A nondescript man in his mid-fifties, Wigny had a background in international and constitutional law, and a PhD from Harvard in international affairs. Indeed, he authored textbooks on the subjects, and tended toward the academic, lecturing his auditors in numbered paragraphs. But he also presumed that his verbal inventions would automatically be transformed into policy deeds. Wigny had something of the character of a shifty and Jesuitical lawyer. When d'Aspremont was promoted to minister of African affairs, Wigny rightly worried that the more forceful aristocrat would take Congo decision-making along a more direct path than the slippery Wigny would have followed.

Baudouin lost the war, and Belgium remained democratic. But he won a significant battle, and put the fear of God into the weak-kneed politicians. Eyskens fought the royal arrogation of national authority, but his new ministry bent to the retrograde policy of the palace. To save constitutional rule in Belgium, the Eyskens administration would take an imperial turn in the Congo, and the forceful ideas of Baudouin would be strengthened.

Whatever determination Baudouin infused into the Eyskens ministers, the international community appeared united against Belgium, and a rout appeared likely. The UN forced Belgium to agree to international stewardship for the Congo that, from the Brussels perspective, kept Lumumba in the saddle. Lumumba expelled the Belgian ambassador from Leopoldville on August 9. From early July about forty-five thousand Belgians had run off or been repatriated. Of the roughly eighty thousand Belgians in the Congo at the time of independence, an estimated thirty or thirty-five thousand remained, twenty thousand of them in Katanga.[33] On August 4 the Belgian troops outside Katanga had been restricted to their bases, and by the end of the month they had left the Congo. The recall of the military from Katanga itself began on August 10 and was completed at the beginning of September. A ranking diplomat watched in Elisabethville as Belgian soldiers left Katanga: "I could not help thinking of the retreat of the legions and the opening to barbarism of a new edge of the Roman Empire."[34]

Yet despite their weakened position, the Belgians saw glimmers of hope that they might carry on victoriously in their former colony. From July 22 to August 8 Lumumba was out of his country, touring the United States, Canada, and parts of Africa. His absence made it easier to encourage antinational sentiment in the Congo. On August 9, in Elisabethville, Albert Kalonji proclaimed the independence of a southern district of Kasai and received d'Aspremont's assistance. The same day Hammarskjöld got a new UN resolution. The peacekeepers would enter Katanga, and the Belgian military would leave, but Tshombe would remain in power, and the status quo between him and Lumumba would not be disturbed; the UN would stay neutral on this "internal" question. The Belgians found some unexpected allies on a widening anti-Lumumba front. Brussels might contrive to maintain its hold after all.

On August 18, just before he won his parliamentary vote of confidence, Eyskens had a conversation with Jef Van Bilsen, a Belgian adviser of Kasa-Vubu. The prime minister gave Van Bilsen, about to fly back to the Congo, an urgent piece of information: tell Kasa-Vubu, the king-like figure, that he had the constitutional prerogative to fire Lumumba.[35] Baudouin admonished the blacks to accept democratic discipline, but refused to take his own advice. Now Eyskens communicated to Kasa-Vubu that the Congo's head of state might do precisely what, according to Eyskens, Baudouin in Belgium could not.

CHAPTER FOUR

The Cold War Comes to Africa

D WIGHT EISENHOWER was having a hard year. Indisputably the most significant world politician, "Ike" had global personal appeal. He had begun his presidency in 1953 by ending the Korean War, which had pitted troops of the United States against those from communist China. Popular and successful in the 1950s, he was finishing his second and constitutionally final term of office that would close in January 1961. As time ran out, however, power seeped away from him. Many critics thought his Republican administration was ending wearily. Eisenhower could not damp down the Cold War, or restrain the dangerous competition of the nuclear arms race. While his prudence was legendary, the president himself felt frustrated. Many times he would deliver ill-humored entreaties and half-frivolous injunctions to his subordinates. His presidency was concluding with little action and a great deal of grumpy talk.

Eisenhower had made his reputation in World War II through an invasion of German-occupied Europe in aid of Britain, France, and the Low Countries. By the end of the war, he was committed to an American role on the Continent. In 1951 he became the first military commander of NATO, the security alliance centered on the Western European countries and the United States. Almost single-handedly Eisenhower dragged his Republican Party to an Atlantic internationalism. NATO shielded the West in its battle against the USSR, but, as important, Eisenhower used NATO to craft a more durable combination of democracies—a European union. NATO had supreme geopolitical importance, and the president took special care to fortify its institutions and to promote cooperation within its cohort.[1]

For Eisenhower this job resembled herding cats, despite his collegial association with Europe's leaders. England under Harold Macmillan's prime ministership cherished a special relationship with the United States and stood off from Europe. Charles de Gaulle had an entirely unrealistic idea about the greatness of France. Konrad Adenauer, whose West Germany had been admitted to NATO in 1955, constantly needed reassurance and often had inappropriate longings for an independent Germany. Eisenhower saw the Dutch and the Belgians as the good soldiers of the alliance, small but buoyed up by the attention they received and eager to please. By urging conciliation, the two countries could increase their weight at the bargaining table.

The rise of emerging nations perplexed and sometimes dismayed the president. The Republicans recognized that the "developing world" influenced the Cold War. Washington also knew that it needed to remind these countries of America's own past as a dependent of England, sympathize with the later colonies, and chaperone them gradually to freedom. Yet Eisenhower could not adjust adroitly to the issues of imperialism. His invaluable NATO colleagues, many old friends, represented the powers forced to disgorge their empires. The United States allowed the British and French—and the Belgians and Dutch—to take the lead in colonial matters. In 1956 the Americans had sabotaged the British and French in a dispute respecting Egypt's Suez Canal. Eisenhower had made an agonizing choice. He had damaged the West in alienating his allies, and would not again act against their direct interests. He never understood, finally, the critical nature of color prejudice. At the end of 1960, because of the president's last-minute personal decision, the United States abstained in an emblematic UN vote condemning colonialism. The entire US delegation had wanted to vote for the resolution, and one member stood up and applauded when it was adopted.[2]

Eisenhower's lack of success in enlisting a group of "modern" Republicans compounded his trials. Instead, Vice President Richard Nixon appeared as the heir apparent. Even after this party warhorse obtained the Republican nomination for the presidency in the summer of 1960, Eisenhower did not esteem Nixon, and unenthusiastically campaigned for the younger man. The American people didn't like Nixon all that much either. In November of 1960 he would lose a close election to an untried Democratic senator, John F. Kennedy. Eisenhower would believe that, because of Nixon, the voters had repudiated the president's legacy. He got it only partially correct. Kennedy convinced a tiny plurality of American voters of the worn-out nature of the administration. Sixty-nine that year, Eisenhower and the men around him were aging, a little long in the tooth, forceful yet stuck with whatever ideas they had acquired since his rise. In his early forties, Kennedy said "we" had to get the country moving again, especially in foreign policy, and proclaimed "a new frontier." Eisenhower surely took a tough enough stance with the Russians—Kennedy knew enough not to attack the former general frontally. Kennedy intimated, however, that the Republicans lacked creativity in dealing with communism. Instead of simply proclaiming the malevolence of the USSR and threatening countries aligned with it, the United States had to show how and why democracy had more attractions. Kennedy would act more flexibly than Eisenhower.

World affairs made Kennedy's point. In far off Southeast Asia, revolutionary fires were burning in Laos and Vietnam. First in command in the Soviet Union, Nikita Khrushchev pledged to fan anticapitalist flames. Eisenhower fussed that matters were getting out of hand. What had seemed a settled world just five years ago had faded away. Eisenhower and his national security managers felt embattled. To citizens in the United States the administration might not have appeared listless, but Republicans looked as if they did not know exactly what to do.

The greatest test lay in Cuba. The United States had historically dictated to this island just off the coast of Florida, but in the late 1950s a revolution had toppled the repressive American-backed regime of Fulgencio Batista. Initially the United States had gingerly acknowledged Cuba's new ruler, Fidel Castro, a bearded wild-looking young man of thirty-four who wore military fatigues. Castro soon proclaimed his loyalty to communism, however, and Khrushchev welcomed him as a partner. Tensions heightened during this era. In April 1961, the United States would fail in a humiliating attempt to overthrow Castro at Cuba's Bay of Pigs, and in 1962 the volcano of the Cold War would erupt in the Cuban Missile Crisis. Even in 1959 and 1960, however, Americans worried about Castro. Policy makers in Washington were more than worried; the communist foothold on America's doorstep enraged them. Frightened national security officials—who now appear to have been unhinged—were tempted to talk about Castro as a target for assassination.

Castro was proof of Kennedy's criticism. Eisenhower had not prevented communism in Cuba. Kennedy pointed to a rising nationalism, especially the surge against European colonialism. The United States had to recall its own origins in the American War of Independence, and show itself a friend to people ruled by others. Then, the United States might constructively guide impulses to self-government. Instead, Eisenhower had stood pat, and his association with the Europeans in NATO had joined him at the hip with empire. On the contrary, Kennedy would convince the colonies that the United States sided with them, and not with the imperialists. Kennedy had an effective critique—especially with Cuba staring Americans in the face. He proclaimed his assessment far more easily than he would ever act on it, for cheering anticolonialism would certainly alienate the Europeans, something Kennedy would not risk.

In 1947 the Andrews Sisters had a hit song, "Civilization," about a girl who wanted to stay in Africa: "Bingo, Bango, Bongo, I Don't Want to Leave the Congo." The singing group the Jayhawks followed this tune in 1956 with their rock 'n' roll record "Stranded in the Jungle," about a teenager trying to get back to the United States for a date. The lyrics suggested the way Africa was coming into the heads of ordinary citizens. Americans learned what they knew about the continent from Tarzan movies.[3] In the late 1950s a new scholarly specialty of African Studies took hold, and the Department of State formed an African section. The knowledge of experts, such as it was, however, hardly reached decision makers, who gave no priority to Africa. Eisenhower tiptoed around the independence of Ghana and Guinea in the late 1950s, and the State Department took its cues from the Europeans. Americans had discovered the Congo in the 1940s and early 1950s because of the necessity of its uranium for nuclear bombs, but for several years other sources had put the Congo on a back burner. At least two top-level governmental discussions of 1960 found that the Congo's uranium no longer had a vital interest for the United States.[4]

In 1960 Kennedy's politicking drew a Republican focus to Africa. By the late 1950s, too, a domestic issue impressed itself on Eisenhower in respect to decolonization. In the United States the civil rights movement called attention to the Jim Crow social system in the South. African Americans often could not vote there, and lived separate, demeaning lives. While civil rights developed into a bigger trouble under Kennedy, even in the last years of the Eisenhower administration the African American fight in the South echoed the African quest to be free of Europe. How could the United States sympathize with anti-imperialism if the country did not allow its own people to vote? Africans pushing for freedom doubted the goodwill of the United States if it kept its own black citizens down.

Kennedy would manage this problem better than Eisenhower. To some extent, age framed the issue. Younger Democrats tended toward indulgent courtesy, pronounced the names of the Africans correctly, and talked about American Negroes. Top Republican officials scarcely knew the location of African places—Mali, Guinea, Nigeria. And who were these people anyway, Lumumba, Kasa-Vubu, Tshombe? Republicans reckoned that the Africans had only recently come "down from the trees"—a favorite phrase that also appeared in both British and French-speaking policy circles. Eisenhower had little sense of the ambitions of people of color anywhere. A genteel disdain also pervaded his civil-rights politics at home. Richard Nixon led the Republicans in his sensitivity to Africa and its connection to domestic issues, although Nixon also regularly spoke about the ignorant natives overseas and, at home, the Colored, or the nigs.[5]

As the independence of the Congo loomed, the Eisenhower administration did the required minimum. At the ceremonies on June 30, Robert Murphy, a diplomat of some ability who had served as ambassador to Belgium from 1949 to 1952, delivered the good wishes of the United States; he had just retired as an under secretary in the Department of State. America upgraded the consulate in the old Belgian Congo but sent an undistinguished career official, Clare Timberlake. Finally, the United

States had launched a CIA post in the Congo, although the "chief of station," Larry Devlin, did not show up until July. Eisenhower gave little thought to the Congo, though the Americans showed the flag in June. They assumed the new nation would remain the purview of the Belgians. During much of 1960, Cuba and Castro absorbed the United States. The Congo only briefly if intensely received attention, but rudely awakened the president from time to time.

The United States Decides on Policy

Kasa-Vubu and Lumumba's supplication to Russia of July 13 was, as we have noted, one of several impulsive cries for help. The cry—and a broader one of July 19—at once prompted American concern about Soviet influence in central Africa. Yet Eisenhower was not interested in a confrontation in the Congo, and he and Secretary of State Christian Herter decided that the UN would forward US interests in this time of uncertainty, when American officials were throwing up various competing proposals.[6] The pro-Western United Nations had large debts to the United States, and in addition the United States would pay for much of the Congo operation of the UN. Its leadership regularly consulted not only with the US delegation to the United Nations in New York, but also with American diplomats in Washington. The peacekeepers would do whatever fighting had to be undertaken, and many of the African nations who contributed troops received training courtesy of the United States and purchased military equipment at a discount. More or less at American bidding, the United Nations might dampen the conflict in the just-born nation. The Americans soon had an understanding that Secretary-General Hammarskjöld would contain Lumumba. Herter and Eisenhower, nonetheless, underestimated the tensions that might flow from a commitment to the UN's diplomacy. To keep Lumumba in his place Hammarskjöld would have to moderate Belgian demands; in backing the UN, the Americans might find themselves at odds with Brussels.

Over and over, the United States called its policy "keeping the Cold War out of the Congo." The expression referred to how the Americans would fight the Cold War there—ensuring that the end of colonialism would not benefit the Soviet Union.

Lumumba made the policy awkward. The Americans knew little about him, but what they did know distressed them. Although he had asked for US help, he had also implied he would take help from communists. While Fidel Castro had at first denied communism, he also had lied. The fast-talking Lumumba looked at the least militant, and in any event untrust-worthy. The revolution in Cuba and the dangerous Castro were the lens through which American decision-makers viewed the Congo. In the middle of July, American intelligence attributed Belgian fears of Lumumba to the fact that Brussels took him for "a budding Castro."[7]

"I Am a Nationalist"

What was Lumumba committed to? At the end of 1958—he was then thirty-three—he had attended a meeting of African politicians in Ghana, the All-African Peoples' Conference. His intelligence and ability impressed the African leaders—especially Ghana's first prime minister, Kwame Nkrumah. Lumumba's inchoate ideas about colonialism and independence crystallized, and he defined his politics via these talks in Ghana. A "Pan-Africanist," he saw the continent as the bearer of its own heritage. Pan-Africanists wanted the Europeans out so that the Africans could foster their own social order. Lumumba later even deliberated with Nkrumah over a union of black African countries—the groundwork of a United States of Africa. Nkrumah occupied a pedestal as a man on the left. However, as intemperate as Lumumba might be—more so than his mentor Nkrumah—Lumumba could not and would not be labeled a Marxist. He wanted technical assistance from Belgium and the West, but would not side with either the United States or the Soviet Union. Lumumba hoped that his Congo would follow this policy of "positive neutralism." He might use nonalignment to curry favors from America or Russia. With their help he would promote a distinctive African Congo.

The French philosopher Jean-Paul Sartre wrote perceptively about French-speaking colonies. He compared Lumumba to Robespierre, the architect of the Terror of the French Revolution of the late eighteenth century. Intrigued by political bloodshed, Sartre intended his comparison as a high compliment to Lumumba, even if he foolishly hinted that

Lumumba had a taste for mass murder. But Sartre grasped another dimension of Lumumba's political personality. Expedient in his dealings with the great powers, the prime minister did not waver in his patriotism. Like the courageous and incorruptible Robespierre, Lumumba believed he could will his peoples into a national accord. Using only his eloquence, he would take the Congolese to an ambitious statehood and make them citizens.[8]

In the commotion of July and August 1960 a variety of Marxist hangers-on did advise Lumumba, but the record shows little to mark him as a revolutionary. On July 22, just before he made a trip to the United States, he publicized a comprehensive financial agreement with a shady American entrepreneur who Lumumba mistakenly thought spoke for US business interests. The prime minister was looking to foil Belgium by replacing the colonizers with Americans, and Union Minière worriedly analyzed the arrangement in these terms.[9] It came to nothing because the entrepreneur was untrustworthy and because the Americans did not want to deal with Lumumba in any case, but the negotiations were hardly the work of a communist. In late August, back in the Congo, Lumumba delivered a bitter radio attack on imperialism. At the same time his government would send 150 students to the USSR, and 300 to the United States, in keeping with an earlier American promise. American policy makers parenthetically but recurrently noted not the communism of Lumumba but his unreliability. He was a man whom they could buy but who would not stay bought. The Central Intelligence Agency's analysts in Washington again and again referred to Lumumba's expediency. The State Department's intelligence division emphasized that nothing substantiated the allegation of Lumumba's communism or communist sympathies, and noted his own description of himself as an African nationalist. Of all the appraisals of Lumumba, the most reasonable was that of a State Department official who wrote: "an unscrupulous opportunist and probably the most able and dynamic politician in the Congo. . . . Ideologically he is probably not faithful to either East or West, nor is he likely to be prejudiced against accepting aid from either side."[10]

The most edifying comment the prime minister made about his values came early on in July 1960, when he warned that he might call in the "Bandung powers." This loose association of African and Asian nations had held a congress in Indonesia in 1955. The group included Pakistan, a partner of the United States, and China, a partner of the USSR. It did not include the important nonaligned European country Yugoslavia.[11] This affiliation most accurately expressed Lumumba's politics—an alliance of nations of color. Such a vision tinted Lumumba's Pan-Africanism.

Another variable finally put the Lumumba ministry in context. Western diplomats were aware that communism in the Congo might have to take a backseat to its quirky governance. In July, before Kasa-Vubu and Lumumba had broken relations with Brussels, an eminent Belgian diplomat arrived in Leopoldville. Another high-level Belgian official greeted him at the airport: "Welcome to the country of Marx—not Karl, but Groucho."[12] The Congo was on a tragic course, but there was also a slapstick ingredient to its politics.

Three Anticommunist Voices

Little of this mattered to important American leaders. Ignoring complexity, people in the Eisenhower administration wanted to move beyond cooperation with the UN and hunted for ways to reduce Lumumba's influence. In addition to State Department diplomats, three intriguing but uninformed men devised actions: Allen Dulles, head of the CIA; Ambassador William Burden in Belgium; and the CIA's man in Leopoldville, Larry Devlin. These officials generated their ideas on the basis of little evidence, and much of it had a bearing different from what they took from it. These functionaries told themselves and others that Lumumba would take Africa to communism, and so they must run him off the rails.

Allen Dulles, long-serving director of the CIA, came from a wealthy family of Princeton graduates. He acquired expertise in clandestine operations during World War II in the Office of Strategic Services (OSS), the predecessor of the CIA. Commentators have noted that Dulles's self-conscious and self-confident ethical absolutism buoyed him in a job that required choices that many others found unpalatable. Historians have also found the man exemplary of the moral complacency that overtook the United States during the competition with the Soviet Union. Dulles compartmentalized his life. Legendary in his ability to keep governmental secrets, he could also be surprisingly indiscreet. Insiders compared his closemouthedness about his job to his notorious philandering. Dulles, friends lamented, seemed to delight in the almost public humiliation of his wife that his dalliances involved. Highly placed bureaucrats moreover complained that he did not competently administer his agency. Dulles, they said, did not attend to the collection and interpretation of information pertinent to national security, but only to the cloak-and-dagger work, where he had a reputation as the consummate spy. By the end of the decade Dulles's management of the CIA was under heavy fire. Like Eisenhower, the director was tired and not doing his homework.

Under Eisenhower, the National Security Council (NSC) had charge of foreign policy. Dulles would often ready briefings for its weekly meetings in the summer of 1960 at the last moment, after hurriedly reading some recent cables, as concerned with his beloved but mediocre Washington Senators baseball team as with the security of the United States. While Dulles had played varsity sports at Princeton, he now had gout, which he relieved in his handsome office by elevating his foot to his desk while he listened to the Senators' afternoon games on the radio and received reports about covert actions.[13]

What little diplomats knew about African politics, or the Congo specifically, hardly percolated up to Dulles, who did not attend to his own analysts on the Congo. He did equate much that was unknown and strange with communism and the Soviet Union, and additionally found it easy to discover threats that only clandestine deeds could foil. Dulles soon detested the militant Lumumba, who could bring to the Congo what Fidel Castro had brought to Cuba. Dulles wanted Lumumba sidetracked, and urged action by the CIA. Dulles might then counter the arguments of bureaucrats who wanted him to manage his department better, stick to intelligence gathering, avoid adventurism, and leave policy to others.

On July 15 Dulles told the NSC of Lumumba's "especially antiwestern" character. Secretary of State Herter said that went "too far." Overall, said Herter, the UN operation satisfied the Belgians—which was untrue—and he asked for caution. The State Department was preparing a report on Africa, and when it was finished, the United States should review its policy. The president was not present at this meeting, but Dulles raised a maximum alarm; the danger of Lumumba could hardly await a diplomatic paper. Less than a week later, on July 21, Dulles remarked to his colleagues in the NSC that in the Congo "a Castro or worse" faced America.[14] Dulles was echoing the ideas of his friend, American ambassador to Belgium William Burden.

Burden was born into the colossally rich Vanderbilt family. He had a background in aviation and finance but for over ten years, from 1950 to 1961, also served on the board of the American Eugenics Society. Unreflective and unintelligent, Burden used his great wealth and the contacts that came from it to secure upper-level governmental experience, socializing with monied internationally oriented Republicans. While he gained expertise in Washington bureaus dealing with air warfare, as a great connoisseur of art and a gourmand, Burden yearned more than anything else to receive the embassy in Paris. There he would have the legacy of American icons such as Benjamin Franklin and Thomas Jefferson, and most lately Burden's old friend Douglas Dillon, who had progressed from ambassador to France to under secretary of state. As Burden's granddaughter would put it, however, "a president would have been mad to appoint a man who was as mentally and physically competent as a bug on Raid." When Eisenhower awarded Burden the distinctly second prize of Belgium toward the end of 1959, his wife complained that the capstone of her husband's career had come with a menial post in a small country. But the Belgians' love of good food and drink came to satisfy the Burdens. In addition to their Cadillac automobile, the couple took with them to Brussels their butler, their French chef, and an enormous quantity of wine. Burden also obtained in Europe a "superb cellar of Bordeaux wines, including fifty cases of irreplaceable Château Blanc, 1947." Two truckloads were delivered to the embassy in Brussels. A number of the family's favorite French masterpieces decorated the embassy and were also lent to museums in Brussels.

Surrounded by a drug-addicted, suicidal, and dysfunctional family, the Burdens' personal lives held difficulties and sadness. Each year the ambassador and his wife spent three weeks in clinics to dry out, and both later died of alcohol-related illnesses.

However, the couple overcame the slight of not receiving Paris. They excelled at dinner parties in Brussels, and adored its high society and the royalty that France lacked. About the only thing the Burdens did not like in Belgium was a shooting match that their bigwig friends organized to kill off hundreds of small animals—"the hunt"; the couple let it be known that they preferred to eat game and not to kill it.[15]

The genuine game was Lumumba. Burden had not expected that Brussels might make its new American ambassador a Franklin, Jefferson, or Dillon. Yet as luck would have it, Burden ended up the right man in the right place at the right time. He had no knowledge of Belgium or the Congo, but was "wisely advised" in Brussels. His memoirs reveal little of policy, more because of the man's own mindlessness than because of any attempt to conceal. His ideas likely derived from the CIA in Brussels, and from his diplomatic staff. In March 1960, he and his wife took a high-powered tourists' journey through the Belgian Congo. The ambassador's visit coincided with the Belgian Sûreté's report to d'Aspremont on Lumumba's supposed communism, and Burden told the Department of State that America could not permit the Congo to go to the left after independence. From mid-July, after Leopoldville fell apart, Burden counseled Washington on Lumumba. On July 19 he told Herter to "destroy" the Lumumba government and to encourage a confederated Congo.[16]

Absorbing the Belgian perspective, Burden barraged Washington with memos asking for greater sympathy for the imperialists, and assistance for the financial troubles attendant on the end of the colonial regime. He understood, he told Secretary Herter, why the United States would look at issues from the point of view of the Congo. Nevertheless, America should instead pressure the UN to support Belgium.[17] At the end of July Burden briefed Dulles when he returned to Washington for discussions. From Europe, Burden would continue as a mouthpiece for the more rabid anticommunism guiding Dulles's reports to the NSC.

Larry Devlin had been a CIA agent from the late 1940s. In 1958 he began spying for the CIA in Brussels, where he had a cover position as an attaché. He recruited Soviets, befriended members of the Belgian Sûreté, and made contacts with the Congo's politicians, who came to Belgium for various deliberations. Devlin chauffeured and guarded Dulles when he called at the Belgian capital. Although Devlin did not take up his post until later, in the second part of 1959 he was appointed the first chief of station to what would be an independent Congo. In March 1960, he went there with Burden, introduced himself to more *évolués,* and then hosted them when they came to Brussels before independence. A charming and efficient man, Devlin returned to Leopoldville more or less permanently in early July just after the Congo went into free fall. A tabula rasa when it came to Africa, Devlin could still produce standard and fervent clichés about Russia. At one point he counted the arrival of "several hundred" Soviet personnel, most of whom the CIA assumed were intelligence officers; an expert on the USSR in the Congo can confirm *three.* Devlin quickly learned, he later related, that his job entailed formulating for the CIA the specific policies he should carry out, for he had the competence.[18]

In the new Congo, fluent French rewarded Devlin, who had married a Frenchwoman and spoke the language well. The country's leaders publicly conversed in French. The United Nations also specified French as one of its languages, but many UN functionaries—including Ralph Bunche—spoke English, which almost no African politicians in the Congo had mastered. Just as the Belgians might employ Flemish as a code when they did not want the locals to understand the whites, the blacks might talk among themselves in an African language like Lingala, which the military used in rudimentary form. Different communities in the Congo did not exchange views easily or straightforwardly. Many deliberations required an interpreter to translate documents and to facilitate discussion.

The Belgians all conversed in French to the Africans, but most of the Africans, even in Katanga, mistrusted the Belgians. Could the Africans turn comfortably to any whites? From the black point of view, the UN and the colonialists each cast doubt on the other. Together they gave Devlin a space. Many of the Africans took Devlin to epitomize the United States. This different, powerful, interest might keep other forces at bay, and the politicians could understand Devlin as well as any European. Some of the Congo's senior officials and politicians, Devlin wrote, quickly became agents: the CIA paid them to inform, or they undertook undercover jobs for him. Devlin did what he could to undermine Lumumba, and almost at once he was suggesting to his new friends that they "get rid of" the prime minister.[19]

Dulles the master of espionage, Burden the diplomat, and Devlin the operative all came to the fore in framing Washington's perception of Lumumba.

Lumumba in Washington

On July 22, Lumumba embarked on a critical trip that took him first to New York to castigate the United Nations for its deficiencies, and then to Washington to secure goodwill and money from the United States. Before Lumumba set foot on US soil, the official policy put him on a leash held by the UN. In Washington Lumumba did not meet with Eisenhower, who maintained his distance on a vacation in Newport, Rhode Island. Instead, Secretary Herter and Under Secretary of State Dillon gave Lumumba a first-class reception. The prime minister received a nineteen-gun salute when he got to Washington. The diplomats put him up at the guest residence for dignitaries, Blair House, across the street from the White House. According to CIA sources Lumumba asked for "a blond girl," and the CIA procured one, although the result of the assignation is unclear.[20] In the negotiations, Herter gave Lumumba nothing and circumvented all queries over aid. The State Department emphasized that the UN would tend to the Congo's legitimate needs, and coordinated this policy with the United Nations.[21] Although the reactions of US diplomats to Lumumba were mixed, he did not get what he wanted. If the prime minister did not get the message, he was a slow learner of international politics: the Congo was to be a ward of the UN.

Then Lumumba took off for Canada, apparently thinking it was exclusively French-speaking. He brusquely negotiated with the Canadians for bilateral assistance that would include Francophone technicians. Ottawa took the US position that all help would come through the UN, and Lumumba changed course and merely tried to attract French-speaking experts to the Congo. A NATO member and modest ally of America, Canada was not known for its extravagant politics. But its representatives found Lumumba "vain, petty, suspicious and perhaps unscrupulous."[22] Moreover, he met with Soviet officials in Ottawa. Now the United States had further confirmation of the danger of the prime minister.

Ambassador Clare Timberlake and CIA station head Devlin had received their postings to the Congo only a few weeks before. Washington took the opportunity of the Lumumba trip to have both of them—as well as Burden—report in person to their bosses.[23] While Herter and Dillon gave Lumumba the runaround, Devlin voiced his anticommunist fears to Dulles. The older and more senior man liked the capable and affable go-getter despite his junior status. The Congo was a blank expanse to Dulles, and he trusted men on the spot. Devlin offered up a frequently repeated analysis to Dulles: if Lumumba succeeded, the subsequent victories of the Soviets would influence all nine countries surrounding the Congo, and would then destabilize northwest Africa. Ultimately Italy and Greece, the southern flank of NATO, would go communist. Devlin later speculated that he was preaching to the converted with his lesson in geopolitics. In any event, noted Devlin, Dulles said the United States could not afford to lose the Congo.[24]

At the NSC meeting of August 1, Dulles again stirred up fears of Lumumba, but may not have gotten what he wanted. Considering a report by the American Joint Chiefs of Staff, the NSC worried that the USSR might send its soldiers to the Congo, and agreed on the possibility of *military* action should a Soviet army intrude. Yet, like many of the NSC's conversations in 1960, these deliberations were hypothetical.[25]

Basing their projections on an interpretation of Cold War events, Dulles, Devlin, and Burden accepted a scenario of "chaos to communism." This set of beliefs generalized about how the USSR manipulated unstable personalities and political situations to make a successful revolution.[26] Lumumba's requests for Soviet aid corroborated this generalization. Nonetheless, through early August, the State Department was fainthearted, and the generals were extreme in their talk of an armed solution. A sober and wary Eisenhower sanctioned only a limited policy of reliance on the UN. Herter explained that the United States would continue to search for "more trustworthy elements" in the Congo as "reinsurance" against Lumumba. But the American position was that the West "must deal with Lumumba as Prime Minister," even if he might be unreliable and unsatisfactory, with unclear sympathies. Dulles and likeminded individuals could not change this policy without the president's approval. As late as the second week in August, the State Department was restraining the anti-Lumumba hard-liners.[27]

The Belgians React

Soon after Lumumba left the United States, the repercussions of his visit were felt all over the world. The American embassy in Brussels reported to Herter the enraged stories in the Belgian press about Lumumba's "preferential" treatment in Washington. When Baudouin had made a royal visit to the United States the year before, he had received a salute of only two guns more than Lumumba's nineteen. Lumumba had slept in the same Blair House bed as Baudouin. The supposed breaches of etiquette and protocol incensed the Belgians. Foreign Minister Wigny personally called Burden and complained.[28]

American policy in New York further maddened Brussels. The United States purposed to impede Lumumba through the UN, and the organization aimed to keep Lumumba in check by ensuring that he could not point to a continued Belgian military presence in the Congo as a way of popularizing his fevered nationalism. With tepid American support, the UN had passed resolutions on July 14 and July 22 that bid the Belgians vacate the Congo. In early August discussion began yet again in the UN's Security Council, and would lead to a further resolution of August 9 indicting Belgium. Henry Cabot Lodge, from an old and distinguished family of Massachusetts Republicans, was the US ambassador to the UN. Well known for his high-handed methods, Lodge may have sympathized with Belgium, but imperiously carried out American goals. Unlike Burden, Lodge adhered to US policy in respect to the United Nations and the Congo. The UN would hedge in Lumumba, but the US ambassador also spoke in favor of the resolutions that blamed Brussels for the Congo's crisis: Hammarskjöld would master Lumumba only if the colonialists were kicked out.

In his usual overbearing way, Lodge told Wigny that the United States could not afford a communist conquest of the Congo just because the Belgians would not move on. When Wigny objected that he might forfeit his career in publicly advocating that Belgium give ground, Lodge told the Belgian that America had lost three hundred thousand—a gross exaggeration—to stymie communism in Korea.[29] In any event, everyone knew that the declarations of the world organization lacked teeth. Designed symbolically, the resolutions expressed recognition of the unsavory nature of empire. Indeed, a few days after the August 9 resolution, the UN would make a deal in Katanga that would give Belgium some leeway there.

The Eyskens government was being pressed on one hand by Baudouin, who wanted Belgium to assert its rights in the former colony, and on the other by Hammarskjöld, who wanted a commitment from Belgium that it would leave. Added to Eyskens's woes was the desertion of the great American ally, first at Blair House, now at the UN. Brussels reacted "furious[ly]." If Belgium's pride were not salvaged, warned Burden, NATO could collapse.[30]

One of Baudouin's hopes for a stronger cabinet, Paul Van Zeeland, told the American embassy in Brussels that Belgians were suffering from "moral shock." They were "bitter, disillusioned and frustrated" by nations they thought "friends and allies." The Belgians granted independence to the Congo, said Zeeland, with "sincere, generous and historically worthy [motives]. . . . Now they are unable to comprehend what has happened to them." Pushed by public opinion, Prime Minister Eyskens, as we have seen, intimated a "revision" of Belgium's NATO military obligation in a press conference on August 9. More portentous for Washington, it was Paul-Henri Spaak, Eisenhower's European associate and the civilian head of NATO, who countered the attacks.[31]

Spaak and Eisenhower

Since August 5, Zeeland and Spaak had been engaged in private dialogues with the king about how a stronger political group could replace the Eyskens ministry. It is hard to believe that the participants were not aware of the effect on the Americans should Spaak leave NATO. Spaak had for some time been grousing over the recalcitrance of France and its president, Charles de Gaulle, in respect to NATO initiatives. Moreover, Spaak was proposing that NATO have its own nuclear weapons. The Americans were hesitating over this proposal, which President Kennedy would later spurn. On July 13, the US ambassador to NATO had urged his colleagues to support anti-Castro policies.[32] If the Americans asked their friends for help, thought Spaak, might not the Europeans expect help in return? The US policy at the UN and the hospitality Lumumba received in Washington made Spaak livid. At the end of July he seethed at a NATO ambassadors' meeting in Paris.[33] American support for the August 9 resolution of the UN pushed him over the edge. On August 10 he drafted an incensed letter to Eisenhower comparing American policy in Cuba to Belgium's in the Congo. What would the president think if the Belgians publicly supported Castro? The westerners must have one another's backs in all parts of the world, or NATO would crash.[34] Spaak was dissuaded from sending his letter, but just before he made the unsuccessful trip to Brussels for a tête-à-tête with the king, he showed the draft to the US ambassador at NATO headquarters in Paris.

Spaak's fluent thoughtfulness on the international policies of the West had gained universal admiration, and his commitment to US-led initiatives for Europe was undeniable. Squat, heavyset, and jowly, he was also a formidable physical presence. Pointing out how the Americans had dismissed the interests of their Belgian ally in the Congo, Spaak announced to the US ambassador that he would resign as NATO's secretary-general. Spaak's work had met with "total checkmate." If NATO's members "would not stand together in time of [the] troubles of one," he wondered whether "the alliance was really worth anything." American policy went against "the roots of [the] NATO concept he had been trying to develop and could force countries like Belgium to neutrality and . . . sponsor the development of more restricted blocs." An irate Spaak focused on Lodge's brusque treatment of Belgian concerns. The NATO chief warned that "the US might someday find itself accused in [the] UN and suggested we look at [the] situation from that point of view."[35]

The warning immediately reverberated through American policymaking circles, drawing concerned reactions. Spaak's continual carping through the rest of the summer and fall would devalue his standing in the Eisenhower administration, but in August his remonstrations shocked and disturbed US officials, who feared Spaak might turn his back on NATO and denounce it publicly. Herter at once replied to the organization's headquarters that Spaak should be told of his "magnificent success."

While the United States would not express an opinion about Spaak in a Belgian government, the Americans would "most earnestly hope" that no other motive might take him from NATO.[36] The American diplomats in NATO and Burden in Brussels worried about a loss in NATO strength. They considered ponying up $25 million or more to Belgium for its contribution to NATO but, with Under Secretary Dillon, agreed that it would look too much as if the US had "guilt feelings" and was "paying off" the Belgians because of the Congo.[37] Dillon wrote to Eisenhower that the hurt involved more a matter of pride than money, and asked the president to entertain Baudouin's brother, who was going to visit the United States in the early fall.[38]

Eisenhower got reports on all these developments, not just Dillon's recommendation of a kiss-and-make-up lunch. On August 10, he discussed with Herter Belgium's disappointment with American policy, and Dillon notified the American ambassadors to the NATO countries about "Belgian disillusionment." On August 11, the day after Spaak's talk with the American representative at NATO, a memo of the conversation was delivered to General Andrew Goodpaster, the secretary of the White House staff and, along with National Security Adviser Gordon Gray, the "principal channel" between Eisenhower and the CIA. On August 16, Eisenhower told a very small group of advisers that he had "very much on his mind . . . how NATO can act in harmony on a world-wide scale."[39] Wanting an increased role for NATO in Western Europe, the president and Herter had been figuring out how to counter de Gaulle's complaints about America's response to colonial issues, and Eisenhower also knew of a flare-up in the ongoing problems with the USSR over Berlin. At the heart of NATO's military approach was the defense of West Berlin, and at any time the USSR might test the alliance in this Cold War cauldron. If European problems became acute, Eisenhower had to have a united front. According to the US military chief of NATO, "Belgium, despite her small size . . . continues to play a key role in NATO."[40] It had to have crossed Eisenhower's mind that Western security arrangements might unravel at a decisive moment. De Gaulle was always a trial, but now the loyal Spaak had poked the nucleus of the president's strategy. How could one black man in Africa wreck the democratic internationalism that Eisenhower had overseen for twenty years?

Eisenhower entertains Spaak at a White House breakfast meeting on October 4.
Eisenhower had known Spaak since World War II. *From left:* Under Secretary
of State Douglas Dillon (who often stood in for Secretary of State Christian
Herter); Under Secretary of State Livingston Merchant (the State Department
representative on the National Security Council committee on covert operations);
Eisenhower; Randolph Burgess, US ambassador to NATO; Secretary-General
Spaak; and Foy Kohler, assistant secretary of state for European affairs.
(*Dwight D. Eisenhower Presidential Library*)

On August 18, Dulles spoke up at an NSC meeting over which Eisenhower presided. Lumumba, remarked Dulles, got "Soviet pay." Under
Secretary of State Dillon joined Dulles. The African, he said, might well
demand that the UN leave the Congo, and then invite the Russians in—to
restore order and expel the Belgians.

Dulles and Dillon prompted Eisenhower's only comments on the
record about Lumumba. Often testy and given at the end of his years
in office to frustrated but empty complaint, the president was still a compelling leader, and no one in the United States had remotely similar prestige. Eisenhower thought it "inconceivable" that Lumumba would force
the UN out. The organization should stay in the Congo even if European

troops—white soldiers who had heretofore had minimal visibility even under UN command—had to do the job, and even if the Russians used such action as the basis for "starting a fight." Dillon told the president that the State Department agreed but that UN ambassador Lodge thought differently. Lodge shared Hammarskjöld's apprehension that either Lumumba or the UN would exit. Perhaps betraying irritation at Lodge's run-in at the UN with America's Belgian allies, Eisenhower contradicted: "Mr. Lodge was wrong to this extent—we were talking about one man forcing us out of the Congo; of Lumumba supported by the Soviets." Nothing indicated, the president continued, that the Congo's people did not want the UN and the maintenance of order. The president must have made his remarks with some force. An NSC action memorandum noted his comments and concluded that the administration, in conformity with Eisenhower's views, would take "appropriate action" to prevent Lumumba, buttressed by the USSR, from ordering the UN out.[41]

Two days later, the State Department argued that the United States "must do everything conceivable, in line with the president's directive, to avoid termination of the UN effort." To cast off Lumumba, the State Department noted, Americans would explicitly construct policies "outside the UN framework."[42] To back up a NATO ally and to ensure that the UN stayed in the Congo, the United States, at the president's behest, would move beyond public sustenance of the UN.

CHAPTER FIVE

Dag Hammarskjöld and the UN

IN THE AFTERMATH of World War I, American president Woodrow
Wilson conceived of a union of the strong and virtuous. This League
of Nations would outlaw war and promote peace and prosperity. Wilson
offered an alternative to the international communism that had taken
root in Russia at the end of the conflict. Both Wilson and the communist
V. I. Lenin blamed the catastrophic war on European rivalries over
colonies. Lenin wanted to overthrow capitalism, out of which imperial
brawls had developed. Wilson spoke for a reformed capitalism—a global
political economy that would sustain free enterprise but repudiate empire. His League of Nations strove for anticolonialism, and he made a
commitment to the League part of the peace treaty. In the end America
rejected Wilson and signed a separate peace with Germany, the principal enemy of the United States. The League crept along in the 1920s and
1930s but had basically ceased to function by the time World War II
began in September 1939. In 1945, as the war ended, the United States
dedicated itself to a successor organization—the United Nations.

Although states constituted the UN, the organization purported to
speak for persons everywhere in a way that transcended nationalism.
The UN expressed humanitarianism, stood up for the inalienable rights
of individuals, and encouraged self-governing societies in all places. It

promised nonaggression and noninterference in the affairs of autonomous countries, which supposedly represented their citizens in a fairer
fashion than they actually did. Theorists envisaged nations ethnically
and racially homogeneous that would embody the preferences of peoples
around the world. Colonies would vanish. Vague and often platitudinous,
these notions still had an inclusive attraction. They also exemplified
Western and peculiarly American ideals, traced easily to the thirteen
English colonies and the founding document of the United States, the Declaration of Independence. French-speaking Europeans—or Lumumba—
discovered the thoughts in the Declaration of the Rights of Man of the
French Revolution, itself influenced by the American Declaration.

In the years after World War II, Americans could more or less rely on
the UN as an instrument of their foreign policy. The rivalry between the
United States and the Soviet Union extended all over the planet. Each
side contested for allies—for democracy over communism in the United
States; or for socialism over capitalism in Russia. In this contest, no fair-
minded witness could doubt where the UN stood. Located in New York
City, the organization received from the United States the lion's share of
its revenue. Although the institution had a bureaucracy of international
civil servants, US nationals and those of America's allies held sway.
While the UN remained scrawny and sometimes feckless, the United
States was in the driver's seat.

The Soviets had a sulky connection to the UN. A General Assembly
included all the nations, but questions of peace and war came to the forefront in the Security Council. To safeguard vital interests after World
War II, the victors had granted themselves special dispensations in the
Security Council. Allied to the United States during most of the war, the
Soviet Union shared these dispensations. The permanent members of
the Security Council could only operate unanimously, and the UN
could not act unless the United States and the Soviet Union agreed. The
communists frequently rejected initiatives. Through a veto power the
USSR put itself out of sync with the UN: the organization identified with
US policies, but the Soviets were protected by their ability to say no.

Did the USSR consequently oppose common human values? To validate this claim would come close to making the United States the unique
home of wisdom and goodness. Some American diplomats held this be-

lief; other diplomats from the United States would have happily had non-Americans agree with the belief. Yet many people mistrusted America, and later historians and commentators have had the same skepticism, not least because from the middle of the nineteenth century, America had only modest anti-imperial credentials. As a great power, the United States had often disregarded Wilson's principles.

Enter Dag Hammarskjöld

In 1953 Dag Hammarskjöld, a Swedish public official, became secretary-general of the United Nations. Forty-seven when he started his job, Hammarskjöld led the UN intelligently and conscientiously. The off-spring of a noble family with a long history of diplomatic service in Sweden, Hammarskjöld assisted in Western economic projects after World War II. He administered the monetary aid Sweden received under the European Recovery Program (the Marshall Plan) set up by the Americans in the late 1940s. Reflective and sagacious, he was devoted to large-scale cooperation and peacekeeping. Observers hoped that with Hammarskjöld as secretary-general, the UN might navigate its own course, free from what Hammarskjöld called the "two blocs." By the late 1950s the prestige of the organization had risen, and diplomats increasingly perceived Hammarskjöld as his own man. He appointed able subordinates, and almost without exception they praised his abilities, his call to service, and his design for the UN.

During the 1950s, room for a more independent United Nations had expanded. The institution stood between Soviet or American coercion and small and weak countries, whose refusal to take sides incensed US officials. Americans said that those who were not with the United States were against it, while the nations that gained their independence from the Western Europeans saw Hammarskjöld's UN as the place where they might raise their own voices. In addition to engaging in a contest for allies everywhere, the two superpowers had fallen into a nuclear arms race. They threatened not just each other but life around the planet, as the Cuban Missile Crisis of 1962 would demonstrate. Because Hammarskjöld adhered to universal values that nationalism did not contaminate, he believed that the UN might prevent the two giants from coming to blows.

By the late 1950s Hammarskjöld believed that the United Nations had freed itself from the orbit of the Americans, and that he might superintend disinterested peacekeeping missions in world trouble spots. As a force that could intercede between Russians and Americans, the UN would equally cultivate the autonomy of colonies. In one of the many times that Hammarskjöld rallied his supporters, he pointed out in late 1960 that the great powers least needed a mighty UN.[1] The impotent and the non-allied had the most to gain from Hammarskjöld's ambition for a sturdy association. To many outside the United States and the Soviet Union, the UN was seen to have more purity than the two superpowers.

The opening session of the General Assembly in September 1960 spoke to the larger-than-life quality of the United Nations for the world's public. That year, giving headaches to American diplomats, seventeen new nations—sixteen of them African—joined the UN. When Soviet premier Nikita Khrushchev and other leading communists decided to grace the United Nations, presidents, kings, dictators, and prime ministers arrived in New York. President Eisenhower addressed the organization. Castro, the Cuban revolutionary and an ally of Khrushchev, appeared. King Hussein of Jordan, Harold Macmillan of England, Gamal Abdel Nasser of the United Arab Republic, Jawaharlal Nehru of India, Kwame Nkrumah of Ghana, Sukarno of Indonesia, Marshal Josip Broz Tito of Yugoslavia, and Sékou Touré of Guinea led their delegations. No one disputed Hammarsjköld's moral authority among these figures. Although the increase in UN membership made control more difficult for the secretary-general, he was determined to make his institution the instrument of a new world order.

In addition to outsize ability, Hammarskjöld had some common faults. He did not suffer fools gladly and often took lasting offense at a supposed slight. Like King Baudouin, who wrote his "Intimate Diary," Hammarskjöld kept a journal that was later published in English as *Markings*. This private book, which reflected his wide-ranging intellect, easily gives the impression that the high-minded Hammarskjöld was priggish and intolerantly staid. At the UN, enemies spread rumors of his homosexuality. No one substantiated these rumors, although his closest friends acknowledged him as a sexually repressed bachelor. While he always strove to do the right thing, the fastidious Hammarskjöld had a wry and intellectually self-deprecating humor. An impeccable dresser and the embodiment of civilization, he entertained at lively parties, distinguished by elegant company and a high level of conversation.

Hammarskjöld and His Colleagues

Hammarskjöld would often elaborate on the demands of his office, and at Oxford University he delivered a lecture, "The International Civil Servant in Law and in Fact."[2] Hammarskjöld believed that his duties under the UN Charter went beyond any "ideological attitude." He could deploy mankind's principles without partiality and objectively. "The common aims" of the UN, "wholly uninfluenced by national or group interests or ideologies," guided the secretary-general. Hammarskjöld averred that he was a "politically celibate," neutral man but not a "political . . . virgin" or "neuter." Acknowledging that he might have his own private preferences, he argued that the humanitarian imperatives of the United Nations called upon his integrity. The tension between preferences and imperatives raised "a question of conscience" that prompted him to make decisions on the basis of international norms. Hammarskjöld often talked about the need for his actions to be "clean." He operated from a realm that might insulate him from the baser instincts that could dirty the statesman. *Markings* gave a philosophical justification to this political ethic. The book adopted a Christian mysticism, and Hammarskjöld's transcendent identification with Christ's redemptive suffering on the cross for fallen mankind assured the secretary-general of his unpolluted honor. Cunning in the work of the Lord, he never had reservations about his ideals, and thought that he might come to self-realization in deeds. Hammarskjöld's actions would embody a life defined by human, not national, interest.

Hammarskjöld's complicated use of language makes it hard to see if he acted on his ideals. In addition to his native Swedish, Hammarskjöld spoke perfect German, English, and French. Though he rarely used the German, he could, for example, translate back and forth between French and English, and the trips he made to the Congo sometimes called on him to do so. But his written English was not only nuanced but also heavy and bureaucratic. His closest aides reported on the similarity of his spoken English, and he would often lose his most patient and sympathetic listener in lengthy elaborations and contorted constructions. Part of this linguistic fussiness reflected Hammarskjöld's subtle mind. His verbal talents additionally made his speech, tedious and convoluted, difficult to interpret.

Perhaps the best evidence about his political inclinations comes from his coworkers in the UN. Hammarskjöld took few if any top civil servants from the Soviet Union or the communist countries because he doubted that these men were loyal to the UN. He often picked policy makers from smaller nations, a bit detached from the Americans. In managing events in the Congo, he overwhelmingly favored certain US nationals in the little group that made UN policy, "the Congo Club."

We have already met Ralph Bunche, whom Hammarskjöld had sent to help the Congo celebrate independence. Bunche stayed on to administer the UN effort. Born into an impoverished black family, he graduated from UCLA as valedictorian of his class through intelligence, hard work, and athletic prowess. Teaching at the all-black Howard University in Washington, D.C., over the next several years, he also studied for a doctorate at Harvard, which he received in 1934 for a dissertation on French West Africa. During World War II, Bunche joined the OSS, the CIA's forerunner, as an analyst of Africa. In 1946 he moved to the UN, with responsibilities for decolonization. His mediation in bringing about an armistice during the Arab-Israeli troubles of the late 1940s had won him a Nobel Prize in 1950. Though a longtime diplomat at the UN, he also stood at the forefront of the civil rights movement in the United States in its early years.

Hammarskjöld dubbed Heinz Wieschoff his African specialist. Trained as an Africanist in Europe, the Austrian Wieschoff had escaped Hitler's Germany. After he emigrated to the United States, he became a naturalized citizen, and held various academic positions as an anthropologist before attaching himself, like Bunche, to the OSS in World War II as an expert on Africa. Wieschoff got off the ground professionally when the UN employed him after the war, and Hammarskjöld favored him.

The Englishman Brian Urquhart was born to a gentrified but eccentric and penurious family. An exclusive "public" school and Oxford

University had educated him before the British army assigned him to intelligence during World War II. Urquhart helped to set up the United Nations in 1945. After the war, he resided permanently in the United States. As an under-secretary-general of the United Nations, he advised secretaries-general before and after Hammarskjöld, and often assisted Ralph Bunche. Urquhart wrote biographies of Hammarskjöld and Bunche, as well as an autobiography. Intellectuals often called upon him to defend Hammarskjöld's stewardship of the United Nations, and of the Congo in particular.[3]

Andrew Cordier served as Hammarskjöld's top associate and had a large role in the Congo. He hailed from a midwestern farm and attended Manchester College in Indiana, a small Protestant school. He earned a PhD in medieval history at the University of Chicago in 1927. After teaching at Manchester, he joined the US State Department during World War II. A self-righteous Protestant and zealous anticommunist, Cordier took part in organizing the UN, and from 1946 worked as a UN under-secretary. He was smart, assiduous, and loyal, and after Hammarskjöld took over at the UN, Cordier proved his worth and quickly won the secretary-general's confidence. By all accounts, however, Cordier was also unlikable and physically unattractive. The most astute observer of the Congo Club, the Irish literary figure and UN diplomat Conor Cruise O'Brien, spoke of Cordier's "massive figure, deliberate movements, and small shrewd eyes."[4] He stood in contrast to the trim and debonair Hammarskjöld. According to critics, when Cordier, a hulk of a man hovering on the untidy, made policy himself, his interlocutors felt an air of the intimidating. For a two-week period in September 1960, Cordier substituted for Bunche as Hammarskjöld's special representative in Leopoldville.

Urquhart did not have the prominence of the American nationals—Cordier, Bunche, and Wieschoff—who advised on the Congo. The Englishman nonetheless exemplified the inclinations of the UN leaders. In other contexts, historians have labeled internationalists of this sort "Cold War liberals." Taking some of the smaller European nations as a model, Hammarskjöld's diplomats ran ahead of opinion in the United States about domestic issues of race and social justice. Yet these officials shared the view of American policy makers about the USSR, although the

UN might petition for less strident initiatives than those that sometimes surfaced in the United States. Anticommunism was more sophisticated at Hammarskjöld's UN, which embraced ideas unexceptional in welfare states such as his own Sweden.

The UN Copes with Lumumba

As the Congo's government nose-dived, the intricate peacekeeping came to embody Hammarskjöld's hopes. His policies would test the UN. On July 20, in New York, Hammarskjöld told the Security Council that the UN sat "at a turn of the road" in respect to its own future, and that of Africa and the entire planet—"strong words," he said, "supported by strong convictions."[5]

These convictions were suspended in a sea of cultural ignorance. On the one hand, westerners laughed because the peoples of the Congo wanted to know which tribe ONUC (Opération des Nations Unies au Congo) was associated with. On the other hand, Urquhart said, "I got to the Congo practically the first day, and I didn't even know which side of Africa it was on. . . . I thought it was on the Indian Ocean, and I was much surprised to discover it was on the Atlantic."[6] Bunche found the Congo's politicians impossible to work with; Lumumba especially tried his patience. The Africans could not confront their own incapacity and expected the UN to accomplish what they could not. Lumumba irascibly demanded that Bunche send troops to Katanga and dispatch the Tshombe regime. From Leopoldville, Bunche cabled over and over about an impossible Lumumba, a "fluent but utterly maniacal child." The prime minister could not keep agreements or even appointments; he altered course precipitously, and often simply lacked the power to run his nation. Yet Bunche despised the Belgians with whom he dealt. The UN knew that the regime in Katanga could not survive without the munificence of Belgium. According to Bunche, only Belgium's "total withdrawal" from Katanga would make for success. If Hammarskjöld could force the Belgians to depart he would have an impeccable anticolonial credential, thought Bunche, and otherwise Lumumba might ask the UN to pull out.[7] Bunche had no time for Lumumba's peremptory demands. Still, more than other members of the Congo Club, the African American Bunche had the most unambiguous view about intolerable Belgian behavior. Soon, exhausted and frustrated, he wanted to end his Congo assignment.

When Lumumba traveled to the United States in the last part of July, the American refusal to finance the Congo was a camouflaged slap in the face from the United States—certainly too camouflaged for Belgium, but a slap nonetheless. Before and after his time in Washington, Lumumba had equally rough sledding at the New York headquarters of the UN. Hammarskjöld had some frosty conversations with Lumumba on July 24, 25, and 26, although their public exchanges did not give away a growing hostility, and the two at least outwardly maintained a show of cordiality. For Hammarskjöld, the new government had to take its medicine. Lumumba's ministry would for a time devolve into a sort of UN trustee-ship until Hammarskjöld and his lieutenants could right the Congo ship of state. Lumumba's vociferous nationalism upset the secretary-general, who wanted his own institution in the limelight. He dreaded an argument with all the Western nations that asked for respectful treatment of the colonialists. Hammarskjöld saw that Lumumba made for an intractable Belgium, and Belgium for an intractable Lumumba. If the UN were to thrive, the secretary-general had to find a way around the two obstructions.

After his deliberations in Washington and Ottawa but before returning to Africa, Lumumba made a last visit to the UN. This time, on August 1, he met with Andrew Cordier, because Hammarskjöld had left for the Congo to see if he could do something about Katanga. Cordier began his interview with Lumumba with a lengthy and condescending exposition. Hammarskjöld's work was "superhuman," "a dramatic chapter of the history of this century." "Strong words," said Cordier, "and I stand behind them." Ignoring the white man's speech, Lumumba made his own long reply. He admonished Cordier and expressed disappointment, telling the underling at least five times that the UN had not evicted the Belgians. "The secretary general has therefore not co-operated with the Government of the Republic of the Congo, and this I must emphasize with all my strength." While Lumumba only hinted to Cordier that the Congo might rescind its invitation to the UN, Lumumba had previously threatened Bunche and later, so Bunche reported, "verged on rage" when the issue came up.[8] Cordier at once forwarded Lumumba's complaints to

Andrew Cordier.
Hammarskjöld's chief
assistant could be a
threatening presence.
(*University Archives,
Columbia University in the
City of New York*)

Hammarskjöld in the Congo, but they did not surprise the secretary-general. Lumumba's ministers in Leopoldville, where Hammarskjöld had disembarked, were at that very moment publicly criticizing Hammarskjöld and the United Nations. For his part, before he went back to the Congo, Lumumba toured various African countries and conferred with a number of friendly leaders. Here he had fewer issues, and to the premiers of several countries he described Belgian activity as the "last somersaults of colonialism."[9] Lumumba set up what was intended as a triumphal conference of African leaders to be held in Leopoldville at the end of August.

Hammarskjöld or Lumumba?

The UN's diplomacy would require all of Hammarskjöld's skills. Perhaps nothing would satisfy the hot-tempered prime minister, but the secretary-general could deflate Lumumba if the UN took a hard line with Belgium. Simultaneously, the peacekeepers could not afford to alienate the United States, which championed the UN but also had sturdy commitments to its NATO partners—the European colonial powers.

At the beginning of August, Hammarskjöld tried to settle with Brussels and Katanga and to take the wind out of Lumumba's sails. Meeting up with Bunche in Leopoldville, Hammarskjöld sent him to Elisabethville to improvise a UN entrée. On August 2, as we have seen, Belgian prime minister Eyskens had no foreknowledge when the Leopoldville radio broadcast that, according to the secretary-general, the UN would take over in Katanga and the Belgian military would leave. Bunche had a difficult visit in Elisabethville on August 4, however, and advised Hammarskjöld to delay plans for Katanga. Suffering a setback, the secretary-general returned to New York on August 6, where he convened a hasty gathering of the Security Council. Three days later, in its August 9 meeting, it voted that the peacekeepers would fan out to the whole of the Congo, but should not disrupt the Congo's internal affairs. The resolution meant that the UN would enter Katanga but that President Tshombe might remain in place. Hammarskjöld left again almost immediately for the Congo, only stopping in Leopoldville for a short time before moving on to Elisabethville to see Tshombe about this latest UN deal.

Deliberating with the secessionists, Hammarskjöld put together a face-saving bargain that got blue helmets into Katanga. While black UN soldiers dispersed over most of the Congo, white Swedes took over in Katanga. They did not encumber the Belgians in Elisabethville, nor would the peacekeepers obstruct the new gendarmerie of Katanga, which the Belgians were creating and which would control part of the city's Luano airport. Hammarskjöld fulfilled the mandate of the UN. Its troops occupied the whole of the Congo, but had not taken sides in the dispute between Lumumba and Tshombe. One could argue that Hammarskjöld's trip produced a racially shaded victory for secession, for

Munongo meets Bunche at Luano airport. On August 4, Godefroid Munongo, Katanga's Secretary of the Interior, *center right,* speaks with Ralph Bunche, *center left.* D'Aspremont, advising Katanga, is extreme right. (*UN Photo*)

the secretary-general had given a license of sorts to the Elisabethville regime. Here Hammarskjöld had taken the advice of Wieschoff, his expert on Africa, who had told the secretary-general to come to terms with Tshombe, a "potentially important conservative . . . counterweight to [the] extremism of Lumumba."[10]

The prime minister arrived back in Leopoldville on August 8 after his two-week trip. He was primed to berate Hammarskjöld about the failure of the UN in Katanga, but did not get the chance. Hammarskjöld avoided Lumumba when he went through Leopoldville to see Tshombe. Furious that the UN had brazenly undercut him in Katanga, Lumumba now refused to confer with Hammarskjöld when the secretary-general left the Congo. Instead, a series of nasty public written exchanges substituted for a meeting.[11] When the secretary-general reached New York on August 16 for yet another Security Council gathering, he did not know what Lumumba would do about the UN's pro-Katanga stance. The prime minister was ominously giving notice about the writ of the UN. Would Lumumba make good on his bluster about the withdrawal of the UN

Hammarskjöld and Tshombe in Katanga. On August 12, in Elisabethville, Hammarskjöld was embarrassed to be pictured with the Belgian-backed leader. (© *BelgaImage*)

force from the Congo? His threats were at that very moment driving the United States to reconsider its policies. Lumumba might order the UN out, and then Hammarskjöld would have to make calamitous decisions. Hammarskjöld had at least temporarily accepted a Belgian presence in Katanga. While most of the new republic looked like a basket case, Elisabethville had a functioning social system, and happy Europeans. A lesson existed here for the secretary-general. On several occasions the Americans had rebuffed Lumumba about various kinds of assistance. Any funds should come through Hammarskjöld. Now, with American help, the secretary-general planned a UN authority that would officially finance the Congo. The handouts would cover all the help Lumumba would get.[12] The invariable "ultimative tone" of Lumumba and his ministers incensed Hammarskjöld. He could not "satisfy a group of child[ren]'s demands," he wrote, when it might "bring havoc in another national situation." From the Congo he had told Cordier of the "mad splendour" of Leopoldville, and of "a story told by an idiot"—Lumumba.[13]

Hammarskjöld had a point. The new prime minister had left the country during a crucial two-week period at the end of July and the beginning of August. During this time the Congo declined, his supporters had no leader, and his opponents coalesced. His enemies in Belgium and the United States—and the UN—had a field day as they fed one another's anxieties about Lumumba's radical politics.

Lumumba Acts on His Own

On August 9, within twenty-four hours of Lumumba's return to Leopold-ville, the southern part of the province of Kasai, bordering on Katanga, declared its independence. The same day, convinced of Belgian intrigues, Lumumba expelled the Belgian ambassador and announced a state of emergency. On August 11, he restricted newspapers and civil liberties, following a precedent set by Belgian colonial rule. While Lumumba wanted to show off the Congo by hosting the African leaders' conference at the end of the month, on August 16 he proclaimed martial law, and began to arrest public figures who disagreed with him. On August 18, CIA agent Devlin described the events by saying that the Congo was "experiencing [a] classic communist effort at [a] takeover."[14] Lumumba's moves were explicable if disturbing. The prime minister typified the escalating distress of someone who had legitimacy but not much power. For Lumumba, dissent fortified the imperialists and the secessionist enemies of the central government, and he knew that his opponents had the endorsement of the secret agencies of foreign powers. His administration just creaked along. A changing group of staffers later reported on the confusion of the ministerial offices: the to-and-fro-ing of camp followers, and Lumumba's need to act as his own secretary, taking and making phone calls, typing up letters and documents, going on errands.

In late August, however, Lumumba managed some decisive action. The Armée Nationale Congolaise, under the leadership of the recently promoted black servicemen Victor Lundula and Joseph Mobutu, would move against the secessionists. Soldiers loyal to Lumumba would quash the rebellion in Kasai, and then do what the UN would not: end the independence of Katanga. The UN mandate might not allow the organization to breach "internal affairs," but the national government itself might do its duty. In Lumumba's eyes, he had the responsibility to defend his country. In the only instance of more than abstract aid, the Soviet Union supplied trucks and planes to Lumumba for the transit of troops, beginning August 18.[15] Although Bunche had no information about the trucks and planes and worried about how the Security Council would respond to their military use, he did not dispute Lumumba's right to the equipment and the right of the USSR to supply it.[16]

The military operation proceeded in disarray. In the breakaway areas Lumumba had as much support as his adversaries, chief of whom was Tshombe in Katanga. In the last week of August, the prime minister's army scored some victories in Kasai, though essentially without a fight as the opposition took flight. But officers could not control their men, who were forced to live off the land without resources. At the end of August in a perplexing battle at Bakwanga in southern Kasai, with which Lumumba had little to do, his troops massacred some two hundred Baluba. In another set of incidents that extended over four days at the close of the month and the beginning of September, Lumumba's soldiers in a search for food indiscriminately killed another forty-five civilians.[17] In this mini-war westerners saw the contriving hand of the communists and Nikita Khrushchev.

Khrushchev

Khrushchev had everything to win and nothing to lose in Africa. Although the continent did not occupy the front lines in the Cold War, the USSR promised to aid revolutions in developing lands. The Europeans dominated Africa south of the Sahara. The Soviet Union had no influence in black Africa, so any gains would cost the West. The Europeans could at best exert friendly persuasion on their former subjects, while Khrushchev could offer Africans an ideology free from imperialism. The socialist way of life proclaimed an end to the humiliation that they endured. The USSR invited the colonies and former colonies to take the step to a soviet form of society and banish exploitative capitalism.

Many Africans, nevertheless, did not want to jeopardize their ties to the former colonial powers. Some Africans were pro-West, and even the most rabid nationalists would not declare for communism. At the same time

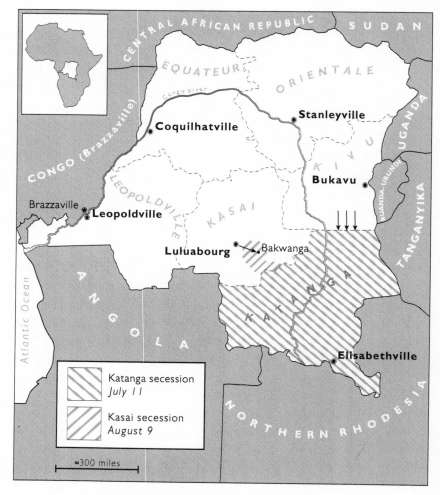

ANC troop movements, August–September 1960

Khrushchev refuted many Western claims about the Congo. He pointed out the anti-Lumumba bias of the UN and its tacit support for Belgium. Yet the Soviet leader was his own worst enemy. This uncouth and pugnacious man alarmed otherwise sympathetic listeners. When he attended the opening of the UN in New York in September 1960, he lurched around, pounding on tables, in one incident using not his fist but his shoe. The Soviets knew how the institution stacked matters against them, and Khrushchev condemned its imperialist ways and attempted to reorient them. Still, it must be remembered that the Soviets worked within the United Nations; Khrushchev never walked out.

Shrill diplomacy only confirmed the hazards of communism and underscored the sour reality of life in the Soviet bloc. America had the moral upper hand in discussions of world politics. No matter how much some Africans favored a centralized economy—socialism—every leader made the point that his country would follow its own, African, path. The Africans—like Lumumba—more usually hewed to a "neutralist" stance that would gain them concessions from both the United States and the USSR, and in many instances leaned toward America. Khrushchev had an uphill climb in Africa.

Russia also postured for effect. Khrushchev competed with the People's Republic of China—Red China or mainland China—for the headship of the communist world. He could rarely appear temporizing or conciliatory, and considered himself a revolutionary, although the Soviets often practiced prudent policy, preserving a status quo, "peaceful coexistence." Khrushchev's place in the international communist movement to some extent required the strident performances that diminished his influence in Africa. Moreover, insecurity motivated Khrushchev's loud mouth. Despite some advertised successes in rocketry, the Soviet Union lagged far behind the United States in the production of atomic arms. Khrushchev knew he did not have many nuclear missiles. Eisenhower believed that he outgunned his enemy, and Kennedy would also—something like ten to one in America's favor, although the USSR thought the deficit greater. Khrushchev might goad the United States, but he could not afford a big ruckus. In the principal theater of Western Europe, even if push came to shove, a massive number of Soviet troops could not offset the nuclear superiority of the United States. The Cuban Missile Crisis of 1962 evinced this truth. The Americans forced the Soviet Union to back down in Cuba, just off the shores of the United States, and the Soviets did not retaliate in West Berlin, literally inside their client of East Germany.

While the USSR had something to gain, it could not match the Americans in Africa, as it could not rival the United States in most places. The Soviets' inexperience of what they called the Dark Continent exceeded even that of the United States. The USSR had little to offer, and geography made the military logistics difficult if not impossible. The gap between

Soviet bombast and reality aside, Khrushchev also harbored a feeling that black Africa was of minor import.

At a significant moment, Khrushchev made a gift of military transport to Lumumba for his late-August attempt to reintegrate south Kasai and Katanga. Later, the communists gave money to Lumumba's successors, but the USSR aided him no further. In part the Soviets understood that unforeseeable difficulties would accompany more meddling. In part Khrushchev did not trust his potential allies, who were more eager for American help than Soviet. In part he intuited the unprofitability of a left-leaning Congo, a source of weakness rather than strength.[18]

Hammarskjöld's Historical Comparison

Matters looked different in New York, where Hammarskjöld found the situation dire. With Khrushchev's help, Lumumba would bring tyranny to the Congo and undermine the United Nations. The secretary-general allowed his historical imagination free rein. Sometimes, he analogized Nkrumah's Pan-Africanism to fascist expansionism, and dubbed Lumumba a Mussolini—"an ignorant pawn" of the Hitler Nkrumah. Overall, however, Lumumba's drive to Katanga altered the secretary-general's metaphorical thinking. Hammarskjöld warned of "incipient genocide" in Kasai, and later described what had taken place as "characteristic of the crime of genocide." With ineffective help from the prime minister's local antagonists, Hammarskjöld found it hard to crush a "Hitler"—Lumumba. Hammarskjöld cabled Cordier that another Munich might be taking place in the Congo, where the UN must prevail in "the showdown" Lumumba had asked for. Cordier too depicted Lumumba as Africa's "little Hitler."[19]

For Hammarskjöld, the clown at the head of a lame and worthless regime had metamorphosed into the most dangerous villain of world history, as the secretary-general compared his own efforts to the Allies in World War II. With Lumumba cautioning that he would ask the UN to make tracks, the Swede agonized that the African was ripping up the UN blueprint for global order.[20]

CHAPTER SIX

The Government Falls

B Y THE BEGINNING of September Lumumba knew about underhanded strategies to supplant him, and dissident black politicians
gathered around Joseph Ileo, president of the Congo's senate. Critics
then and later saw paranoia in Lumumba's fevered complaints about his
enemies. But he had no friends among the UN leaders. The Belgians were
undermining him. American officials in Leopoldville and Washington
wanted to bring him down. Lumumba's enemies were real.

After Kasa-Vubu and Lumumba had broken off relations with Brussels, Belgian diplomats had congregated in Brazzaville, across the Congo
River, where they stimulated as many anti-Lumumba efforts as they
could. At the end of August, they reported to Brussels on their ongoing
discussions with whites and blacks in Leopoldville about how to overthrow Lumumba "in accord with our wishes." The plotters would follow
"a legal scheme." Article 45 of the *loi fondamentale* allowed a censure
vote in either house of the parliament to discredit a minister. Dissident
politicians, supported by demonstrations from the unions, would generate a vote of no confidence in the senate against some members of the
Lumumba cabinet. Then Kasa-Vubu would ask for the resignation of the
prime minister. The operation was coordinated by Benoît Verhaegen, a
professor at Lovanium, the Catholic university in Leopoldville, and

deputy chief of staff of the Congo's minister of economic planning. Verhaegen was descended from a well-to-do Belgian family, fought in Korea as a volunteer, and had lectured in political science at Lovanium since 1958. He urgently asked Brussels for additional funds to make the ouster successful. According to the Belgians in Brazzaville, Kasa-Vubu had not yet given his approval and was worrying about how he would intervene. Brazzaville intended to work up a memo for the president on his constitutional prerogatives. Belgian foreign minister Wigny objected on September 1: "Speak, do not write and never sign." Wigny also advised the conspirators *not* to use the procedure of an antigovernment vote (Article 45) since it was too risky. Lumumba might win the parliamentary debate. It would be easier, cabled Wigny, to use Article 22, which said that the chief of state appoints and revokes the ministers; Kasa-Vubu had the right to dismiss the government even without a no-confidence vote in the parliament. We think that this notion occurred to Wigny just because he had seen how close Baudouin had come in Belgium to getting rid of a legitimate ministry on the basis of the same article in the Belgian constitution. Now Wigny wrote that Kasa-Vubu must not hesitate. The president had not only the power but also the moral obligation to act. In Belgium Wigny had taken just the opposite position in respect to Baudouin. The schemers planned a new ministry, with Lumumba in opposition. They worried, however, that Lumumba would not join the game and would instead declare a rival government in his stronghold of Stanleyville.[1]

How realistic were these machinations? As matters turned out, when Kasa-Vubu was informed of them, he acted on his own. In the United Nations he also identified a new and eager helpmate.

UN Representatives

In June 1960 Ralph Bunche had hit the ground running. He attended the independence ceremonies at the end of the month, drew up the Congo's application for UN membership, and coordinated the technical assistance that Lumumba might claim. Prior briefing had not prepared Bunche for the extension of his mission and the overwhelming UN undertaking. The job grew moment by moment as he established a command post, introduced a set of military forces from a first group of ten nations, set up a UN civilian administration, and dealt with demanding but unstable politicians. In two months, they had worn him out. Particularly fed up with the unmanageable Lumumba, Bunche wanted to get home, look at colleges with his son, and resume his old job as assistant to Hammarskjöld in New York.

Hammarskjöld sought a new representative, and found one in Rajeshwar Dayal. An Indian diplomat of unusual perspicacity, Dayal would develop into the sharpest observer in the Congo. He had previously served India in the UN, which had later employed him on "loan" from his own land. The secretary-general now again asked for him on loan. He wanted Dayal in New York for an orientation, then in place as his special representative in Leopoldville by the end of August, when Bunche would return to the United States. On August 25 Bunche wired Hammarskjöld that Lumumba would no longer see him, and pleaded for Dayal to come at once. Bunche wrote in his diary that he had last spoken to the "Jungle demagogue" and "Congolese Ogre" on August 12. While willing to take on the job, Dayal had to delay his New York stopover until the start of September and so would not get to Leopoldville until a few days later.[2]

Under these circumstances Hammarskjöld temporarily swapped Bunche for Cordier. Cordier landed at Leopoldville on August 28, and Bunche flew out two days later. By September 1 Bunche was back at the UN headquarters; Dayal had made it to New York a couple of days earlier. He consulted with the Congo Club and with Bunche, and took off for Leopoldville on the evening of September 4.

As matters turned out, Lumumba reached a crossroads on Cordier's brief watch. When Cordier deplaned on August 28, rumors filled Leopoldville about disputes between Kasa-Vubu and Lumumba, and about the West's diplomatic and clandestine attempts to have Kasa-Vubu sponsor a new government and to terminate the Lumumba prime ministership.

The Policy Line

Kasa-Vubu had uneasily allied himself with Lumumba. In July the army's breakdown and the flat-footed Belgian response made a tenuous bond between the two men. While Kasa-Vubu despised the treatment that he had received as president at the hands of Katanga's elite, he had a commitment to ethnic regionalism, and thus something in common with Tshombe. The breakdown of public services, the despotic rule in August, and the winds of civil war gave the president further anxieties. Belgian advisers constantly told him to save the situation from Lumumba, and the ABAKO leadership also expressed its fears. So he pondered the removal of the prime minister.

Cordier and Hammarskjöld had worked closely together, and Cordier agreed with a policy line that Hammarskjöld expounded. They had promulgated three goals: maintaining law and order, underwriting democracy, and staying out of internal affairs. Hammarskjöld would encourage the Congo's integration into the world community and prevent the reestablishment of colonialism. Yet he believed that the UN would only succeed if it clipped Lumumba's wings or switched the prime minister for a more docile type; then a more reasonable Congo might emerge, and, according to the secretary-general, the Belgians would step back. The UN had an aim inconsistent with its pledges. Hammarskjöld wanted to "chasten" the Lumumba government, as he often said. In its own best interests, the Congo would move along a path that the secretary-general had in mind.

In Leopoldville, African leaders had just ended their conference, which had achieved little. At the opening on August 25, an anti-Lumumba demonstration instigated by the CIA had turned violent and damaged the reputation of the prime minister. Devlin wrote that "the reality of the Congo situation" entangled the African delegates.[3] They still did not want to throw Lumumba overboard, and parleyed with Cordier on September 1. Lobbying for better relations between the UN and Lumumba, the African luminaries also wanted the UN to patch up grievances between Lumumba and Kasa-Vubu. When Hammarskjöld learned of these ideas, he cabled Cordier that a "spirit of reconciliation" had "gone far too far on the line of compromise." The UN might pay "lip service" to the desires of an "utterly incompetent" government "utterly incapable of acting." But "Congolese pipedreams" should not distract Cordier. Moreover, Lumumba and his ministers had a "complete misconception of [their] rights in relation to the UN and their own role in the world." Lumumba himself would have to be "forced to constitutionality."[4]

On the evening of September 3, Kasa-Vubu summoned Cordier. The president contemplated dismissing Lumumba. While Cordier related that he withheld comment, the turn of events pleased him, as his communication later that night with Hammarskjöld via teleprinter intimated. They discerned a great opportunity in Kasa-Vubu's declaration of intent. The two UN officials agreed that they shared the same goal and did not have to hash it out in detail. As one official put it, Hammarskjöld used "language . . . typical of him."[5] Even "hypothetical discussion" of possible moves, said the secretary-general, would put the UN in a "most exposed position," and Cordier should rely on the knowledge the two men had "of each other's point of view." Hammarskjöld did note that the "complete disintegration of authority" would entitle the representative to "greater freedom of action in protection of law and order." "The degree of disintegration . . . widening your rights is necessarily [a] question of judgment." "We cross our fingers," Hammarskjöld ended his electronic conversation: "The whole team . . . joins me in good wishes. Dayal is here too getting baptized to his future life. . . . He is still wet."[6]

Cordier and Kasa-Vubu had more meetings over the next two days, September 4 and 5, although Cordier later wrote several times that they discussed nothing of substance.[7] On September 4, the UN military in Leopoldville practiced various emergency responses. The next day, Dayal's plane arrived in the morning, and later that day Hammarskjöld reiterated his attitude by cable to Dayal and Cordier. He wanted them "to follow the line . . . that . . . liberal interpretation" of principles is "automatically widened." They should find the "proper balance between strictly legal and extraordinary emergency latitudes." He allowed himself an "irresponsible observation": "responsible people on the spot may permit themselves, within [the] framework of principles which are imperative, what I could not justify doing myself—taking the risk of being disowned when it no longer matters."[8]

The Work of September 5

A few minutes before 8 P.M. on September 5, Kasa-Vubu sent his Belgian adviser Jef Van Bilsen to Cordier with a formal written exhortation:

Cordier should close the airports and monitor the Leopoldville radio station.[9] Then, at 8:12, Kasa-Vubu appeared at the station. He was a poor public performer, and read a speech in halting French in a squeaky voice. He nervously asserted that he was sacking Lumumba, erroneously calling him the "prime mayor" instead of the "prime minister." Kasa-Vubu's limitations did not alter the explosive import of his talk. Joseph Ileo, president of the Congo's senate, was designated the new prime minister.[10] Kasa-Vubu thus plunged the Congo into turmoil.

While the president went home to rest, incommunicado until the following afternoon, Lumumba spoke on the radio three times in the next nine hours. He did not just defend his government but also declared that Kasa-Vubu was deposed. In between his addresses to the public, Lumumba and his ministers thrashed matters out through the night. On September 6 the politicians scurried back and forth among their offices, the Western embassies, and UN headquarters. In evaluating the political outburst, Hammarskjöld told Cordier to "tak[e] into account the views of the president," although Cordier himself dealt more with what Kasa-Vubu "wanted" and "requested." Moreover, while the UN should appear equidistant between the two rivals, the secretary-general would have Cordier "liaison" with Kasa-Vubu if necessary. The representative should avoid Lumumba: "you will not and cannot see him." "By God," said Hammarskjöld, "nothing should be done to give certain people prestige."[11] Devlin accurately reported to Washington on Kasa-Vubu's plans, "coordinated" "at [the] highest levels" with the UN. The United Nations in Leopoldville kept a list of fourteen letters from Lumumba in the first two weeks of the crisis that it did not answer, though some were written and received when he unquestionably had the title of prime minister.[12]

Cordier immediately implemented Kasa-Vubu's written solicitations. Three days before, Cordier had been negotiating with Lumumba's government to retain some indisputable air rights for the UN. Now on the evening of September 5, right after Kasa-Vubu spoke, the UN took over the airports, and completed a shutdown before midnight. Cordier also placed the radio station under guard at once, as Kasa-Vubu had asked. Lumumba was able to use it only because Kasa-Vubu had not stipulated its closure and just wanted it monitored. The next afternoon the president sent an emissary to Cordier with an oral message requiring a firmer policy. The UN representative moved on this message at once, and the Leopoldville station went off the air at 12:30 P.M. on September 6.[13] A more effective radio personality than the Congo's other politicians, Lumumba could no longer benefit from the medium. Continuous and strident anti-Lumumba broadcasts came from across the river, where Fulbert Youlou governed Congo (Brazzaville). Fearful of clamorous nationalism in Africa, Youlou opened his county to Kasa-Vubu and to anti-Lumumba groups. More important, without the airports, Lumumba could not fly his military into Leopoldville from other parts of the country.

At the beginning of September Hammarskjöld had selected Jean David, a Haitian diplomat, as an official UN contact with Kasa-Vubu. The president would employ David as an aide. After Kasa-Vubu dismissed the prime minister, David operated as the go-between. He might broker a deal between Kasa-Vubu and Lumumba that would bring the prime minister to heel. The two would "cooperate." The UN would oversee all assistance to the Congo and would vet Lumumba's political appointments. In the parliament, Ileo would stand up and decline the prime ministership "in the interests of general peace." If Lumumba went along, Cordier or Dayal would reopen the radio and airport. Hammarskjöld called this the "David line." As Cordier and Dayal informed the secretary-general, "We have given David strongest green light."[14]

UN officials told the world and sometimes each other that the radio blackouts and shutdown of air travel broadly applied the principle of maintaining law and order. Cordier's stand would prevent a civil war during an abnormal time. But Cordier's repeated telexes to New York before the shutdowns told of a nationwide serenity. The UN had no problem of law and order, just Kasa-Vubu's appeals. The telegrams mentioning tensions came *after* Cordier stopped air traffic.[15] Moreover, in Tshombe's stronghold of Elisabethville, officials of the United Nations protested that tampering with the airports would cause the *breakdown* of law and order. International diplomats begged their bosses, Cordier and Hammarskjöld, not to close the Elisabethville airport of Luano lest blood be shed. The UN authorities worried that Katanga's soldiers might attack the peacekeepers. Hammarskjöld instructed his people to pretend to the end, but to yield if Tshombe used Luano and forced the

UN hand. An annoyed Hammarskjöld telegraphed that in contesting the shutdown Tshombe did "not understand his best interests." That is, the secessionists should appreciate the UN coercion of Lumumba. In the end, Tshombe successfully kept Luano open, while Lumumba could not break the hold of the blue helmets on the Leopoldville airport.[16]

UN civil servants cabled the same sorts of protests in Stanleyville, Lumumba's home base. There, Brian Urquhart, the prolific apologist for the UN's actions, was temporarily observing for Cordier. At the time, Urquhart worried that an airport closure might bring mayhem, and found the situation "unintelligible." He later wrote that UN policies made a lot of sense.[17]

What was Dayal, the new representative, doing? His memoirs recalled that he did not anticipate the events of the night of September 5 and 6. Had he known of them he would have reassessed matters and deferred his journey from New York to "realign . . . my sights." General Indar Rikhye, another Indian adviser to the secretary-general, wrote later that Dayal almost "exploded." New York, Dayal said, had given him almost no inkling of this crisis. Now he found the temporary head, Cordier, making policy. Rikhye added that Dayal thought of not taking up the job. When did Dayal want to take over, Cordier asked him in the early morning of September 6. According to Dayal's later account, Cordier had "taken initiatives"—which he surely had—and the Indian told Cordier to see them through. According to Dayal, again, Cordier promptly agreed. Dayal said he was "physically present but without authority."[18]

In his memoirs Dayal forgot that he had been in the UN cable office in New York on September 3, when the Congo Club discussed the proposed change in government by teleprinter. Dayal knew as much as anyone about the unfolding politics of the Congo. He also forgot to note that when his flight touched down on the morning of September 5, he at once had the title of special representative and spent the day in Leopoldville. Dayal may or may not have approved of what Cordier was going to do or was doing, but Dayal knew what was going on. He also declined to assume responsibility himself by introducing different policies. By November, when Dayal himself was pressed, he maintained his bona fides by boasting that *he* had been responsible for "deflating" Lumumba.[19]

So much for Dayal's hand-wringing. "Dayal and I have agreed to carefully calculate timing transfer," wrote Cordier, "on ground that I am expendable." Dayal, who first delayed his takeover until September 7, did not step in until the next day. Because of what Cordier had done, Hammarskjöld concluded, Cordier should leave that day. The secretary-general expressed his "warmest gratitude for Cordier's wisdom and courage."[20]

Dayal later wrote that Cordier's decisions "cast a malevolent spell" over the mission, and that their injurious effects proved "Sisyphean."[21] At least five times over the years, the American revisited his actions in an attempt to justify them.[22] At variance with the contemporary evidence and his intent to bulldoze Lumumba, Cordier's reconstructions were self-serving. After Lumumba's death had been cataloged as a world historical moment, no one—Hammarskjöld, Cordier, and Dayal among the UN men—wanted anything to do with it. But at the time the effort to devalue Lumumba drew in everyone.

The Constitutional Question

When the UN interfered in the Congo's domestic politics, it hurled itself into a raging dispute about the procedures that defined the newborn nation. Hammarskjöld, Cordier, and Dayal confronted the partiality of their mission. Both Belgium and the Congo had accepted the *loi fondamentale* at least as an interim framework. The document had already determined the selection of Kasa-Vubu and Lumumba. The Congo's parliament had elected Kasa-Vubu as president, and he had a term of office. According to the central Article 22, copied from the Belgian constitution, "The chief of state names and revokes the prime minister and the ministers." Kasa-Vubu would have a king's formal duties in giving his consent to the various administrations that might come or go.[23] Should the prime minister and his cabinet lose the votes necessary to control the legislature, they would present their resignations to Kasa-Vubu, who would appoint another politician to form a new administration.

Less than a month before, the Belgian king, according to that same article, requested the resignation of the Eyskens government; Baudouin wanted stronger anti-Lumumba policies. The Eyskens ministry had a safe parliamentary majority, and resisted. The Belgian ministers indicated that in the Congo the king-like figure Kasa-Vubu had powers they had just denied to Baudouin. Eyskens had told Kasa-Vubu's adviser, Van Bilsen, that Kasa-Vubu had the authority. Wigny enjoined the Belgians to persuade Kasa-Vubu to unseat Lumumba. Van Bilsen had reflected "Could the president just do that?" Didn't Kasa-Vubu need "a legal reason"?[24] Unsurprisingly, a wacky double standard worked itself out.

The Belgian constitution did mandate that any act of the head of state had to be issued with the written consent of a legitimate minister who thereby became accountable. So did the *loi fondamentale*. According to the Congo's constitution, only when Kasa-Vubu had the signature of a minister on his decree could the successor administration of Joseph Ileo take over. According to Belgian tradition, an administration began as soon as the king appointed the new ministry and before parliamentary approval. A government went immediately into effect. The old cabinet went out of office even if the new one did not appeal at once to the legislature for a vote of confidence, but there actually had to be a new cabinet—men named to positions of ministerial responsibility, with one of them designated as prime minister.

Because the legalities formed the basis of the UN line, focus on them is important. Kasa-Vubu had rights. But he did not ask advice from the Congo's politicians; instead the imperial power with which he had cut connections prodded him. Ileo had no hope of gaining a legislative majority. Kasa-Vubu had every reason to think that Lumumba would triumph in a legislative vote. Many of the Western diplomats did not want the parliament to convene for this reason—the legislators would vote an Ileo government down. The president also designated Ileo as prime minister before he had come up with a cabinet. And, finally, Kasa-Vubu spoke without having a minister put his name on a decree of dismissal. *The firing was invalid,* as indeed Van Bilsen had warned Kasa-Vubu. When the president had dispatched Van Bilsen to Cordier, the Belgian told Kasa-Vubu: You can't do this without a signature.[25] Kasa-Vubu acted as a chief, not as a chief of state.

The events pointed to the president's indifference to Western-style politics and his own self-regard. Nonchalant about a system of which he knew little, Kasa-Vubu may also not have shared Belgium's goal. He may just have wanted to intimidate Lumumba and produce a more acquiescent ministry. The UN had a similar intent when it urged the "David line." Two reasons explained the buffoonish takeover. First, the West cobbled together a pretext to sink Lumumba. Second, Kasa-Vubu did not aim for Lumumba's disappearance from the scene.

Lumumba made the illegality of Kasa-Vubu's ploy clear in a letter to Hammarskjöld delivered to Cordier at 4 A.M. on September 6, noting the constitutional deficit again on the radio an hour and a half later. American ambassador Timberlake had lamented in August: "No one with national stature" opposed Lumumba. Kasa-Vubu was "a political zero . . . naïve, not very bright, lazy . . . content to appear occasionally in his new general's uniform." Now the American ambassador wrote that Lumumba revealed "brilliant broken field running," while Kasa-Vubu "acts more like a vegetable."[26]

On Wednesday afternoon, September 7, in the Congo's house of representatives, Lumumba yet again explained the illegality of Kasa-Vubu's action. His virtuoso presentation showed his grasp of Western legislative procedures and affronted Western diplomats with its tactical acuity. "It is not Lumumba they are out to destroy," he told the House, "but you and the future of Africa."[27] Hammarskjöld wired Cordier that Kasa-Vubu needed some minister's signature for the "legal effectiveness" of the transfer of power. The UN legal division consistently took this position: Lumumba remained until Kasa-Vubu had a written endorsement of his decision. On September 9, Hammarskjöld repeated the need for a politician to sign off for the new government to be legitimate.[28]

The mid-afternoon of September 6 would be the earliest time Kasa-Vubu could have legally selected Ileo. By then the Western powers had gotten a better grip on the constitutional issues and rallied their African collaborators—perhaps because Lumumba had made his mastery of the law so public. That afternoon Kasa-Vubu obtained the needed signature—actually two signatures—from Minister of Foreign Affairs Justin Bomboko, and Albert Delvaux, who had a job comparable to that of ambassador to Belgium and was in that capacity also a minister. With the signatures, Kasa-Vubu made a more constitutionally sensible announcement on Brazzaville radio, at 4 P.M. on September 6.[29] At least in theory it could be argued that Lumumba had been terminated. Nonetheless, since Ileo had not gathered a cabinet, no administration existed. The Lumumba ministry would have to serve until Ileo had become indeed the prime minister of a group of politicians.

Here we enter deep waters. It is our considered judgment that in part the dismissal was illegitimate, but most of all that the procedures made no sense. The Belgians and the United Nations were trying to throw some legal set of formulas over what Wigny himself called, more than once, a coup. Wigny dreamed up every argument he could to justify the gimmickry of September 5. He generated the constitutional language to make sense of Ileo's investiture, and instructed Kasa-Vubu on how to install the new government. The administration had full jurisdiction once inducted by the president, said Wigny, and could wait for a favorable moment to ask for its vote of confidence. On September 8, after each branch of the Congolese legislature had supported Lumumba, Wigny was furious. The Africans had not delayed a vote as the foreign minister had advised, and Wigny wrote that the "coup d'état" had only reinforced Lumumba's authority and legitimacy. "This is really serious," he said, "and makes me pessimistic." The CIA told Vice President Nixon that Kasa-Vubu's "precipitate action has at least seriously jeopardized the plan for ousting Lumumba by constitutional means."[30]

On September 10 or 11, a list of names apparently got written down, which might be taken as the start of an Ileo regime, although he did not broadcast his choice of ministers until the evening of September 12. A new government existed, but could carry on only if the parliament approved in due course. That day Hammarskjöld lost sleep in New York worrying about when the parliament might approve the new cabinet.[31]

September 10 would be the first time for a legitimate transfer to have occurred, and so for five days Cordier took instructions from politicians who had no justifiable authority. He had closed the radio station and shut the airports because Kasa-Vubu asked him. The UN had no problem of law and order, and Lumumba, the only candidate for legal prime minister, opposed the decisions, while Cordier allowed the secessionist Tshombe to defy them.

Western Collusion

The Belgians advised Kasa-Vubu about what they considered a coup d'état, but Kasa-Vubu used the UN to carry it out. In the aftermath of Kasa-Vubu's radio performance, the Belgians thanked the Americans for egging on Hammarskjöld, yet while Washington supported the coup, it did not intervene as had Belgium.[32] The UN led the way, although Hammarskjöld did discuss his outlook with the Americans and presumed himself in concert with them. Whether Cordier's throwing his weight around was good or bad, the UN had violated its mandate, and meant to overturn Lumumba. Hammarskjöld had written that the prime minister must be "forced to constitutionality"; then the secretary-general had pushed Lumumba out of office by unconstitutional means.

When Bunche first went to the Congo, he sought guidance from the US State Department,[33] and from the end of June Hammarskjöld's other assistants from the United States had regularly shared intelligence with Ambassador Lodge and the American delegation at the UN. Now, in September, the Congo Club showed messages to the American diplomatic corps in New York as they came off the teleprinter from Leopoldville, and the secretary-general joined the informers.[34] The evening of September 5, Americans learned that Cordier had received Ileo and lectured him on politics. Soviet apparatchiks at the UN could not have betrayed its secrets to the USSR more fully or with greater alacrity than Hammarskjöld and the Congo Club did to the United States. Lumumba—still prime minister—could not get to Cordier, as Heinz Wieschoff, the former OSS official now with the UN, told the Americans on September 6. Cordier treated Lumumba as a private citizen and refused to see him. In contrast to the UN, the American embassy in Leopoldville remained unsure. On September 9, Timberlake hosted a meeting between Lumumba and illustrious visiting American diplomat Averell Harriman. The prime minister gave Harriman a ninety-minute address on politics, and was respected as "Prime Minister."[35] The UN showed more hostility to Lumumba than did the United States.

At one point in the tense moments back in New York, as the men of the United Nations waited for word of Cordier's work, Wieschoff complained to the Americans. The UN had found it difficult to keep pro-Lumumba

members of the ANC off the streets and away from parliament when Lumumba's feeble political opponents stayed in bed. "How can you make a
revolution with such material?" queried Wieschoff. Through the Belgians, Wieschoff also suggested that Kasa-Vubu jail Lumumba: the UN
would not interpose itself, unless the Africans threatened to lynch the
prime minister. Hammarskjöld joined his staff in divulging particulars
to the United States but confided to his American friends that his hands
must be "absolutely clean." On September 7, he said he was trying to
unseat Lumumba, and stood behind Kasa-Vubu, but did not want to
compromise the "UN position and himself." He was pursuing "gamesman-
ship," said the secretary-general, "how to win without actually cheating."
"Several times" during this conversation, noted the American memorandum, Hammarskjöld referred to his posture as "extra-constitutional."
He would "break" Lumumba, Hammarskjöld told Lodge on September 9,
just before the secretary-general reported to the Security Council.[36]

What did Hammarskjöld report to the council? He had, he said, told
Cordier "to avoid any action . . . which directly or indirectly, openly or
by implication . . . would pass judgment on . . . either one of the parties." Cordier had never "consult[ed]" with Kasa-Vubu, and had never
"consulted" with Hammarskjöld himself, although the secretary-general
endorsed Cordier's actions. The UN, Hammarskjöld concluded, had
conducted itself with "utter discretion and impartiality." He later wrote
Dayal that he had to present the UN with "the naked realities" of the
Congo "girl," "stripping her not . . . to tease but to force [member] governments" out of their unreal attitudes.[37]

Principles Do Not Change

The secretary-general was no more than human, and had a personality
and political beliefs that shaped his decision making. He first of all conducted *Western* diplomacy and acted with the United States in mind.
The USSR and its defenders plainly saw this, and this orientation explained why many Western commentators thought Hammarskjöld ad-
mirable. To find him pro-Western or anti-Soviet should not surprise us.
This predisposition did not dishonor him and in many ways had much
to recommend it. In early September the secretary-general additionally

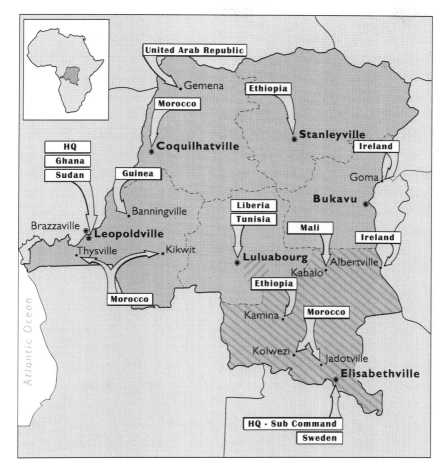

UN soldiers, October 1960

made a bid to give his Western-sponsored institution real clout in the world. At first he had refused to intrude in the Congo's affairs, and so had strengthened Tshombe against Lumumba; then he *had* intruded to impair Lumumba in Leopoldville. We have here distasteful but perhaps typical international politics.

More peculiarly, Hammarskjöld demonstrated an inability to understand himself. The ideals of the UN did not pour forth from him as from a sterile vessel. Yet Hammarskjöld was no simple hypocrite. He did not see the gap between his often expressed ideals as they applied to the Congo and the policies he employed there. Nor did he consciously lie.

Nor did a dash of cynicism lurk in Hammarskjöld. The secretary-general had instead the blemish of many didactic individuals and could not conceive that politics could tarnish him. Hammarskjöld could not grasp how he might sometimes fall away from his ideals.

Conor Cruise O'Brien, the Irish man of letters, for some time in late 1961 represented Hammarskjöld in Katanga. After O'Brien left the UN, he wrote a stunning indictment of the UN's intervention in the Congo in a play, *Murderous Angels*. The UN thought about silencing O'Brien because of the potency of the accusation. Even in this production, however, O'Brien mitigated the responsibility of the secretary-general: Hammarskjöld shrank from a dreadful collision between the Soviet Union and the United States. For Hammarskjöld, claimed O'Brien, atomic war might come about if he did not remove Lumumba. Some such long-term issues might have weighed down Hammarskjöld, and for a few days in August 1960 a "pint size Korea" worried him.[38] But even the most frightening documents in American and UN archives never mention a nuclear face-off as a result of events in the Congo.

When the UN was invited into the Congo, Lumumba and his peers showed they were not master in their own house. Moreover, the United Nations faced a daunting task. One could see the muddle of the regime of Kasa-Vubu and Lumumba even before Western agents motivated Kasa-Vubu to destroy it. Although the UN did its best to flatten Lumumba, Hammarskjöld was less a kingmaker than he thought, and the peacekeepers were not the force in world affairs the secretary-general dreamed they would be. Lumumba may not have stayed in power with Hammarskjöld's neutrality, or even approval. Had the prime minister retained his office, no one knows if he would have ruled effectively or benignly. Nonetheless, Hammarskjöld did not just offer peace on earth to persons of good will. From the thirty-eighth floor of UN headquarters in New York, he esteemed himself as schoolmaster of the Congo, made up reasons for his policies as he went along, and did what he could to kill the Lumumba government.

CHAPTER SEVEN

Mobutu

O N THE EVENING of September 14, nine days after Kasa-Vubu dismissed Lumumba, the military figure Joseph Mobutu proclaimed on the radio in French that he was "neutralizing" Kasa-Vubu, the two competing governments, and the parliament. The short speech was recorded, but Mobutu followed up with an explanatory press conference at the fancy Regina Hotel in downtown Leopoldville. There had been advance word, and reporters filled the ballroom. For the time being, said Mobutu, Kasa-Vubu and Lumumba would not rule. The army would give them a time-out, an armistice, until the end of December, when they might agree on one acceptable administration. Mobutu asked some of the Congo's university students to form a technical cadre to oversee public affairs till the end of the year. The colonel closed his press briefing with the declaration that he would order the envoys of the communist nations of Czechoslovakia and the USSR to leave, and would close their embassies. On September 19 a "College of Commissioners" came into being, composed of more than thirty graduates.[1]

A protégé of Lumumba in the Mouvement National Congolais, Mobutu had experience as a journalist and had ranked as a sergeant in the headquarters of the old Force Publique. In June 1960 he was promoted to

secretary of state in Lumumba's cabinet. In the bedlam of independence, Mobutu owed his rise to the prime minister, who had lifted him
to a colonelcy. Although Victor Lundula got the command of the ANC,
the Armée Nationale Congolaise, Lumumba had wanted Mobutu for
this job.[2] But Mobutu, who was named chief of staff, would not give his
fealty to Lumumba. When the dust settled in 1965, Mobutu established
a tyranny that endured for thirty years.

What happened has allowed historians wrongly to look back on the
beginning of a Mobutu dictatorship. As many people on the scene have
testified, however, Mobutu was a skinny, quivering twenty-nine-year-old
on September 14. Nine days before, on the evening of September 5, he
had not thrown his lot in with Kasa-Vubu, Ileo, and Bomboko, but had
met with Lumumba and his government. Locked in his residence, Kasa-
Vubu had refused to see Mobutu that night.[3]

Mobutu's Mentor, Ben Hammou Kettani

In early September the UN general from Morocco, Ben Hammou Kettani, advised Mobutu. Morocco had gained its independence from France
in the mid-1950s, and in its dangerous and unsteady postcolonial politics
General Kettani was an important personage, navigating between tradi-
tionalists and more left-leaning modernists.[4] Much evidence indicates
that Kettani wanted Mobutu to behave in the Congo as the general had
in Morocco: Mobutu should restrain the soldiers and keep the ANC
neutral in the crisis but work for a stable political solution. Kasa-Vubu's
onetime Belgian adviser, Jef Van Bilsen, believed that General Kettani's
impact on Mobutu had produced the colonel's contorted entrance into
the Congo's politics, and Clare Timberlake reported that Mobutu liked
and trusted Kettani.[5] At the same time Mobutu's officers pressed him
about the irresponsibility of the politicians—Kasa-Vubu, Lumumba, and
Ileo. Distraught, Mobutu considered resigning.[6] Indecisive, often over-
whelmed and perplexed, he had nationalist inclinations and felt a duty to
his land. The soon-to-be designated "strongman" worried about communism and an erratic Lumumba. What should Mobutu do? He wanted
to do the right thing and did not know who was the legitimate prime
minister—Lumumba or Ileo. Mobutu did know that the anarchy of early

Mobutu press conference. On September 14, the colonel answers questions after his announcement of "neutralization" of the politicians. (© *BelgaImage*)

September should not continue. Two opposed regimes existed, and therefore nothing lawful.

The politicians, Mobutu thought, should agree on one stable administration before the start of the year. Meanwhile, he would keep the army out of the struggle that was tearing the ANC into pieces. Politicians openly vying for contingents of soldiers compounded the troubles of the military, and Mobutu looked to the UN and Kettani for assistance in bringing into being a more disciplined force. Indeed, Kasa-Vubu told Timberlake that Kettani would help to "reorient" the army.[7] For Mobutu, this reconstituted force would empower the commissioners, the interim order of technocrats. The colonel would orchestrate some settlement.

He implied that Kasa-Vubu's pronouncement was temporary and not definitive. Mobutu perhaps followed Kasa-Vubu *and* Hammarskjöld, who looked to a hemmed-in Lumumba. In an interview on September 19, Mobutu said that Kettani was "my military advisor and my best friend" and had wanted to take him to see Kasa-Vubu, but Mobutu "did not agree": "I cannot take sides with Kasa-Vubu or where will be my honor as a soldier?"[8] Timberlake repeatedly worried to Washington about Kettani's impact on Mobutu.[9]

Mobutu evidenced his priorities in the subsequent "deneutralization" of Kasa-Vubu after the president swore in the College of Commissioners on September 29. A symbol, not a constituent of the partisan strife, the president should merely preside *over* the system in which Lumumba and Ileo would compete. It is not surprising that Mobutu was confused. He may have demonstrated a dark side in his initial foray into politics, but his actions nonetheless made more constructive sense than scholars have realized.

The mischief of the next month corroborates this interpretation. Since westerners thought Lumumba could cling to power because of his clout with the ANC, some observers believed Mobutu aided Lumumba; others thought Mobutu was not taking sides between Lumumba and Kasa-Vubu. High officials in Belgium and the State Department in Washington scrambled to categorize Mobutu, and to learn of his politics. Contradictory appraisals—including those by Timberlake—flew back and forth across the Atlantic.[10]

Men with guns and ammunition rose up as the supreme mediators in the Congo, but while some three thousand troops in Leopoldville took orders from Mobutu, he did not control the ANC. Moreover, he did not neutralize the politicians. For three weeks, and even more, a search continued to bring Kasa-Vubu and Lumumba together. Through Jean David the UN negotiated with the pair. Dayal described several similar attempts. Kettani nudged Mobutu in the direction of a compromise between Lumumba and Kasa-Vubu. Kasa-Vubu himself had not made up his mind that Lumumba should cede the premiership. These varied efforts came close to brokering a reconciliation, but at the last minute Kasa-Vubu backed off from arrangements with the prime minister, probably yielding to pressures from the United

States and Belgium.[11] Mobutu hardly defined matters but, as just another member of the cast, joined the Kafkaesque drama.

Palavering

Western diplomats fabricated and evaded. The Africans in politics now bloomed with their own version of deeds and public talk. They would say whatever seemed right at the moment, but ignore what they had said at the next. They would browbeat one day, and abjectly apologize on the next; demand on one occasion, and retreat on the same issue soon after. The performances altogether flummoxed the outside diplomats, and the Africans may have aimed at befuddlement. Yet they often acted this way to one another: they would compromise and arrogate, welcome and re-buff, in rapid succession. Even arrests and counter-arrests went along with peacemaking and deliberation. The Congo's politicians wanted covenants more or less acceptable to everyone. When matters got out of hand, the techniques drove Western military authorities to distraction. African soldiers on a military expedition would often not fight. Hostile groups of armed men would look at the circumstances, guess what might happen, and then broker with their erstwhile enemies before they had recourse to guns. Sometimes discussion broke down, and individuals would lose their lives in a tremor of violence, or infantry would indulge in a seemingly random killing spree.

For lack of a better word we describe this political style as *palavering.* The practice was not democratic, although it pursued accommodation, and its aggression was usually scrappy. Dayal and Timberlake homed in on the phenomenon thus: the Africans were "inclined [to] talk much, [and] do little in [a] constructive sense but attack whatever they dislike[d] at the moment."[12] Palavering was at issue when Kasa-Vubu went on the radio on September 5. Mobutu was rehearsing the same sort of politics on September 14, and for several weeks thereafter. Now introduce Belgium and the United States. They wanted no part of this sort of hem-ming and hawing if it would include Lumumba, and did everything they could to hinder it. The westerners succeeded in putting off a settlement between Lumumba and Kasa-Vubu. Yet while the Americans and the

Belgians could break up any entente with Lumumba, they could not get an entente without him. When they began to see their predicament in October, some weeks after Mobutu's edict, they gravitated to the colonel as a more permanent manager of an authoritarian army-led government of the sort that the West knew so well.

With Mobutu, the Europeans and Americans had a military as opposed to a constitutional solution to Lumumba. The foreigners additionally encouraged the violence of palavering—if not the talk—in the form of the obliteration of Lumumba. Many distractions filled this long and slow Western learning process. Mobutu proved wobbly, and the prattle *cum* battle went on. In time, however, the West, and especially the United States, would get fed up with African palavering.

Two Other Mentors: Devlin and Louis Marlière

In September 1960 Mobutu created the College of Commissioners because he suspected that the Ileo government would not go into office. The Congo had to have an administration while Lumumba and Kasa-Vubu ironed out their differences. Lumumba and his friends belittled Mobutu, however, and when Kasa-Vubu saw that an Ileo regime was going nowhere, the president used his ceremonial status to support Mobutu. An estrangement between Mobutu and Lumumba grew, but Lumumba's overconfidence and Kasa-Vubu's persistence alone were not enough to bring it about.

The CIA's Larry Devlin had barely connected with Mobutu, but his acquaintance initiated the consolidation of a group of politicians who looked to the United States and not Belgium. Devlin ingratiated himself with the blacks who he had reason to believe felt uncomfortable with Lumumba, or whom he believed he could induce to feel uncomfortable. Unlike Tshombe, these men were unwilling to work hand-in-glove with the Belgians but wanted some sort of loosely unified Congo. Even Kasa-Vubu did not oppose some such outcome. These Africans additionally felt that none of them had much of a chance if Lumumba triumphed, and so all of them might be tempted to strangle his leadership.

The CIA's influence on Mobutu in September, however, is overestimated.[13] Devlin sang his own praises in respect to September 14. According to one of Devlin's often repeated stories, Mobutu would neutralize Lumumba only if the United States backed the colonel. According to Devlin, again, he went out on a limb and promised American recognition of the new military regime.[14] But the chief of station had no standing to make such a promise, and no one in Washington had a sense of Mobutu's ideas. It was not even clear whether the army was under his control. The contemporary evidence tells us that Devlin exaggerated his importance, although he met with the colonel before September 14. Mobutu asked Devlin for money and, while often displaying anti-Lumumba sentiments, also told the American more than once that the army should stay out of politics. Lobbying Mobutu on September 21, Devlin cabled Washington that the colonel was like a man in a "trance," and he worried a week later about a "weakening" Mobutu. Devlin also claimed that he had persuaded Mobutu *not* to engage in hasty military action for fear that it would fail and further cloud any claims to have a legal government in the Congo. As the CIA briefed the American NSC, "confusion" surrounded Mobutu's actions.[15] The CIA did not control Mobutu as Devlin related, and in any event the African had little authority and conflicting inclinations in the late summer and early fall of 1960. Although the CIA was starting to fund Mobutu and the officers he could buy with American dollars, the UN paid the ANC in Leopoldville in early September.[16]

Moreover, while the Belgians focused on Kasa-Vubu, they had not ceded Mobutu to Kettani or Devlin. They had an important asset in Colonel Louis Marlière, former chief of staff of the Force Publique, who had stayed in Brazzaville after the diplomatic rupture between Leopoldville and Brussels. Marlière and Mobutu had strong personal and even family ties from the period in which they worked together at the headquarters of the old Force Publique. The Belgian officer was godfather to Mobutu's oldest son, and at the end of August Mobutu had asked for the return of Marlière.[17] The Belgian wanted to drive a wedge between the UN and Mobutu, who initially put his faith in the international organization and General Kettani for the improvement of the ANC. When it struck Mobutu that the UN might want to disarm the ANC—a motley bunch in the eyes of Dayal—Marlière readied trainers and matériel. Marlière encouraged the colonel's ambition to turn the ANC into a predictable instrument but one that relied on Belgium and not Kettani. The influence of Marlière cannot be quantified, but he informed Brussels of Mobutu's uncertainty and was easily closer to Mobutu than Devlin was.

Over time Devlin did gain the confidence of Mobutu. Although the CIA paid many African leaders, Mobutu became America's chief "contact," as Devlin called him. Devlin moreover worked with Mobutu's College of Commissioners. Various commissioners received CIA largesse. Devlin gave them "advice and guidance," and they delivered "intelligence on their plans and objectives." Chief among them was former Lumumba foreign minister Justin Bomboko, who had signed Kasa-Vubu's notice of dismissal and who got designated president of the commissioners. Devlin also employed Victor Nendaka, whom prime-minister-in waiting Ileo had named the new head of the Sûreté. Nendaka had informed on Lumumba to the Belgians and Americans after the roundtable in January–February of 1960, when Brussels was working itself into a frenzy over Lumumba's supposed sympathies for the USSR. In March, Devlin had wined and dined Nendaka in Brussels while the African badmouthed Lumumba for hours. Devlin found Nendaka "crafty, devious, and articulate . . . by no means . . . sincere." After he later joined the CIA's Africans in Leopoldville, Nendaka, said Devlin, was "a tremendous ally," and Bomboko and Nendaka "key allies."[18]

Because they all inclined toward the United States, Washington labeled this faction "moderates," a soothing usage on par with "keeping the Cold War out of the Congo." In time, with finances and aggressive advice from Western security services, Mobutu, along with Kasa-Vubu, came to have no interest in sharing authority with the renegade Lumumba. Because Mobutu had driven off the Soviet Union, little chance existed that anti-westerners would challenge him in Leopoldville.

Arresting Lumumba?

While Mobutu was on the fence, and an unknown quantity, the Belgians were assisting Kasa-Vubu in his constitutional exploits. The president had uncertain anti-Lumumba principles, but they were firmer than Mobutu's, though the idleness of Kasa-Vubu made him undependable. Belgians lectured the president on how he might put Lumumba in jail. As a member of parliament, Lumumba had a prima facie exemption from prosecution under the *loi fondamentale*. Yet Kasa-Vubu could argue that Lumumba was not entitled to that exemption, for he was a rebel. The cashiered Lumumba had not facilitated the transfer of power to his successor but instead had persevered about his supposed rights. In fact as the events of early September unfolded, Lumumba had even declared Kasa-Vubu out of office.

In the last part of August Lumumba had begun to turn the screws on his political opponents, and the Western diplomats had condemned his maneuvers. Now the same men pressed Lumumba's opponents to employ such tactics. Poked by the whites, Kasa-Vubu tried to have Lumumba apprehended on September 12, a week after the dismissal and before Mobutu entered the equation. Lumumba's top officer, General Victor Lundula, thwarted this attempt, and on Belgian advice Kasa-Vubu fired Lundula. On September 15, after Mobutu's announcement, Baluba soldiers who were hostile to Lumumba attacked him when he went to Mobutu's headquarters; Ghanaian UN troops stopped the attack. This first round of political hostage-taking nonetheless only began a tournament by politicians and would-be military figures to put one another out of commission. Incarceration was often followed by discharge because the UN was allowed to frustrate warrants—an example of palavering. Although people with some judicial legitimacy pursued Lumumba in the last two weeks of September, the UN guarded Mobutu, Kasa-Vubu, and Lumumba, and each was scared of what the other two might do. On September 23 Lumumba's cabinet ministers Antoine Gizenga and Maurice Mpolo were arrested and scheduled for a transfer to Katanga. But the following day, under UN pressure, Mobutu liberated the Lumumba clique. Palavering started at Kasa-Vubu's residence. André Lahaye, a Belgian Sûreté agent in the area, cabled Brussels: "We fear that all will end with a general reconciliation." Soon another message followed: "Predominant influence of Kettani and Dayal on Mobutu is clear." Timberlake voiced an identical worry to the State Department. At the end of the month a Belgian emissary reported that an unsure Mobutu feared that a segment of the army would put him aside. On October 4 Mobutu refused to execute an order from the College of Commissioners to detain Lumumba although they talked of resigning.[19]

Mobutu still did not have the upper hand over his soldiers, and learned that the UN did not intend to train them. Indeed, Dayal wanted the ANC disarmed. Kasa-Vubu and Mobutu had been barking up the wrong tree in looking to the UN, which was ending its brief partnership with anyone who was not Lumumba. At the same time, Mobutu got money from the CIA, and Devlin whispered in his ear that only with Lumumba gone could the government in Leopoldville steady itself. More important, from the Belgians, Mobutu got promises on how he would get help to strengthen the army.

The UN Vacillates

Khrushchev arrived in New York on September 19 for the formal start of the UN General Assembly, and the USSR assailed the UN's favoritism to the West. In a notorious speech of September 23, he shouted at Hammarskjöld and demanded new leadership. Khrushchev would not give an inch, and with some very boorish manners went far beyond the bounds of diplomatic decorum.

The onslaught on Hammarskjöld's probity combined with the more subtle pressure of many of the African and Asian nations, whose weight had grown dramatically in the world organization. They put their faith in the UN as the best guarantor of aboveboard policies. They were also convinced that Hammarskjöld had acquitted himself improperly in dislodging Lumumba. The secretary-general had heeded the European imperialists, who had a silent partner in the United States. The Africans and Asians wanted Hammarskjöld to succor Africa more boldly. Had the Africans and Asians known that Hammarskjöld had taken the lead in the demolition of the elected government, they might have reacted differently. In the last analysis, however, these Africans and Asians would bet on the Europeans, the Americans, and the UN in preference to the communists.

Still self-deluding but more conscious of his anemic resources, Hammarskjöld altered course. He now had to resuscitate Lumumba and pressure Belgium. He had effectively relinquished his confidence in an independent UN course, and acted as what he was: the impresario of a rickety institution buffeted by the demands that various factions made on it. As he told the UN General Assembly on September 26, "Use whatever word you like, independence, impartiality, objectivity—they all describe essential aspects of what, without exception, must be the attitude

of the secretary general. Such an attitude . . . may at any stage become
an obstacle for those who work for certain political aims which would be
better served or more easily achieved if the secretary general compromised with this attitude."[20]

Belgium and the United States did have clear political aims. The Belgians, however, had little clout with the United Nations. On the other
hand, after the initial period of hesitation in its embassy in the Congo,
the United States came out for Ileo. In New York, on September 26, the
same day that Hammarskjöld proclaimed "impartiality," Secretary of
State Herter talked to the secretary-general about Lumumba's imprisonment. The legal division of the American Department of State thought
the Lumumba cabinet had a good claim to be regarded as a caretaker
ministry and, the lawyers thought, parliamentary immunity should protect Lumumba himself. Herter may not have seen the legal opinion, and
in any event argued for the arrest of Lumumba. The UN, said Herter,
should side with those of the Congo's politicians who aimed to put
Lumumba away. Hammarskjöld accurately replied that many of the
Africans, including Mobutu, did not want to go after the Congo's number-
one figure, but Hammarskjöld also resorted to evasion, if not outright
untruth. He and Dayal, said the secretary-general, agreed on the danger
of Lumumba. Hammarskjöld blamed the failure to arrest Lumumba on
the black politicians, who had not produced a legitimate warrant. Dayal
carried on this line of reasoning for a time. He was steadfast in his respect for a warrant, but the politicians had come up with nothing valid.[21]
Since the UN officials argued that an illegal government had made the
warrants worthless, such a government could hardly author a sound one.

Soon, however, Hammarskjöld found other grounds. He could not permit, he said, the jailing of Lumumba. Lumumba's claim to be prime minister was as good as anyone else's in the dim politics of the Congo. Maybe,
said Hammarskjöld, he should not interpret the Congo's constitution as a
Belgian document, whereby Ileo immediately became prime minister.
Perhaps, the secretary-general suggested, the Congo exemplified a more
general European constitutionalism, whereby Lumumba remained the
head of an outgoing government until Ileo went to the parliament.[22]

This interpretation did not go far enough. The United Nations had
imposed itself on the Congo; the secretary-general had wanted Lumumba

subservient to the UN. Now more than once, however, Hammarskjöld told American officials that the UN had to act on the "basis of principles." These principles had previously favored Kasa-Vubu. Now they favored Lumumba. For by nonintervention in internal politics, said Hammarskjöld, UN forces had kept Lumumba out of jail. The secretary-general told the Americans that he could not "choose men, nor their inclinations, but rather must take [an] objective stand." Hammarskjöld must "keep clean on the record." He "pointedly remarked" that the UN should permit no outside influences. The United States and the UN, Hammarskjöld told a variety of Americans, abided by "different philosophies." In truth the United Nations had reconsidered its policy and now wanted a political place for Lumumba. The Americans reflected with contempt that a partial Hammarskjöld had taken refuge in "impartiality."[23]

By the end of September the UN was working not to frustrate Lumumba, but to increase his legitimacy. What Cordier had done frightened Hammarskjöld, and Dayal willingly shifted policy, converting himself into the chief custodian of Lumumba's rights. Relations between the UN and the Congo's de facto rulers, or at least Leopoldville's de facto rulers, worsened. In August, Lumumba would only treat with Bunche, Hammarskjöld, or Cordier to rebuke them. After a brief honeymoon, Mobutu and Kasa-Vubu also found the UN a sniping organization. They fought with Dayal. Dayal, in addition to finding the commissioners irresponsible outlaws, derided them as a "useless group of amateur youngsters," and Mobutu as a "coward and a weakling."[24] Although the Congo's leaders did not order the UN to leave, they did believe its representative to be patronizing and opposed to their government—their appraisal of Dayal correct in both instances.

The Spectacle Continues

On October 9, the maybe-ex prime minister left his house and campaigned for his views in the *cité* of Leopoldville. Once again, on the small stage of the capital's beer halls, Lumumba raised his voice to will a nation into being. The next day, Mobutu made the move that defined his swing to the anti-Lumumba camp. Units of the ANC that he controlled—some two hundred soldiers from Thysville—appeared around the prime minister's residence, which had UN guards. Ordering an arrest, Mobutu squared off against the peacekeepers, but the colonel's forces retreated. Another example of palavering: Mobutu's ANC feared a fight. Later, Mobutu blamed Kasa-Vubu for what had happened, and the ANC declared that it had not tried to jail Lumumba but only to limit him to his domicile. Louis Marlière, the Belgian adviser to Mobutu, had been shoring him up by promising that Belgium would train cadets for the colonel, if only he would show some fortitude by proceeding with this arrest. Mobutu would be able to beef up his ANC without UN aid. At the beginning of October, before Mobutu had attempted to arrest Lumumba, Marlière complained to Brussels that events were "passing" the colonel, who was "desperate," "on the brink of a nervous breakdown." After the failed attempt Marlière wrote that Mobutu was in danger of "neutralizing" himself.[25]

It became still plainer that no constitutional compromise would occur, and that Mobutu was a cog in the anti-Lumumba machine. Lumumba's detractors pushed Hammarskjöld more. The ANC loosely surrounded the UN troops protecting Lumumba's residence. Although not yet choking, the noose was tightening. The ANC harassed the prime minister's family and staff. More a prisoner, Lumumba saw his hold on affairs lessened. More important, the sparring of October 10 led Hammarskjöld to change course again. Dayal formally took the position that the UN would only shield Lumumba at his home, despite the fact that the Kasa-Vubu/Mobutu regime and Western diplomats now targeted him for imprisonment. The UN would allow the prime minister to be delivered to his enemies should he exit his compound.[26] Hammarskjöld's dislike of Lumumba was patent. Nonetheless, the secretary-general told Western diplomats that the Congo must have some sort of de jure government. They should keep Lumumba off the tracks, but must do it in some kind of quasi-legal fashion.[27]

The westerners could not meet Hammarskjöld's demand, although the outlines of a de facto administration emerged. Kasa-Vubu was the "deneutralized" head with some real power. He presided over a weird administration composed of Belgian mentors, young graduates in the College of Commissioners, political hangers-on from the parliament, and UN functionaries. Taking on new importance was Justin Bomboko, named president of the College of Commissioners and its spokesman for foreign policy. Mobutu was the real riddle. He gave the regime whatever military strength it had, but only slowly materialized as the chief lodestar of Western faith and as a callous antagonist of Lumumba. On November 21, Kasa-Vubu's chief supporter in the military, Colonel Justin Kokolo, commander of the military camp in Leopoldville, was killed in a murderous exchange between the ANC and some UN Tunisian forces. Kokolo had controlled some three thousand men, and Kasa-Vubu now had less independence. He was forced to rely more on Mobutu.

As Mobutu's star rose, Dayal's derision became less tolerable—as much to Mobutu as to his Western backers. The special representative wrote to Hammarskjöld:

> The Treasury is empty, there is no administration worth the name, unemployment is increasing, there is no judiciary or magistracy, no tax collections, no schools are functioning, and . . . shortages everywhere. . . . I have made unceasing appeals to the leaders to take heed of the catastrophic situation. I have not succeeded in drawing their attention to these urgent problems and away from the bitterness of their party strife and the clash of personal interests. . . . With complete and utter recklessness, the political struggle—if it can be so called—is going on without logic or sense. Meanwhile the country is hurtling headlong on the road to disintegration and chaos.[28]

Belgians and Americans bemoaned the ability of Lumumba and denigrated the anti-Lumumba Africans when they acted autonomously. Nonetheless, Western patronage reinforced the junta in Leopoldville, although this favor could not make the rule of Kasa-Vubu and his comrades robust or acceptable to the UN, to many African and Asian nations, or even to the political class in the Congo. It was a pity, said one of the Congo's functionaries, "that some of our high leaders are being bribed by whites." The bribery had resulted "in all this internal strife" when the disputes could be "settled amicably."[29] Would the prime minister reestablish himself in the face of the timid opposition and the UN's ambivalence? Again and again through October and into November officials of the United States and Belgium worked themselves into a lather mulling over a return by Lumumba to government. Along with Kasa-

Vubu, Mobutu did not want to mobilize the Congo's legislature to attempt Ileo's validation. The president and the colonel were not stupid. The elected politicians still esteemed Lumumba, and so far as the people had a choice in the Congo, they chose Lumumba. Naturally, the Western democracies wanted nothing to do with a reopened parliament. They took every opportunity to buck up Mobutu and Kasa-Vubu with good words—and real money—when Mobutu showed signs of faltering, which he did almost daily.

CHAPTER EIGHT

Africans against Lumumba

Lumumba's murder brought him laurels he might never otherwise have acquired. History is unlikely to have revered him as an epic figure had he lived longer. Few African politicians who actually wielded power for any length of time in the twentieth century have escaped the stain of corruption, accusations of neocolonialism, the taint of warmongering, or the label of ineffectiveness. Had Lumumba survived, would he be regarded as a Mobutu? Lumumba prevailed in death as he did not in life, especially as a crusader for Africa; in 1960 an array of Africans opposed him. They exhibited mixed motives and assorted political aptitudes. Unless the imperial belief that Africans robotically did the bidding of whites is accepted, we need to examine the agency of Lumumba's indigenous enemies. Some Africans on the continent and some in the Congo set themselves against Lumumba. The mental world of his adversaries bears exploration, for they sought a passageway for Africa that might take them away from the dangers of war—with one another, and with Europeans. On the one hand, these Africans did not have a Western ideal of governance. On the other hand, these men looked to the West for help to carve out their own way.

Friends and Enemies in Africa

When Lumumba formed his ministry, nonaligned Africans and much of the non-Western world cheered. In his two jail sentences he had earned authentic anticolonial credentials. He also had grace, intelligence, and flair—best briefly signified when he introduced his cabinet, ending with: "and the prime minister, your servant, Lumumba." On the left his friends included Gamal Abdel Nasser of the United Arab Republic, Kwame Nkrumah of Ghana, and Sékou Touré of Guinea. Less strident leaders like Jawaharlal Nehru of India and Mongi Slim of Tunisia might criticize Lumumba but also took pride in this spokesman for a world shedding the European empires.

Lumumba had complex adversaries among people of color. Some, like those in Liberia, founded by former slaves from the United States, lined up with America in a knee-jerk reaction to Lumumba's combative, non-subservient politics. Nigeria and Sierra Leone joined Liberia. In Brazzaville, Fulbert Youlou, who took over in the old French Congo in August 1960, gave the Belgians and Lumumba's local foes a sanctuary. Moreover, Youlou did not just represent himself. The "Brazzaville group" from former French West Africa eschewed Lumumba's view that Africa wanted no tutelage from the West.

A former Roman Catholic priest, Abbé Youlou made his way in the pre-independence French Congo. Youlou embraced the Franco-African community that de Gaulle offered in 1958, and came forward as the Brazzaville politician whom France favored. Youlou nonetheless did not rise merely as an accomplice to the French after they had given up their colonies. Like many Francophone Africans, he did not want to stick his finger in de Gaulle's eye, and commentators have accused Youlou and his peers of subservience to colonialism. African politicians benefited European whites. A few Africans, say critics, lived in vulgar affluence, but left their countrymen little better off than under French rule. Yet Youlou believed that the French Congo could hardly govern itself without some kind of guardianship from France, and could face disaster with French enmity. Though perhaps fainthearted, Youlou comprehended that he needed the French to take the inhabitants of his Congo beyond their status as subjects. He appreciated that France wanted to use his new country, but also determined that he might use France in turn.

Youlou's connection to Kasa-Vubu added another variable. Both men belonged to the Kongo people, and each had wished for the restoration of an independent Kongo state. Before June 30, Kasa-Vubu had abandoned his separatist position for a sort of Congo federation, although his followers still hoped for an autonomous Kongo. While Youlou and Kasa-Vubu often had family quarrels in the late 1950s, Youlou campaigned for Kasa-Vubu as the Congo reached independence. After June 1960 and then after Youlou took office in Congo (Brazzaville) in August, he worked to debilitate Lumumba and to preclude his return after the overthrow in September. Youlou looked toward a confederated Congo that would allow Congo (Brazzaville), Leopoldville province, and Angola to come together. After Lumumba was in trouble beyond doubt, it seemed that a sturdier Congo (Leopoldville) might come out of the clutter. Youlou then tipped away from Kasa-Vubu and Mobutu. Above all else Youlou did not want a strong Congo on his border.[1]

A new Kongo state would have revolutionized Africa. From the perspective of Youlou, Lumumba was in the hands of the imperialists who had originated the "nations" of the sort Lumumba wanted to rule. The restoration of precolonial principalities epitomized not just romance about Africa and mythmaking about how peoples might have lived before the late nineteenth century. Youlou wanted a sovereign Africa unpalatable to nationalists like Lumumba. Consequently, after the Belgian Congo got its own government, Youlou wanted not just to take Lumumba down, but also wanted a return to a regional autonomy that antedated European rule.

The Leopoldville Opposition

Lumumba's allies in 1960 are unfairly characterized as fair-weather friends. Some strong nationalists, like Maurice Mpolo, minister of youth and sports in the cabinet, and Joseph Okito, vice president of the senate, would die with him. Others like Thomas Kanza, the Congo's first university graduate in 1956 and sometime ambassador to the UN, stayed alive, but trod a narrow line in fealty to Lumumba. Cléophas Kamitatu, the president of the provincial government of Leopoldville, would remain loyal to the prime minister despite pressure from Mobutu and Kasa-Vubu.[2] Still others, like Antoine Gizenga, the deputy prime minister, stuck to Lumumba's nationalism by escaping to Stanleyville, a Lumumba citadel, after the constitutional upheaval in September 1960. From there, by the end of the year, Gizenga would pull together forces in an attempt to restore the prime minister. As a result of Gizenga's operations, Anicet Kashamura, Lumumba's minister of information, would seize power in Kivu province in December.

At the same time, many of Lumumba's enemies in Leopoldville had once associated with him. These men were a mixed group, some former followers in the MNC, and some convenient comrades during the brief struggle from the late 1950s until June 1960, or even into the early period of the Lumumba government. Most had claims to be nationalists; all were more cautious than Lumumba, or at least suspicious of his intemperate and disorganized politics. By September 1960 fear of where Lumumba might take them kept his opponents together. Perhaps he would usher them into the tyranny that whites had forecast. More likely, he would rush them into an unknown territory, where they would lose financial support from the West and be constrained to run their own affairs when they knew they could not. These men were also ambitious, and Lumumba's preeminence would limit their advance; power seeking motivated their rivalry. Rapacious Western diplomacy worked on African minds, but also verified Lumumba's wildest accusations about those leagued against him. Yet Lumumba had deficiencies that drove away some who would otherwise have clung to him. He wrestled with his own demons in trying not to alienate other politicians. They were unprincipled in their hostility. They acknowledged his gifts and sponsorship, and would have joined Lumumba if they had thought circumstances would have tempered him and allowed a substantial place for them.

Kasa-Vubu shared Lumumba's distaste for the heavy-handedness of Belgian interference and the pro-Belgian spirit in Katanga. But in the late summer of 1960 as Kasa-Vubu fell away from Lumumba, the president proved a slothful adversary. Mobutu, a nationalist and former disciple of Lumumba in the MNC, was a different case. The Western powers had thrust Mobutu into the limelight. They victimized the young man. He too wound up hating Lumumba, but in 1960 deserved pity more than disparagement. Joseph Ileo, the president of the senate, was a former colleague of Lumumba in the MNC and had shown some courage as an anti-Lumumba voice in the legislature. For some time he hung around as prime-minister-designate. But he never developed a significant following and did not play much of a role in de facto governance after September 5.

Two other men had equal significance and fewer scruples. We have already met Justin Bomboko from Équateur. Foreign minister under Lumumba, he became the chief foreign policy spokesman for the Leopoldville politicians who resisted Lumumba after the coup in September. Opportunism and identification with Brussels drove Bomboko. He resembled Kasa-Vubu and Mobutu in his concern about Lumumba's goals. Bomboko, however, had a greater sense of self-advancement, and had the attributes of a conventional sly politician, learning a deadly game.

Yet another political type rose up in the deceiver Victor Nendaka, whom Ileo named director of the Sûreté. A risk-taking business entrepreneur, Nendaka got into politics in his mid-thirties, and worked for the MNC in 1959 and early 1960, but broke with Lumumba before the May elections of 1960. Nendaka thought Lumumba a communist, and Lumumba believed Nendaka undermined the MNC. Nendaka's own party did not succeed in gaining a parliamentary seat, and the triumphant coalition of the MNC-Lumumba forced him into the shadows at independence. After Kasa-Vubu gave notice to Lumumba in September, Nendaka rushed back into politics as head of the Congo's security service. In Leopoldville this organization amounted to a secret police force smiled on by Belgians and Americans. Nendaka showed some real skills, and in his new job his ability to take advantage of the timidity of others, his furtiveness, and his hostility to Lumumba all received a focus.

The Leopoldville competitors only slowly jelled. Even when they did, they had little positive to offer. As a collective, they had minimal qualities of democratic popularity, although they could produce destructive effects.

Secessionist Enemies

Lumumba faced two sorts of African opponents in the Congo. The faction in Leopoldville had some commitment to Congolese nationalism. Mortal enemies outside the city had few ties to the central government. They shrank from Lumumba's grab for power that might destroy the ethnic regions from which they originated. These men saw their future in a number of lands in a new central Africa that would reimpose indigenous authority and annul the geography of the Belgian Congo. Simultaneously these nonnationalist Africans broke bread with Belgians who hated Lumumba.

Some contemporary scholars will not use *tribalism* to describe developments in Africa because of the brutish and ahistorical connotation of the term, yet it cannot be entirely dismissed. Tribalism notes cultural conventions that separated or joined more or less homogeneous peoples. Certainly, Belgians had earlier manipulated the personalities of various groups. The Europeans exploited identities and differences, exaggerated them at times, and fixed on stereotypes. But none of this implies that the realities were illusory. All African leaders saw that the chasm between Western civic commitments and local fidelities made their experiment in independent political life precarious. Lumumba did not just make up his disdain for time-honored chieftaincies and petty empires; he pointed to the Congo's weaknesses, and one of them he called *tribalism*.[3]

Lumumba's more principled and unrelenting antagonists distanced themselves from Leopoldville. To consider these politicians in Katanga and in Kasai, we must, in however simplified form, take up the difficult problems of tribal, regional, or ethnic conflict.

Évolués had founded the MNC in 1958, with Lumumba its head. Although he spoke against rigid racial nationalism, he said that "a man without any nationalist tendencies is a man without a soul."[4] Nonetheless, the Congo's obdurate divisions baffled Lumumba, and by the middle of 1959 his party had divided over centralization. In Kasai, Lumumba at first worked with Albert Kalonji, an accountant in Luluabourg, the capital of the province. Kalonji headed the MNC there and was a member of the Baluba from Kasai. His people had a strong identity, maintained their own language, and aroused the suspicion of others. Unsurprisingly,

Kalonji identified the MNC in Kasai as a Baluba association, a commitment Lumumba opposed. By the end of 1959 an MNC-Kalonji came into being, centered on the Baluba, in contrast to the unitarian MNC, now the MNC-Lumumba. Kalonji had his peculiarities, but held the devotion of the Kasai Baluba. On a smaller, less sophisticated stage Kalonji had some of the same populist qualities as Lumumba, but spoke out most against him.

At the end of 1959, bitter and violent conflicts occurred in Kasai between the Baluba and the other main ethnic group in the province, the Lulua. Frightened Baluba began to migrate from Luluabourg and its surroundings to their homeland in the south, around the city of Bakwanga. The elections of May 1960 added to the disturbances. Although the MNC-Kalonji was the largest political party in Kasai, the MNC-Lumumba formed a common front with all the other parties, and this coalition controlled the new provincial legislature. Kalonji threatened that the Kasai Baluba would set up their own government in the south. The announcement propelled more Baluba to Bakwanga. When Lumumba put together his national government, he again ignored Kalonji. On August 9—Katanga had already seceded—Kalonji made good his threat, and declared independence. More Baluba left for the Bakwanga area, creating a huge refugee problem and troubling the UN, which tried to prevent escalating reprisals on each side. For Lumumba a renegade south Kasai exacerbated the disintegration of the nation. Kalonji's scanty holdings occupied only one of the province of Kasai's four districts, but this part of south Kasai was the second-richest mineral-producing area after Katanga, and was home to the Congo's diamond mines run by the Belgian Forminière Company. Kalonji expected that the diamonds would see him through and planned, however uncomfortably, to connect with Katanga to his south. For Lumumba, Kalonji stood for the worst sort of ethnic localism, and from Lumumba's perspective Kalonji was responsible for the continuing violence that Baluba tribalism created. Several months later Kalonji made himself the king of the Kasai Baluba and associated himself with idiosyncratic spiritual beliefs.

When Lumumba attempted to invade Katanga at the end of August, the route went through south Kasai. Kalonji's regime would fall before Tshombe's, and on August 26, with only a brief exchange, Bakwanga surrendered as Lumumba's army drew near. Kalonji took refuge in Elis-abethville. Then, at the very end of the month, bloody skirmishes oc-curred in the region, and Lumumba's Armée Nationale Congolaise ram-paged against Baluba in southern Kasai. These were the conflicts that Hammarskjöld characterized as genocidal. Whether or not Kalonji listened to the secretary-general, he now saw Lumumba as a deadly enemy. In the last week of September, shortly after Lumumba's dismissal, Kasa-Vubu and Mobutu ended the invasion of Kasai and Katanga and withdrew their troops. Kasa-Vubu asked the UN to set up a neutral zone around Bakwanga. Belgian officers, however, assisted Kasai Baluba with weap-ons. Kalonji climbed back to power in his mini-state. Without renouncing secession, he accepted the post of minister of justice in the Ileo govern-ment, and was primed to go after Lumumba.

Katanga's Friends and Enemies

Deadly rivalries also made matters complex in Katanga. The province had many divisions, although it roughly split between north and south. In the south of Katanga, home to Union Minière, and especially in the towns, the multiethnic Conakat political party prevailed, and after July 11 its leader Tshombe ruled the breakaway regime that spoke for all of Katanga. The Conakat had first defined itself as a movement to limit the rights of immigrant Baluba who had trekked from Kasai to Katanga. Tshombe's Conakat nurtured all of Katanga against outsiders.[5]

Born into a wealthy family of merchants, Tshombe married the daugh-ter of a Lunda chief and ultimately aimed for a kingdom that, with some kind of European aid, would go its own way in a new Africa. He hewed to pragmatism, although two of his ministers gave the regime an ideo-logical posture. Minister of the Interior Godefroid Munongo had bick-ered with Tshombe in Katanga—Munongo first led the Conakat. The grandson of a Bayeke king, Munongo had no time for democracy, or a Westernized Congo. He wanted to return to an old-time domain in south-ern Katanga and restore the customary chiefs, who did not need votes to govern. After the secession Tshombe and Munongo worked closely if self-interestedly in Elisabethville. Munongo was the will behind the de-cision in July 1960 to close the Elisabethville airport to Kasa-Vubu and

Lumumba. Making Ralph Bunche's visit uncomfortable in August, Munongo then secured Hammarskjöld's capitulation to Katanga. As one expert said, Munongo was "forceful, aggressive, and brutal."[6]

The other noteworthy minister, Jean-Baptist Kibwe, had a lesser reputation than Munongo. In May 1960 Katanga had elected Kibwe to its provincial assembly, although he was dedicated to Katanga's independence. When Katanga seceded in July, Tshombe named Kibwe minister of finance. He soon journeyed outside the Congo to procure benefactors—in August he and other members of Katanga's delegation met with Baudouin in Brussels. Munongo and Kibwe both believed in an antimodern Katanga. For each man, Lumumba typified the European nationalist impulse that would brush traditions aside. Tshombe and Munongo doggedly opposed Lumumba from the first. After his attempted invasion of Katanga in late August, they abominated the prime minister.

Tshombe, Munongo, and Kibwe had an intricate alliance with the Belgians. The leaders of Katanga tried to hold themselves aloof from Brussels and from the whites in Elisabethville. The Europeans in Katanga worked for the rights of the *colons* as well as for the decentralization of the Congo, taking as an example the settler regimes that had developed in the English colonies in southern Africa. The Belgians in Elisabethville wanted such a government in an autonomous Katanga that would yet be bound to Brussels. By the late 1950s the program of the locals meshed with that of the Europeans, who promised Tshombe a kind of home rule. Through him the Europeans would reinforce a separate Katanga. Tshombe and his peers consciously exploited the Europeans to maintain anti-Lumumba power in Katanga, aware that the Belgians in Elisabethville exploited them in turn. To hedge their bets, Munongo and Kibwe pushed Tshombe to call on French technical and military expertise to offset the influence of Brussels.

Tshombe had assets the Europeans needed. After Katanga declared its sovereignty, his charm and glamour gave legitimacy to the unrecognized but operative government. In some ways he personified an African diplomacy. While Western officials could say yes and no at the same time, Tshombe could do that and more: he could stonewall, not show up, fabricate, voice contradictory positions without embarrassment, refuse to see even august personnel or send them off on a fool's errand, give away points in negotiation and later refuse to give them away, and dismiss inconsistencies—all with a cordial affection. His skills did much to keep the disaffiliated administration on an even keel. After independence, Katanga had an up-and-running government; with European advice, the economy generated profits, even if most of them still went to the whites.

Minister of the Interior Munongo was perhaps the indispensable person. He ruthlessly ran Katanga's Sûreté and influenced its police force. Kibwe, cunning in his management of the economy and in his politics, contributed too. Tshombe gave the regime an acceptable popular appearance. All three argued that Lumumba's African nationalism was communist. For Katanga, centralization equaled Soviet tyranny. They drummed up part of this rhetoric to get the positive attention of the United States. But Katanga's secessionists also viewed communism—like the constitutional democracy for which they felt distaste—as a *Western* virus against which they should inoculate Africa. This dislike of commitments they perceived as un-African may have sat uneasily with the religion Tshombe espoused, an African version of evangelical Protestantism. All told, the government in Katanga had a peculiar Afro-centric vision. It brought together anti-individualism and anti-Western politics, and a religiosity that integrated African and European traditions.

Jason Sendwe

In the north and in Katanga's urban centers the resident Baluba stood out and vexed the Elisabethville regime. These Baluba had an association that eventually grew into a political party, the Balubakat. The power of the Balubakat came mainly from its attractive leader, Jason Sendwe. The Americans thought him friendly and pleasant, but stupid and inept, but he did not act dumb, and was constantly in the picture. Sendwe was a medical assistant. He had been a boyhood friend of Tshombe, and was like him a Methodist. At first he followed Tshombe's xenophobic politics.[7] Even before independence, however, the Balubakat felt that Tshombe's dislike of the Baluba immigrants would extend to the Baluba who made their homes in Katanga. Sendwe reckoned that Conakat supremacy might injure the Baluba of Katanga. Tshombe's connection to the *colons* also discomfited Sendwe. Underneath, Tshombe might have abhorred the Europeans, but he harped on an Afro-Belgian community and was, for Sendwe, in bed with the colonizers. In the elections of May 1960 the Balubakat challenged the Conakat. Conakat won overall control but in a close call. Each party had about equal strength, although Tshombe drew more on south Katanga, and the Balubakat on the north.

Although the proportional balloting helped, the elections of May 1960 had sent Sendwe to the national legislature as a representative from Elisabethville, and showed Tshombe's slender hold even in the cities of south Katanga. Complicated political negotiations allowed Tshombe to exclude the Balubakat from the provincial government. But in Leopoldville, Lumumba appointed Sendwe state commissioner for Katanga. Even after Katanga seceded in mid-July, Tshombe continued to appreciate Sendwe and still wanted a coalition that would bring in Sendwe as vice president of an independent Katanga. Now in Leopoldville, Sendwe refused and confirmed the split between the two leaders.

At the end of August when Lumumba's military had gone after the insurgencies in Kasai and Katanga, the march against Katanga had come through southern Kasai. Another part of the operation to the east had called for Sendwe to captain the ANC from Kivu Province just to the northeast of Katanga. This military detachment would join up with Baluba supporters in north Katanga. After Kasa-Vubu forced out Lumumba, Leopoldville's military operations were disorganized, and the invasion ended. Although the anti-Tshombe forces left northern Katanga, the region was in rebellion from then on, and the Baluba upheaval exposed the boundary of Tshombe's Katanga. Tshombe had limited jurisdiction in the north, and while he ruled firmly in the south, he was always threatened by Sendwe's popularity.[8] The north welcomed Sendwe, a bearer of nationalism; and his adherents sang of Lumumba and Sendwe as "liberators of our country."[9] Sendwe would protect the Baluba people from Tshombe, and jeopardized Tshombe's Katanga as much as Lumumba did, more so since Sendwe commanded devotion so near to Elisabethville.

Sendwe walked a tightrope. An antagonist of Tshombe, he had something in common with Leopoldville. Yet he was too friendly with Lumumba for the likes of Kasa-Vubu and Mobutu. On October 16 Mobutu

Mobutu finds common ground with Tshombe. In civilian clothes and a bow tie,
Mobutu made dramatic arrangements with Tshombe in Katanga on October 16.
(*Time & Life Pictures/Getty Images/Photo by Terrence Spencer*)

palavered with Tshombe in Elisabethville, and it looked like Leopoldville
and Elisabethville would link up on the basis of their distaste for
Lumumba and Sendwe. We have only a white official's account of the
deliberations, but apparently in three months Tshombe would provide
Leopoldville with cash, while Mobutu indicated that he would "neutralize Lumumba completely, and if possible physically."[10] Three days after
this arrangement was made, on October 19, Leopoldville politicians
jailed Sendwe. The arrest appeared to seal the bargain. Then the UN
got Sendwe out of the lockup, arguing he had "parliamentary immunity." Now a peacemaker under UN sponsorship, he got to tour north
Katanga, urging the Baluba to refrain from bloodletting. Sendwe's people greeted him ecstatically. The performance reminded commentators
of Lumumba's effect on ordinary folks, and tensions declined in the area
that the UN safeguarded from warfare. Tshombe censured the UN interference and labeled Sendwe a "public danger."[11]

Sendwe had humiliated Tshombe, and someone—perhaps Mobutu—
had double-crossed Katanga. On the scene in Katanga, Sendwe gave the

lie to Tshombe's claims to dictate outside the south of the province, and indicated Lumumba's strength on the doorsteps of the seceders. Kasa-Vubu, Mobutu, and the commissioners in Leopoldville found in Sendwe a pawn who might come in handy negotiating with Katanga. But Sendwe did not act like a pawn. At least in Katanga he was in a class with Lumumba on this dangerous chessboard, and Belgium and the United States feared that the more acceptable nationalism of Sendwe might dislodge Tshombe.[12] For his part, Tshombe could find no one to trust.

CHAPTER NINE

The Central Intelligence Agency

THE CIA had an exaggerated reputation for providing instant answers for troubling issues. In the late 1940s, America had formed
the Central Intelligence Agency as part of the fight against the Soviets.
The CIA gathered information, but had a security dimension that grew
rapidly, despite the hostility of other governmental departments. By the
mid-1950s the Cold War had enveloped American politics, and the
Eisenhower administration relied more and more on the organization to
put out of commission or hijack regimes that the United States disliked.
The Agency engaged in underhanded tactics, dirty tricks, and antidemocratic activities in covert operations. In extreme circumstances, policy
makers might even mandate that the CIA permanently cripple, imprison,
or exile enemies thought to be drifting dangerously close to communism
or the USSR.

Tensions between America and Russia might spiral into a civilization-
ending thermonuclear war, and for Eisenhower undercover enterprises
offered a comparatively humane way to keep the peace in certain parts of
the world. The CIA justified hidden escapades by arguing that they
would avoid a "hot war." The USSR and the United States might cir-
cumvent a showdown if they struggled for advantage out of sight. The
president could turn his eyes away from the ambiguities of efforts that

chipped away at democratic ideals. If the CIA uprooted or banished a few foreigners, the United States paid a tiny moral price for the greater good of finding a way around a confrontation. Even if these people lost their lives because the CIA made unsavory decisions, the president still faced a small cost. Despite receiving criticism, Eisenhower let the Agency get away with murder—at first figuratively, then literally.

A decisive event occurred when Fidel Castro took power in Cuba in 1959. Officials seethed at the success of a communist revolution so near to home. Accustomed to dictating events in Cuba, the Americans found Castro absolutely unacceptable and made up their minds first to depose the man himself, and second to prevent more like him. Many historians have found the concern over Cuba by Eisenhower, and still more by his successor John Kennedy, obsessive, and possibly "crazy." The CIA ultimately oversaw a whole menu of loony plots to kill Castro. In any event, after he popped up on the world scene in 1959 and 1960, assassination was on the minds and in the discussions of leaders. The option found a kind of acceptance. By the time Kennedy took office in January 1961, the CIA felt comfortable enough to form an "Executive Action" program, ZR/Rifle, that would approve and carry out executions. ZR/Rifle showed that murder had moved from the disallowed, to the atypical and ad hoc, to the bureaucratized.[1]

Morals and Politics

Historians and citizens interested in these matters are blessed by the 1975 report of a U.S. Senate committee set up to investigate suspect government actions: the Senate Select Committee to Study Governmental Operations with Respect to Intelligence Activities. The committee's hearings took place in the wake of the scandals in the administration of Richard Nixon, who had finally won election in 1968. The committee unearthed documentary sources for understanding the history of intelligence. The hearings also promoted a forum that compelled spies and high functionaries to speak about their participation in murders, and launched the publication of many tell-all memoirs. But this retrospective testimony cannot be read as if the men involved were just stating facts. The figures of speech and systematic euphemism demand attention.

The Senate committee wanted to know if national security administrators really proposed to kill foreign executives. Sometimes the people interrogated acknowledged that the world crises of the 1950s and 1960s might have necessitated questionable action. Nevertheless, the officials said that they only spoke of such action in a roundabout way; they needed to give statesmen "plausible deniability." For example, by speaking of "high authority," or "thinking in high quarters," or "my associates," these men buffered the president.[2]

Democracies engage in public diplomacy, in which policies are discussed with citizens. The ethics involved are familiar in everyday life and proceed on the basis of accepted notions of right and wrong. Thus, on September 22, 1960, Eisenhower, sometimes called the moral leader of the free world, made a speech at the opening of the UN session, when the Congo had the globe's attention. Eisenhower implored the membership to bolster the UN's African effort, which had the interests of all of humanity at heart. "The United Nations," he said, "was not conceived as an Olympian organ to amplify the propaganda tunes of individual nations." *Five times,* in separate parts of his address, Eisenhower admonished governments to refrain from mucking about in the internal affairs of the Congo, as he said in one place, "by subversion, force, propaganda, or any other means . . . or by inciting its . . . peoples to violence against each other."[3]

Yet in the month before his speech, the CIA had used all of the specific forms of interference Eisenhower mentioned—subversion, force, propaganda, and the inciting of domestic violence. Do we simply throw up our hands at this grotesque duplicity? Can Eisenhower's words and actions be made consistent? Simply to talk about lying in politics misconstrues what is going on.

International affairs require another sort of morality from that exhibited at the UN. Eisenhower could not deal with Lumumba as he would with his butler or his brother. The president was constrained to act in ways that might conflict with personal ethics. This argument can be put in different, related ways. What is appropriate for a private individual differs from political obligation. The president might have to organize bad things to accomplish good, or choose among lesser evils. A transcendent end might justify doubtful means. Commentators call this the problem of "dirty hands."[4]

This is easily comprehended on one level. Eisenhower was a top leader of the American army in World War II, and supervised enormous bloodletting. War is to be deprecated, but its ways impose themselves on the usual disinclination to kill people. Philosophers of politics say that even outside of war, human beings *cannot* govern unsullied. Politics *demands* heartless and unlawful undertakings antithetical to individual virtue. Only simpletons presume that the same rules apply in personal and civic life, for diabolical forces lurk in the political. Hammarskjöld is an exceptional case. Unlike most public men, who have a sense—disillusioned or tragic—of being pulled in two ways, the secretary-general never understood the forces at work on his moral compass.

Political theorists also admit a central paradox. Although politics and morality function in different spheres, defined by different laws, the two spheres somehow touch one another. Political action does not move choices to a place where conventional morality has no footing. Political ethics do not vanquish individual ethics but are rather somehow uneasily allied with them. "Reasons of state" may justify some disagreeable decisions, but politicians cannot do whatever they want. National security officials must walk a narrow line between what political morality can legitimate and what is out of bounds. This line, on which assassination lies, is subject to religious or moral evaluation. Most people would accept the use of covert operations aimed at killing Hitler, but might stumble over efforts to put out a contract on Dwight Eisenhower or Paul-Henri Spaak. These statesmen take on some of the most difficult tasks given to human beings, and so deserve gratitude; they also may merit the severest criticism when they wrongly cross a line.

For such men the area between political and personal morality holds extreme danger. Suppose that, after Eisenhower spoke at the UN, Khrushchev had stood up and given irrefutable proof of illicit American intrusions in the Congo. Something like this had occurred just a bit earlier when the United States had launched the U-2 spy planes over Russia. The Soviets shot one down in May 1960, and the president dissembled about the incident. Then Khrushchev produced the pilot, who had miraculously survived the crash. Khrushchev exposed Eisenhower's equivocations and diminished his stature. The embarrassment contributed to the lackluster end of the American administration, during which time the president clung to entrenched policies, and stumbled in carrying them out.

So when CIA advisers talked about "plausible deniability" in the Senate hearings, they were outlining a strategy of high politics as it interacted with ordinary life. One had to safeguard people like Eisenhower. "Plausible deniability" made for coded speech when articulating policy because it might have to be discussed in public as a matter of personal morality.

The World of the CIA

According to plausible deniability, the national security bureaucrats claimed that if they did not utter certain words, they could say that they wanted something other than murder. But this logic has something odd about it. Whatever words were spoken, the English context made their meaning transparent. "Executive Action" equaled *murder;* "elimination" equaled *murder;* "getting rid of" equaled *murder.* The Americans who testified before the Senate committee in 1975 were not in 1960 protecting themselves or the president from some later possible accusation that they were having someone murdered. Under scrutiny, the documents unmistakably talk murder. The homicidal idioms have plain meaning, just as "high authority," "my associate," or "thinking in high quarters" refers to Eisenhower. Historical examination breaks down plausible deniability as a strategy.

Richard Bissell held the second place in the CIA, and Allen Dulles marked Bissell as his successor. In 1961, however, an Agency disaster failed to depose Castro in the Bay of Pigs invasion, and Bissell lost his job, as did Dulles. When Bissell came before the Senate committee in 1975 (Dulles had long since died), he demonstrated some bitterness. A most aggressive undercover professional, he was uniquely willing to make gritty assertions about the world of intelligence. Bissell told the committee that no lack of clarity resulted from circumlocution. It had, he said, "obvious" meaning. "The director [in this case Dulles] is being told, get rid of the guy, and if you have to use extreme means up to and including assassination, go ahead." Talking around an issue, Bissell went on, did not make it obscure; it was "perfectly clear." "If it is gobbledygook," he concluded, "it is on a good high level."[5]

These secondary matters of ambiguity should not obscure another sort of verbal jujitsu. American politicians might use a range of words to talk about ending the career of an opponent who might be scapegoated, humiliated, undercut, exposed, investigated, subpoenaed, harassed, or gotten. No one, however, would use the word "eliminate," for that would mean *murder*. Here the English differs from the French, where "éliminer" has a wider nonlethal set of connotations. Another range of words is associated with different sorts of ways of ending the life of other persons. No one involved in government would voice phrases like "waste," "off," "give cement shoes to," or "take for a ride"—verbs frequently employed (at least in the movies) by criminals in various disputes. CIA functionaries would have laughed over talk about Lumumba's passing away. "Killing" is the preferred word that soldiers use in battle. When higher-ups order murder in conditions of war, they favor "execute." National security managers might be willing to say "assassination," which connotes the murder of a person of rank for a political reason. One member of the Senate committee asked Bissell, "How many murders did you contemplate . . . assassinations, I am sorry."[6] Primarily, the language about deliberately ending a life warrants the goal, softens the blow, in a range of different circumstances.

Frequently in the committee hearings, bureaucrats said that they did not remember what occurred, or that no discussion of killing had taken place, that the United States and its hirelings did not consort with murderers. After brooding about murder for three months in 1960, these men said: "I never heard any discussion of assassination attempts"; "Even after I reviewed the documents . . . I was unable to recall"; "I have no knowledge"; "I never heard. . . . I do not recall"; "I do not have any specific recollection"; "I still have no direct recollection."[7] In 1960, Chief of Operations Richard Helms worked with Bissell and later ran the CIA himself. Here is what he had to say about Lumumba:

> I am relatively certain that he represented something that the United States government didn't like but I can't remember anymore what it

was. Was he a rightist or a leftist? . . . Actually what was wrong with Lumumba? Why didn't we like him?[8]

Sometimes people don't remember, and some officials may have kept away from the murder. And sometimes these servants of the state really wanted to guard significant secrets. But overall, in their lack of recall, their expression of rectitude, and tasteful language, these men were judicious in a specific way. The officials safeguarded *themselves* from a full grasp of what they were undertaking. They did not want, even as men involved in the rough and nasty world of international affairs, to address openly what they were about. Words helped them disguise many things they did on the job. The CIA later politely described its bribery of politicians as "subvention." When foreign politicians were persuaded to hand enemies of Americans over to killers—that was "rendition."[9] The CIA's continued censorship of its documents is known as "redaction" or "sanitation."

The murder of another human being necessitates some sort of linguistic safety net. Bureaucrats employed language to stifle the claims of conscience. Although using an equivocal phrase does not necessarily mean that Americans chose the unconscionable, they opted for roundabout language over and over again in elaborating their decision making. Even though realpolitik might legitimate what they did, these men never wanted to face that they were turning their hands to murder.

Between individual morality and political morality, a nontrivial but irregular contrast exists, and both historians and decision makers call upon it. In addition to this disjunction, the language presents another issue. It shows the inability to meet head-on what one has stepped into in the terrain of politics. The language allowed the officials a certain comfort level when they reflected on their jobs. As Agatha Christie has written about murder, "Fortunately words, ingeniously used, will serve to mask the ugliness of naked facts."[10] Our analysis holds special importance for members of the national security elite who said yes or no in Washington in the fall of 1960. In the comfort of air-conditioned offices where they wore their jackets and ties on even the steamiest days, these men stayed away from the dirt and misery of the Congo, and so too did their conversations.

The CIA benefited from substantial amounts of money and the planet-spanning bureaucracies of the United States. The Ivy League, especially Princeton and Yale, graduated many of its employees. But they did not all have prepossessing gifts. These clubby men had not always gone to these universities because of merit, however defined, but because of money or family connection. As a group, they were not particularly intelligent, talented, or able. Yet with authority over secret operations and with little oversight, the Agency came to have great power. In addition to its own language, the Agency developed eerie procedures and observances. As romanticized as a James Bond movie, the CIA's self-image whitewashed the pathological characters regularly in its employ. Men with problems of substance abuse or the complications of casual romances plagued superiors, but were tolerated on the rationale of "boys will be boys." At their best these functionaries exhibited discretion and competence. But the secret societies of Ivy League undergraduates also come to mind. Of course the Congo had more at stake than late adolescent fun; these civil servants were engaged in life-ending affairs.

Later, for over half a century, the Agency kept its records from the prying eyes of historians and the public, and fought a never-ending battle to nullify inquiry about itself. Perhaps fancy theories about the difference between morals and politics are moot. These bureaucrats use every tool to prevent embarrassment and indignity to themselves and their predecessors.

The Struggle for Control of Policy

Brussels had irately responded to Lumumba's visit to America and to the UN's assumption of authority in the Congo. The anger of Belgium's politicians threatened the Western alliance, and the ferocious criticism of NATO Secretary-General Paul-Henri Spaak troubled Eisenhower. At the same time the clash between Lumumba and Hammarskjöld put the UN operation in the Congo at risk and favored the Russians. All these issues incited Eisenhower's eruption in the National Security Council on August 18. The record quoted the president as saying that the United States must prevent Lumumba from pushing the United Nations out of the Congo. The staff member responsible for writing up the memorandum for the meeting, Robert Johnson, distinctly remembered that the president gave "an order for the assassination of Lumumba." "There was no discussion," he added; "the meeting simply moved on."[11] When interrogated by the Senate committee, many officials could not recall exactly what the president said, and some flat-out denied that he called for murder. Most agreed that the written record would not contain raw language. In any event, the American government was at once spurred to movement.

We have already seen that in early September the United Nations assisted in dislodging Lumumba from the prime ministership, and that in September, October, and November the result was even more turmoil among the local politicians. Amid this disarray, however, US policy now took a new direction, without much notice of the shifting scene we have already explored in the Congo itself. We must revisit the autumn of 1960, when Americans paid little attention to the minutiae of the Congo's politics.

Eisenhower's words first of all energized the continual battle within his administration over whether the military, the diplomats, or the spies would control foreign policy, although other agencies were often involved in addition to the Departments of Defense and State and the CIA. This fight went on and on, and was resolved differently depending on the time and the problem, but a basic matter was the competence of Allen Dulles. The president's irritation on August 18 fueled government-wide concerns about the ability of Dulles in running the Agency. He was supposed to garner intelligence, but obtaining information had few attractions for Dulles, who liked the work of subversion and who, critics claimed, had allowed the CIA to run amok. The director got his grip on the federal bureaucracy because of the overwrought fear of communism, and the CIA's supposed ability cheaply, clandestinely, and efficiently to immobilize evildoers. From 1956 on, however, a "Board of Consultants on Foreign Intelligence Activities" had been recommending changes, underscoring even earlier reports to Eisenhower about Dulles's ineptness. No one had any idea of how valuable the covert operations of the CIA actually were, or whether money was spent prudently. The board wanted real supervision and

Allen Dulles. The head of the CIA was revered within his organization, suspect outside it. (*Princeton University Library*)

accountability, and an end to Lone Ranger escapades, which seemed dubious and dangerous to American prestige. Dulles had responded by promising improvements but not delivering.

The oversight committee also intimated that the close connection between the CIA and the Department of State prevented the worst abuses. The State Department gave some mature overall government direction to CIA work because Allen Dulles and Secretary of State John Foster Dulles were brothers. Then, in April 1959, John Foster Dulles resigned because of illness and died soon thereafter. A new group took over in the State Department. John Foster Dulles no longer shielded his brother, and in 1959 and 1960 the criticism of the CIA increased. We believe that, even with Castro to point to, in 1960 Allen Dulles wanted to make himself and his bureaucracy indispensable to the president as the cost-effective way to achieve certain policy goals overseas. Dulles had a vested interest in the sort of communism that the CIA might foil through undercover tactics. In any event, he did not have the will or the ability to restructure his Agency to make it look less like a rogue elephant to the board of consultants. They denigrated the effectiveness of clandestine effort, took issue with a number of "major covert action[s]," and wanted the CIA out of this line of work. Dulles stalled. As Eisenhower's term of office concluded, an obviously upset president was worrying about the CIA. In the final analysis, however, he bore responsibility for not reining in the Agency. For well over four years Eisenhower had given it wide leeway. In the fall of 1960, his genuine fears about Castro and his short fuse about Lumumba actually led him to push for CIA action.[12]

Project Wizard

On August 23, less than a week after the president had ordered the US government to go after Lumumba, the State Department called a meeting with the CIA to propose an "interagency" team, including the Defense Department, to discuss options "outside the UN framework." The State Department wanted to learn what the CIA was up to, and the new committee would coordinate action.[13] The military always looked to a fight. The diplomats usually wanted more discussion, while the CIA had secret exploits up its sleeve. Who would make decisions, and what would they be? Whatever Dulles and his assistants told the State Department on August 23, over the preceding two weeks the CIA had revised its strategies for Leopoldville.

Project Wizard had come into being. It grew out of Devlin's ideas but also out of proposals of the Brussels CIA. Eisenhower's fit of temper threw Wizard into high gear. On August 18, immediately after Eisenhower said that Lumumba should not be permitted to throw the UN out, the president had met with National Security Adviser Gordon Gray. The next day the CIA cabled Devlin to move forward with various ramped-up dirty tricks. Ultimate formal approval of the government's most unpleasant jobs came through a standing four-person subcommittee of the National Security Council, the "Special Group." In addition to a note taker, it consisted of a top man of the Department of State and of Defense; Dulles; and Gordon Gray, who spoke for the president.[14] On August 25, Dulles had his regular meeting with the Special Group. He outlined the mounting anti-Lumumba exercises of Project Wizard in the recent past. But the national security adviser was not satisfied with the CIA, and put Dulles on notice that Wizard was not sufficient. "His associates," said Gray, had "extremely strong feelings" about the need for "straightforward action." Gray wondered if the CIA was doing enough. After some discussion, the Special Group agreed not to "rule out 'consideration' of any particular kind of activity which might contribute to getting rid of Lumumba."[15]

The next day Dulles himself wired Devlin about the "removal" of Lumumba as "an urgent and prime objective." With a State Department nod, Dulles allowed Devlin some freedom of operation and stipulated "more aggressive action if it can remain covert." The CIA also awarded Leopoldville an additional $100,000 to accomplish these goals should a "target of opportunity" present itself and should Devlin not have time to sound out either the embassy in the Congo or the CIA at home.[16] By the end of August Devlin was accelerating his stealthy activity at the same time that Hammarskjöld's own fevered agitation about Lumumba was escalating.

By the beginning of September, when Kasa-Vubu pitched Lumumba out, the Congo's president had the help of Belgian and UN authorities and quite possibly support from other imperial powers, and also the goodwill of the CIA. At this time too the Americans put Joseph Ileo, Kasa-Vubu's choice for prime minister, on the payroll, although he had already been funded to secure his election as president of the Congo's senate.[17]

Even when these forces had pushed Lumumba to the wall, the Americans continued to think of him as a threat. On September 6, the day after Kasa-Vubu's radio address, Devlin wrote, "Lumumba in opposition is almost as dangerous as in office." Deposing Lumumba, Dulles told an NSC meeting on September 7, did not diminish the menace. The African "always seemed to come out on top in each of these struggles." The memorandum of that meeting does not record that Eisenhower spoke. The next day, however, in a Special Group meeting, Gray again reminded Dulles that the president wanted "people in the field" to know that they should take "vigorous action." The CIA in Washington then nagged Devlin in Leopoldville about Lumumba's overriding "talents and dynamism." Even if it seemed he had lost, he could "reestablish . . . his position."[18]

In the NSC on September 21, Dulles gave officials, including Eisenhower, an up-to-date summary. Kasa-Vubu had axed Lumumba, and Mobutu had contrived a military solution. Yet stories of a settlement floated around, and Lumumba still had a political presence. Dulles parroted Devlin: "Lumumba was not yet disposed of and remained a grave danger as long as he was not disposed of."[19] Meanwhile, UN representative Rajeshwar Dayal gave some protection to Lumumba. UN troops surrounded the prime minister's house, and forestalled action by components of the army unfriendly to Lumumba. Because of the UN, the risk from Lumumba appeared even more substantial. The United Nations, Devlin wired, had given Lumumba an "opportunity [to] organize [a] counter attack." The "only solution is [to] remove him from [the] scene soonest."[20] Mobutu had sent the diplomats of the USSR packing, but if the Americans were to put down communism, they had to stamp out Lumumba. Each Western tactical success fed a demand for a further and more immutable solution.

The Decision to Kill

On September 19, two days before Dulles had advised the NSC on Lumumba, the director and his immediate subordinates launched a top-secret communication channel to Devlin called PROP, which would only discuss assassination. Through PROP Devlin would report progress and receive orders of the highest priority. On September 19, PROP announced that a special agent was flying to Leopoldville. Sydney Gottlieb, who was Richard Bissell's assistant for scientific matters, stuttered and had a clubfoot. Known as "Dr. Death," Gottlieb cut a strange figure even in the macabre world of the CIA in the 1950s and 1960s. He carried poisons to Devlin. On arrival, Gottlieb told Devlin that Allen Dulles had "instructions from President Eisenhower." "I am giving you instructions on highest authority," said Gottlieb, according to Devlin, "to assassinate Lumumba any way you can." On several occasions Devlin recalled that he believed Gottlieb: "They were serious about it . . . it was clear that the policy decision to assassinate Lumumba had been made."[21]

Just at that time King Baudouin declared to the world his engagement to Fabiola. No one was quite sure if protocol permitted an American president to offer his felicitations. Ambassador Burden in Brussels pushed the State Department. And so on the same day that PROP informed Devlin of Gottlieb's visit, Eisenhower cabled the king his congratulations: "the American people join the people of Belgium in rejoicing at this happy news."[22]

Analysis

How should these events be interpreted? No responsible leaders in the United States had much knowledge of the Congo. Nonetheless, officials closest to the president outside the CIA, the CIA itself, the American ambassador to Belgium, and the agent in the field all propelled one another into grim tirades that compared Lumumba to Hitler or Castro. By mid-August, these officials would pay any price to have Lumumba out.

Stimulated by the Senate committee's interest, many commentators have wondered whether the plotting implicated Eisenhower. In 1960, the president was almost seventy, battered by twenty years of demanding public life. He was increasingly cantankerous, more and more out of sync with new-style politics, and discouraged by his inability to end his presidency on a high note. John Kennedy's campaign had nailed some truths about the end of the Eisenhower era. The president now often used the National Security Council as a venue for cranky policy chats. One scholar has called the president "the kibitzer in chief"—he often sounded like a grouchy bystander to events and not the person in charge. Moreover, historians know well that the president never had an itchy trigger finger; he detested military solutions, especially on the margins.

After August 18, we believe, the president told National Security Adviser Gordon Gray more than once with annoyance and impatience that Lumumba must go. But Eisenhower did not have a considered policy in mind with his order. Nor did a generic anticommunism motivate the president. Then why did he want to have the luckless Lumumba killed? Why not Nkrumah or any other African who might have asked for Soviet help? Lumumba was no threat himself, and hardly merited execution. As one earlier historian wrote, "How far beyond the dreams of a barefoot jungle postal clerk in 1956, that in a few short years he would be dangerous to the peace and safety of the world!"[23]

Spaak's defection from NATO was on the president's mind. In a sustained bad humor and dismayed that Lumumba might set NATO on the rocks, Eisenhower was prompted to go on the offensive when he learned that Lumumba might also turn the UN out. This was a job for the CIA, but the president had no idea about the Agency's resources in the Congo, and Dulles exaggerated about them.[24]

Despite the CIA's initial promotion of the danger of Lumumba, Dulles in Washington also acted slowly. Others, and not just Devlin, had to goad the top of the Agency to carry out the president's wishes. Gray told the Senate committee in 1975 that he had no "independent recollection" about Lumumba. Yet another man with a convenient memory when it came to the murder, Gray swore that "I don't remember sufficiently what was being discussed in the National Security Council to give meaningful explanation in response to questions put to me." At the same time, when confronted with the appropriate memos, Gray allowed that Dulles could have taken assassination as a "possibility," even though Dulles, it appears, consistently thought of murder as one of the things the United States should not undertake.[25] Dillon also recalled that the CIA had prudential objections to a murder.[26] The CIA did not conclusively respond until September 19, over a month after the NSC meeting of August 18; over three weeks after the Special Group reached its verdict on August 26 to look into murder; and eleven days after Gray's second complaint.

Dulles only moved when browbeaten. We believe that Eisenhower endorsed an assassination more than the head of the CIA. We must distinguish between the interest Dulles had in hidden goings-on, and a taste for killing. He sounded alarms about communism so the president would give the CIA a free hand with covert operations. The director liked to talk tough, and now his big mouth had gotten him into the business of murder. He was not eager to step into this stygian river, but once Dulles left dry land, his Agency would rush on in this malodorous stream, heedless of change of circumstance, and taking lack of further discussion as license.

A last factor also needs to be mentioned. Policy makers were beyond rage at Castro, whom they believed encouraged smaller nations to play the USSR against the United States. The Americans also expected their NATO allies to help tighten the screws on Cuba. Yet the United States had not ripened its initial plans to kill Castro, which by a few months preceded those to kill Lumumba. Then discussions of both proposed executions overlapped. We believe that Eisenhower evinced a sort of moral fair-mindedness after Spaak invited the president to compare the United States' Castro to Belgium's Lumumba. Spaak reminded him that America also had a "colony." If the president expected his European allies to take his side in Cuba, he should take theirs in the Congo. Eisenhower reasoned, we believe, that if Castro had to go, Lumumba had to go also. The two stratagems had a certain parity to the president.

It is moreover possible that Dulles wanted to go slow with Lumumba in part because he had just committed himself to doing in Castro, a foe of greater import; the CIA might have wanted to see how it went with the first priority. On the other hand the chronology of the CIA's initial murder attempts in the late summer and fall of 1960 has a narrative line: the Agency devoted more effort to Lumumba, and less to Castro. The Cuban received modest attention earlier in 1960 and then more sustained notice in 1961, after Kennedy took office and Lumumba was dead. It may be that the CIA decided on Lumumba as a test case—in the muddy politics of the Congo, the CIA could always blame the Belgians, get away with more, and risk less. The Agency could apply any lessons learned to Castro.[27]

What did English King Henry II mean toward the end of the twelfth century when he declared of the Archbishop of Canterbury, Thomas à Becket: "Will no one rid me of this turbulent priest"? Did Eisenhower truly mean to order the killing of Lumumba? We think so, but the question does not hold first importance. Lumumba was sort of collateral damage, but sovereign authority cannot claim that words uttered on a supposed whim or in exasperation should not be taken seriously. Eisenhower was president. His officials responded.

Assassination Plans

Over the next months, as the CIA deprecated the morality of the "nefarious plotting" of other countries on behalf of Lumumba, and his use of "goon squads," the Agency cast about for ways to murder the man, and Devlin took the bit in his teeth. He was no Allen Dulles. From July Devlin had intimated that the CIA should do away with Lumumba, and had boosted various schemes. After Washington decided to assassinate, Devlin made eight separate suggestions over a three-week period on how the Americans might accomplish the murder, and he enlisted others to help. His bosses at the Agency declined the suggestions as too chancy.[28]

CIA turncoats, among others, have testified that in the immediate aftermath of the assassination Devlin boasted to people in the Agency about his role in the murder. However, on several occasions over the next forty years Devlin reflected differently on the record about his responsibilities. He repeatedly justified his decisions as a dimension of Cold War fears. The pressures of the time, he recalled, may have magnified those fears, but realism warranted secret operations against Lumumba. Nonetheless, Devlin distinguished between liability for assassinating Lumumba and placing him in harm's way. Devlin did the latter. He would shuffle Lumumba outside of UN protection. The locals themselves might then do him in, or they would jail him, put him before a judge, and sentence him to death. Devlin explained his policy formulaically: "Let the Africans handle this in their own fashion." Washington, Devlin repeatedly said, wanted the murder, and he circumvented his superiors. These points first appear in his recollections before the Senate committee in 1975, and recur in public interviews in the early twenty-first century, and in his autobiographical account of 2007.

Like Cordier, Devlin told a story about his own decency over and over. He had a practical concern, he told the Senate committee. "Fanatic Lumumbists" might believe he did kill the prime minister, and decide to "eliminate" Devlin himself. "It is not much fun to know that somebody is out to kill you." The scientist with the poison, Sydney Gottlieb, was also worried when his activities got minimal exposure from the committee. Maybe the publicity would endanger him and his family, or harm his reputation "perhaps irrevocably." Devlin also had a motive in addition to his personal safety. He wanted to assure his audiences that he had not been involved in the repellent work of assassination. Devlin could only justify assassination had Lumumba held the same danger as Hitler, but Devlin did not equate Lumumba with Hitler.

The station chief's memory and his memoirs do not elicit trust. As a facet of putting his own stamp on CIA policy, he repeatedly said in 1960 that Lumumba's triumph would mean Hitler-like expansion with the fall of central Africa, northwest Africa, Greece, and Italy to communism. He feared that with Lumumba in the saddle, the Congo would follow the "Cuban path [and] . . . all Africa fall under influences if not control of anti-Western nations." Devlin also asserted more than once that he had received a presidential order to murder. As the Senate committee noted, Devlin's testimony in 1975 did not comport with the secret documents. "The cables portray [Devlin] as taking an affirmative, aggressive attitude toward the assignment, while he testified that his pursuit of the operation was less vigorous."[29]

It was not faulty recollections that led Devlin to smudge the truth. In 1960 he persisted in trying to finish off Lumumba and immediately and immodestly took credit when the African was killed; he later persisted in denying that he tried. Once the enormity of Lumumba's murder had sunk in, Devlin—like the men of the UN—did whatever he could to separate himself from what had happened. His own account tripped him up. His desire to validate his credentials in the Agency, and to promote himself as the power behind the throne, conflicted with his narrative of moral courage.

Hit Men

Murderous intent does not translate directly into effective action, and in the Congo the CIA was as much about braggadocio as competence. Gottlieb did not appear in Leopoldville until September 26. That day, Devlin cabled Washington that he and Gottlieb were functioning "on the same wave-length." As a priority, the two proposed that Devlin rustle up an agent who had access to Lumumba and his entourage at the prime minister's home. Devlin, or one of his operatives, would ensure that Lumumba ingested poison, and the cause of death would seem to derive from some common disease prevalent in Africa. Devlin also told Washington that Mobutu was "weakening" under pressure to compromise with Lumumba and that circumstances demanded the "most rapid action." Gottlieb went back to the United States on October 5. The Agency intimated that if Devlin needed reinforcements, he might get assistance from "a third country national"—a citizen from some other country whom no one could associate with the United States.[30]

In August the State Department had asked Eisenhower to host King Baudouin's brother Albert when he holidayed in America in the autumn; it would help make up for the slights to the Belgians. Wigny had opposed this trip. He said it would clear the Americans of blame too easily; it was "unthinkable that the prince would occupy the same bed as Lumumba."[31] Where Albert and his wife, Paola, slept is unknown, but they ignored Wigny and toured Washington in early October. On October 4 Eisenhower breakfasted with Spaak in the capital and discussed NATO matters. On October 7, the president and his wife, Mamie, gave a luncheon at the White House for Albert and Paola. Eisenhower stood up and made remarks "cementing the bonds of friendship" that brought the two countries together. "The bonds have been formed . . . by ideals commonly held, and by blood shed in a common cause; they have linked our two countries in an alliance of the spirit and—when necessary—an alliance of the sword. . . . I would like to propose a toast: to Baudouin I, king of the Belgians."[32] That same day Devlin reported that he had discussed with an agent how to bootleg Gottlieb's poison into the prime minister's residence, and perhaps stick it in the food.[33]

In mid-October Devlin lamented that no one could be found to "penetrate" the house. Washington proposed a commando raid on the dwelling, or better still a raid on Lumumba should he go into Leopoldville, although by this time—courtesy of Mobutu's troops and the UN—he could not leave the residence. If a local assassin might implicate the CIA, the Agency could send the "qualified third party country national." Devlin noted that if headquarters thought his own choices dangerous, he must have such an outside person. If Devlin thought the third-party national was working out, Washington added, the Agency might send another senior agent from the United States who would, under Devlin, run the assassination.[34] The reasoning seems to have been that the plot risked Devlin's exposure, and so the Agency wanted the greatest possible space between Devlin and the actual assailants.

After some delay, Justin O'Donnell, a senior case officer from CIA headquarters, got to Leopoldville on November 3. O'Donnell would oversee the murder and report to Devlin. In asking for O'Donnell after Washington's encouragement, Devlin let headquarters know that he still had the poisons, but also wanted a "high powered foreign make rifle with telescopic scope and silencer." Devlin had discussed a rifle with Gottlieb back in September, and also with David Doyle, who came to the Congo as Devlin's new officer in Katanga, where the CIA opened a base. Now Devlin asked for the rifle in writing a week after an unusual appearance by Lumumba on the balcony of his residence when he spoke to a crowd below.[35]

Dulles had chosen O'Donnell, but in Washington he had initially refused the assignment. Why did he get on a plane? Dulles, himself a reliable bureaucrat who carried out orders, did not want to risk his neck over a job about which he was not 100 percent certain. O'Donnell was unlikely to perform with distinction, but just for that reason he may have been considered a good choice. Devlin recalled that O'Donnell "did not seem to do anything most of the time, and I didn't take him seriously. He spent a lot of time drinking." At the same time, while he objected to murder himself, he did not oppose actions that would deliver Lumumba to Kasa-Vubu and Mobutu. O'Donnell thought they would do to Lumumba just what O'Donnell himself would not. Later in November, O'Donnell wanted to create an observation post near the house. The CIA would lure Lumumba outside, where he could be captured and delivered to his African enemies. But Devlin worried to Washington that it was proving hard even to glimpse "the target."[36]

While O'Donnell mirrored Dulles's scruples, Richard Bissell, number two in the CIA, screwed his courage to the sticking point. Like Devlin, he was more willing to go for the kill, and soon Washington offered Devlin two untraceable assistants through Bissell. The first was WI/ROGUE, a soldier of fortune, forger, and bank robber. Washington recommended him with a certain verve:

> [ROGUE] is indeed aware of the precepts of right and wrong, but if he is given an assignment which may be morally wrong in the eyes of the world, but necessary because his case officer ordered him to carry it out, then it is right, and he will dutifully undertake appropriate action for its execution without pangs of conscience. In a word, he can rationalize all actions.[37]

Were the men of the CIA saying that ROGUE would do what the CIA knew to be wrong? That the CIA could not rationalize all actions? That it was OK to have the morally bankrupt do your murders for you?

The CIA also prepared another agent and third-country national, QJ/WIN. CIA hands described WIN as an unscrupulous criminal type; they could count on him for anything.[38] The CIA let WIN know of "a large element of personal risk" in his assignment but did not tell him precisely what it wanted him to do. "It was thought best to withhold our true, specific requirements pending the final decision" to use him. The CIA, however, did have him round up other suitable people once he got to the Congo. Washington had almost certainly selected WIN to work under O'Donnell on the assassination. ROGUE was more a freelancer whose specific role was unclear. On November 2, the day before O'Donnell got to Leopoldville, Washington cabled that WIN would soon arrive. But he had not reached the Congo by mid-November, although Devlin repeatedly called for his "immediate" posting. WIN did not get on the ground until November 21—as it turned out, two weeks before ROGUE.[39]

By the time the United States had matured its plans to kill Lumumba, his comings and goings had been restricted, and Devlin and his contract murderers could not get close to him. There is some evidence—and much speculation—that the security forces of other imperial powers— the French and the British—were also scheming to dispatch Lumumba.[40] But their activities and those of the CIA in October and November had come to nothing.

CHAPTER TEN

The Return of the Belgians

C OUNT D'ASPREMONT TOOK OVER the ministry of African affairs in September when Kasa-Vubu appointed Ileo and Mobutu "neutralized" the politicians. At the same time that the United States brutally simplified its approach to the Congo, the upsets in Leopoldville complicated diplomacy in Brussels. Belgians flowed back to the Congo, some relieved that Lumumba was gone, some determined to prevent his resurgence. In his mammoth memoirs Prime Minister Eyskens echoed the official Belgian mantra: Brussels stuck to its "prior stance of no interference in the Congo's internal affairs." For the period after the fall of Lumumba, "We didn't throw in our lot exclusively with any one of the competing politicians."[1] One half-truth piled on another created a tangle of misrepresentation designed to prove Eyskens's evenhandedness.

Because Kasa-Vubu and Lumumba had severed diplomacy with Brussels, the hub of the Belgian bustle was Brazzaville in the French Congo, just across the river from Leopoldville, where Marcel Dupret was serving as consul general. Brussels upgraded the consulate to an embassy on November 28, the formal independence day of Congo (Brazzaville). Like many other Belgians in this story, Ambassador Dupret was a veteran of World War II, a royalist and a fervent anticommunist. His embassy offered Joseph Ileo and other politicians, in particular Albert Kalonji and prominent officials from Katanga, all the facilities they needed. The telephone line of the colonial period between the Brazzaville consulate and the residence of the former governor-general in Leopoldville, now the residence of President Kasa-Vubu, continued to operate. Messages from Kasa-Vubu and Ileo for the UN or heads of state were sent via the telex of the Brazzaville embassy.

At the same time, the Belgians underestimated the Africans and were often unaware of what was going on. Perhaps Kasa-Vubu and Ileo were not as slothful as the whites claimed. No doubt the native politicians acted on their own. Although Brussels thought that it could steer them, the Africans maneuvered Belgium in turn, in a game that had no rules. That was why the September 5 dismissal of Lumumba came as a surprise, even though the undertaking was prepared with Belgian assistance on-site and explained with Belgian legalese. Dupret cabled Minister of Foreign Affairs Pierre Wigny (in French): "The scenario for the elimination of Lumumba has unfolded 48 hours too early."[2]

Although Kasa-Vubu was usually considered malleable, the Congo's president nurtured an anti-Belgian resentment. He had only two Belgians in his entourage, but both repeatedly made their mark. Jef Van Bilsen, a professor at the University Institute for Overseas Regions in Antwerp, advised the ABAKO leader from 1959 on, and Kasa-Vubu officially appointed him at independence as his counselor. As we have seen, Van Bilsen delivered Kasa-Vubu's message to Cordier on September 5. Thereafter Lumumba and his followers wanted to dislodge the Belgian. The president's men in turn felt that Van Bilsen was damaged goods, and no longer welcomed him after Kasa-Vubu designated Ileo as prime minister. Worried about his personal safety, Van Bilsen left Leopoldville shortly after. He traveled as an informal ambassador to argue Kasa-Vubu's case in New York, Brussels, and Elisabethville. At the end of September he revisited Leopoldville for a few days. To Van Bilsen's disappointment, the president—apparently under duress—tentatively ended their collaboration. In a twenty-two-page letter of October 2 intercepted by the UN, Van Bilsen lectured Kasa-Vubu and told him "not to accept any compromise before you have complete control. . . . The major problem for the moment is . . . to succeed in imposing your 'legal government' and to eliminate totally the former government and its allies."[3]

The other Belgian, Georges Denis, a former lawyer in the colonial administration, mentored Kasa-Vubu's cabinet on matters of law. After September 5 Denis ensconced himself in the presidential residence for over a month. On September 16 the first of several of his personal accounts of events went to Wigny. Denis emphasized that Lumumba must go to jail, if Kasa-Vubu were to triumph: "The length of the crisis is regrettable but not irremediable. The wise but languid African does not worry about our western interest in speed and logic. The first and unique problem was and remains the elimination of one man, Lumumba. To this end we need the army." And he concluded his message: "I am aware of my involvement in a fundamental contest for the ideal of a free West."[4]

Brussels initially bet the house on Ileo. Because he had authored a famous manifesto for independence, he had credentials as a nationalist. As president of the senate, he had criticized Lumumba. Most important he was a practicing Catholic and friend of the black bishop in Leopoldville, which elevated him in Belgian eyes. Ileo served on the board of the Catholic University of Lovanium in the capital, and he could count on the support of the Christian labor union and of the most important newspaper, *Courrier d'Afrique,* which Belgian money kept in business.[5] The Belgians had more commerce with Ileo than with Kasa-Vubu. The would-be prime minister crossed over to Brazzaville periodically and discussed affairs with Belgian diplomats. Eventually, they found him disappointing—another African who appeared lackadaisical.

As Ileo looked more and more like a losing horse, Belgium put its money on the commissioners. Young and inexperienced university graduates or still students, the commissioners had received, or were receiving, their education in Belgium or at Lovanium. The two main figures among the commissioners campaigned for Belgium. Their president, Justin Bomboko, had studied at the Free University of Brussels and had always pursued a pro-Belgian track. The vice president, Albert Ndele, the former chief of staff to the minister of finance in the Lumumba government, maintained good relations with his alma mater as one of the first African alumni of the Catholic University of Louvain in Belgium. Other commissioners, such as Fernand Kazadi, studied at Lovanium, and their professors influenced them. One of these lecturers, Benoît Verhaegen, had already used his position to plan Lumumba's overthrow. Alois Kabangi, one of the moderate ministers in the Lumumba government who had drifted away from the prime minister at the end of August, had employed Verhaegen as deputy chief of staff. Now Verhaegen had the same position with Joseph Mbeka, commissioner of economic affairs and planning, another alumnus of the Catholic University of Louvain who had himself been Kabangi's chief of staff.[6]

Yet Belgium and the Republic of the Congo had no diplomatic ties, and the commissioners were not a de jure government. This led to peculiar situations. In August, at a Geneva conference, Brussels and the new republic had devised the liquidation of the Central Bank of the Belgian Congo and Ruanda-Urundi. It had not yet happened, and the bank was still active as the Congo's national bank, under the guardianship of the Belgian minister of African affairs, now d'Aspremont. By September Leopoldville's budget was a complete disaster. To help keep afloat the Congo's treasury at the end of September and to allow the commissioners to pay the salaries of the ANC and civil servants, d'Aspremont approved an increase of $10 million in the Congo's debt limit.[7]

By mid-September more and more Belgians were coming back to Leopoldville: men who had waited across the border for conditions to improve, but also officials who had gone home. In Brussels a recruiting agency, "The International Center for Cooperation," did a land-office business. The commissioners delivered lists that advertised governmental posts to this center, and it covered up the restoration of the colonial bureaucrats. One of Verhaegen's principal jobs for Commissioner Mbeka was matching up jobs and candidates through the center, and informing Brussels of progress.[8] Of course the novel immigration did not go unnoticed, as old hands landed in key positions. UN representative Dayal immediately sensed that the wind had changed and warned Hammarskjöld. "Mobutu's commissioners . . . are mostly still university students, under the thumb of Belgian professors who are already interfering with previously made UN plans . . . apparently on the assumption that things are on the way back to the good old pre-independence days." And two weeks later: "The Belgians are returning in large numbers and are forming a screen around the commissioners rendering access to them difficult. . . . The aim seems to be to prove their indispensability and thus to demonstrate [the] UN's redundancy." Dayal feared that the commissioners would force the UN into pushing papers while the Belgians defined strategic policies.[9]

No Return for Lumumba

Diplomacy in Brussels and the efforts of the Belgians in the Congo aimed for accord among Kasa-Vubu, Mobutu, and Bomboko to isolate Lumumba. They should give no room to the dethroned prime minister, and Belgian fears soon fixated on Lumumba's rehabilitation. All of Belgian influence checked any cooperation with Lumumba.[10]

As soon as he learned of Lumumba's reaction to his dismissal, Wigny pressed for an arrest. According to the Belgian minister of foreign affairs, Lumumba had become a rebel no longer entitled to parliamentary immunity, and had "to be made harmless" *(mettre hors d'état de nuire)*. Three times that morning of September 6—at 9:35, 10:10, and 11:45—Wigny cabled Brazzaville the same urgent message: "Success of Kasa-Vubu's political operation necessitates that by preemptive arrest Lumumba be made harmless."[11] The night of September 6, Kasa-Vubu, assisted by Denis, summoned to his residence the principal jurist in the Congo, the white chief prosecutor, René Rom. Before his appointment by Lumumba, Rom had been a lawyer and had defended Lumumba in the Stanleyville trial. Under pressure, he now produced a warrant for the prime minister.[12] The warrant would become the subject of quarrels, theft, and other disputes for weeks. On September 10, Wigny underlined again the importance of a quick arrest. Through September, however, Lumumba had the run of Leopoldville. Belgian diplomats noted the problem on September 16, after two failed attempts to jail Lumumba. "General symptom: the lack of will to act, which explains why Lumumba has not yet been made harmless. . . . The fundamental issue must thus be to set Lumumba aside with a strong unified effort against him by the natives."[13] Wigny continued to defend the legality of an arrest even after October 10 when the UN determined that the nonconstitutional regime of commissioners could not—because of that fact—produce a valid warrant for Lumumba's detention.[14]

Brussels reacted alertly to any sign of a settlement that would let Lumumba or his allies have a say. Late in September Wigny saw Bomboko in New York at the UN. "Reconciliation is not a compromise but a certain disaster," Wigny informed Brussels.[15] In a letter to Tshombe, who could have been expected to be angry about the financial support for Leopoldville, d'Aspremont justified his monetary policy: "It seems to me evident that the most effective way we can act against Lumumba is to assist, within the limits of the possible and the reasonable, Leo's [Leopoldville's] actual authorities, who are trying to eliminate Lumumba from the public life of the Congo."[16] In early October rumor had it that a new government in Leopoldville was forming with members from all camps, including some of Lumumba's men as well as Munongo, Katanga's minister of the interior. D'Aspremont cabled Ambassador Rothschild, his successor as head of the technical mission in Elisabethville, and told him to scotch the plan. D'Aspremont thought this inclusive ministry unlikely, but dangerous since "even indirectly it tends to elevate Lumumba." Rothschild was assigned to warn Munongo off the initiative, "because"—d'Aspremont closed his telex of October 6 (in French)—"in the interests of the Congo, Katanga, and Belgium the principal objective is obviously the definitive elimination of Lumumba." In this controversial sentence some people have seen an order to kill. However, one does not order a diplomat to kill someone and copy the ministry of foreign affairs. In essence the telex had a simple message: tip off Munongo that a new and worrisome government is in the making and warn him against this initiative, because even a hint of Lumumba's return is unacceptable. The minister's words did reflect a general mood. Lumumba had to be kept down. On October 6 d'Aspremont found it sufficient to discourage a new government.[17] Out of sight, Brussels employed other tactics.

Secret Deeds

Obscurity hangs over many bonds between Brussels and the Congo in this period. Contacts, advisers, mediators, and troublemakers all came and went in the foggy area of two countries with an unkempt diplomatic connection, called "empiric" cooperation in the documents. Moreover, Kasa-Vubu and members of the College of Commissioners made anti-Belgian statements for domestic consumption.[18] Behind even these murky politics, however, were more secret and often outré machinations that were undisclosed even to most members of the cabinet in Brussels.

When Eyskens had shuffled his ministers on September 3, Count d'Aspremont's elevation drew much criticism. He had a reputation as a man of too much force, and the Socialist opposition branded him "the man of the large business corporations." Wigny, who had just gone through two months of heavy discussion with Minister of Defense Gilson and who had regretted d'Aspremont's too-visible activity as chief of the technical mission in Katanga, was disillusioned and envisioned another period of difficulty. He demanded that he be put in charge of the Congo. Eyskens accepted the demand at a cabinet meeting of September 6, but Wigny continued to have trouble holding the reins of policy, and indeed often found that he did not have matters under control. Not until February 1961, when the issues had become a public embarrassment, did Eyskens establish a Congo Committee inside the government.[19]

The ministry of African affairs, which had become paralyzed under De Schryver, revived under d'Aspremont, who behaved as if decolonization had not taken place, and as if Wigny were a schoolboy. In Katanga representatives of the ministries of foreign and of African affairs seldom got along. Wigny also did not know that d'Aspremont had given major responsibilities to Major Jules Loos. Loos advised d'Aspremont's ministry on the military, and during the colonial period had specific duties. A man of long-standing service in the Belgian Congo, Loos recruited Belgian officers for the Force Publique and requisitioned its weapons, ammunition, and uniforms. Now the job gained new significance by virtue of the cooperation Belgium offered the armed forces of Katanga. In Brussels Loos became responsible for the roughly two hundred Belgian officers in Katanga's just-formed gendarmerie. On top of that, supported by d'Aspremont, Loos assumed yet another duty. He directed the Belgian martial presence in Leopoldville and drew up policy for the reform of Mobutu's ANC.[20] He had been brooding over a plan, "Operation L.," which aimed at the elimination of Lumumba, perhaps by placing contaminated drugs in his residence.[21]

Loos's contact in Leopoldville was Colonel Louis Marlière. After Belgium-Congo relations were cut in July, this ex-chief of staff of the Force Publique had initially remained in Leopoldville as Mobutu's friend and consultant. On August 18, after the Belgian embassy had closed, Marlière was one of the last Belgian officers to cross to Brazzaville. Three weeks later, after Kasa-Vubu dumped Lumumba, Marlière again had influence back in Leopoldville. He knew the ANC, its African officers and garrisons, its strengths and especially its infirmities better than anyone. Secret cable traffic between Loos and Marlière flourished, as they scrutinized various clandestine operations that involved Mobutu and his troops. Marlière's first intervention would have an impact. On September 12 he met in Brazzaville with would-be prime minister Ileo, who feared that the ANC would not obey him. Marlière came up with a solution: read General Lundula the riot act and dispose of him if he refused to follow orders. Ileo at once phoned Kasa-Vubu. Lundula did not get read the riot act, but learned by radio the next day that the president had stripped him of command of the ANC.[22] The road was cleared for Mobutu, and Lundula would later join Gizenga in Stanleyville.

Marlière was not the only man with secrets at the office of the Belgian consul general in Brazzaville. In July 1960, Brussels had sent over André Lahaye, alias Agent 070a of the Belgian Sûreté. An inheritance of the colonial period, the Sûreté in the Congo had collapsed in early July when Lumumba fired and exiled its Belgian chief, Colonel Frédéric Vandewalle, and when many Belgian agents left the country. In Belgium the Sûreté was a section of the Ministry of Justice. Its administrator Ludo Caeymaex reported to various ministers in Brussels depending on the nature of the information that was available to him. Caeymaex assigned Lahaye, himself an ex-director of the colonial security service, to organize the repatriation of the Belgian spies, but Lahaye stayed on with a far vaguer job description. More or less daily he wired intelligence to Brussels. Close commitments grew up between Lahaye and the American (and French) secret agents. The documentation remains—as usual in this type of setting—brief and enigmatic. "I've been contacted by a man to whom you have given a medallion of Leopold II that has a hidden penknife," Agent 070a wrote on August 10 to his chief in Brussels. The contact was Larry Devlin, whom the Sûreté referred to as "Raymond."[23]

Marlière and Lahaye first had separate roles but slowly harmonized in a duet in their own room with radio equipment at the Brazzaville embassy. Lahaye delivered intelligence; Marlière acted on it. From September on Marlière figured in several covert operations, such as weapons drops, to guarantee that Lumumba would stay on the outs. The most intriguing effort was Action 58916, named after telex 589 of September 16, wherein Loos first put forward the idea. A series of enigmatic cables over the next three-plus weeks told about 58916. Marlière was somehow to get Lumumba (code-name Joseph) into the custody of his enemies, but except in an emergency d'Aspremont was to judge the opportunity. On October 1 Marlière indicated that the right time had come; what did Brussels think? To avoid leaks, Loos and another emissary of d'Aspremont's traveled to Pointe Noire in Congo (Brazzaville) to consult with Marlière.[24]

The movements of Edouard Pilaet, alias Alex Lapite, alias Achilles, evidenced that 58916's options included the cutthroat. A former resistance fighter, Pilaet had cover as a representative of Antwerp's diamond industry, Forminière, but was actually an intelligence officer in a private network of Forminière's. Achilles had insinuated himself into the underground world of d'Aspremont and Loos under the framework of Action 58916 and would eventually become a serious nuisance to Marlière. As Achilles described his assignment: "Above all I understood my duty as a merciless struggle, without abatement or doubt, that would result in solution or reconciliation—the disappearance of Patrice or of our own forces." Unlike Marlière, Achilles felt that it was not time to act, because the organization had an amateurish character. "My view after a dozen days of observation and of contact is that the time is not ripe to go after our beautiful game, whom I will call *le perdreau*." *Perdreau*, partridge, is the French for the Dutch *patrijs*, which gives us Patrice. After this telegram, the details of this intrigue are lost.[25]

Bribery and financial shenanigans surfaced as tools that might accomplish Belgian aims. D'Aspremont had secret money at his disposal. As a result of decisions made by the government in August and September, the minister of African affairs received $1 million that he could allocate at his own discretion. The money did not have to be accounted for and was beyond the control of parliament, even though the amount was part of the state budget. A staff member of the minister did the bookkeeping for the funds with precision, as the parliamentary inquiry of 2001 brought to light. Men such as Bomboko received quite a bit of cash. This largesse did not flow unconditionally. One of the politicians would "get no more money if he proposes or participates in a government with Lumumba."[26]

After his collaboration with General Kettani had come to little, Mobutu looked for trained officers and supplies outside of UN auspices.

By the end of September the money to pay his soldiers was lacking. D'Aspremont made $400,000 from his hidden funds available to Marlière for the ANC. The commissioners could only use the disbursement if Lumumba was "effectively neutralized." D'Aspremont's decisions about the Central Bank of the Congo around the same time made the subsidy redundant. But the Belgians were forging a path toward more intense cooperation with Mobutu.

On October 6, at the request of Mobutu, Marlière moved back to Leopoldville. D'Aspremont cabled "I agree with your return to Leo as an unofficial, repeat unofficial, counselor of Mobutu. Do not put on the uniform."[27] Lahaye followed on October 10 as the adviser of Damien Kandolo, commissioner of domestic affairs. Lahaye also had his hand in the newly created Congo Sûreté, which by this time had fallen into Victor Nendaka's waiting arms.

Marlière came to an agreement with Mobutu that Lumumba would be arrested in exchange for a form of Belgian military aid. Marlière reported to Brussels: "I believe that the training [of African officers] would be more profitable than a subsidy, and I insist that you take the trainees. The only possible opposition is the UN. But we must send them [the trainees] as civilians, without the UN's knowledge." He added that "the maneuver to put Lumumba aside can be resumed. The essential aspect of the operation is that Mobutu shows authority. At the same time as a guarantee, I ask you to approve the training of the cadets."[28]

On October 10, as we have seen, Mobutu tried to arrest Lumumba using men from Camp Hardy, the Thysville garrison south of Leopoldville. Then Mobutu backtracked, although a precedent had been set, and Marlière worked on the collaboration. Around that time four Belgian officers arrived at Camp Hardy as army trainers. Kettani and Dayal soon learned about Marlière's "secret" activities, and a new crisis with the UN was precipitated.

Sinking in the Swamp of Katanga

While the politics of Leopoldville complicated the lives of Belgian officials, Katanga simultaneously challenged them in different ways once Lumumba was provisionally out of power. The secessionist province was no longer the placid refuge that the Belgians had praised in July.

Although the coup of September 5 had made for a short-lived reconciliation between Leopoldville and Elisabethville, the tide had turned quickly.
Tshombe equivocally spoke on September 6 about a confederation, inspired by Ambassador Rothschild. But he took back his words later. Katanga turned down Ileo's invitation to become part of the government in
Leopoldville. Tshombe and his peers demanded upfront recognition of
their independence. They did not want to dance to Leopoldville's tune,
even less than previously, since its governance looked even more disorganized after September 5.

Once again an undecided Brussels sent mixed signals. In serious
trouble, the Belgian politicians faced a dilemma. They had supported
Katanga against Leopoldville to demolish Lumumba. Once that goal
had been reached, reconciliation with Leopoldville became obvious. To
stick with Katanga would make future relations with the Kasa-Vubu and
Mobutu group impossible. Choosing Leopoldville, however, meant of-
fending Katanga. Brussels tried to win over both parties, although the
ministries of foreign and African affairs each sailed a different course.
Wigny wanted to normalize relations with Leopoldville. Seconded by
Rothschild, d'Aspremont believed in Katanga and in Tshombe's leadership in the reconstruction of a Western-oriented Congo. The African
affairs minister suspected that the former colony would continue to "ex-
plode," and that after Kalonji's Kasai, Kivu too would choose Katanga's
side.[29] D'Aspremont counted on his personal relationship with Tshombe
to move the resource-rich state to flexibility and acceptance of a loose
confederation, whatever that might mean. D'Aspremont overestimated
his influence, however, and did not see the contradictions in his task. He
created an indomitable Tshombe, but then boosted Mobutu, and thus
Leopoldville, via Marlière.

Katanga's politicians did not know much about the wheeling and dealing in Brussels, but they knew enough to get the idea. Belgium's "double
play" offended them as much as it did the men in Leopoldville. Tshombe
and those around him quickly caught on to the tricks of diplomacy and,
perhaps inspired by their local Belgian advisers, blackmailed Brussels
with fierce statements. Évariste Kimba, Katanga's newly appointed minister of foreign affairs, rebuked the Belgian delegation to the UN because
of Wigny's "hostile attitude" toward Elisabethville's autonomy. In the

first half of October Tshombe aired his criticism openly in three consecutive letters to Eyskens and blamed Brussels for "forsaking the cause of Katanga."[30]

Tshombe's irritation produced the dissolution of the Belgian technical mission. On October 16 it closed down, and Rothschild left for Brussels. Elisabethville no longer wanted to hear about a mission that supposedly had Katanga's interests at heart but had to get direction from Europe. Tshombe, Munongo, Kibwe, and Kimba despised the Belgians who held Katanga hostage and who refused to acknowledge the new state. Nonetheless, realism dictated toleration of the Belgians, because without their officers and the executives of the Union Minière, the Katangan excellencies would have to pack their bags.[31]

The end of the technical mission suited the Belgians fine.[32] In fact, little or nothing changed. The mines of Union Minière flooded the Tshombe regime with riches. White advisers studded the government. Most cabinet chiefs were Belgians. Administration, police, and security services depended on white officials, and a delegation of the National Bank of Belgium camped in Elisabethville to ready Katanga's own currency. Through a new agency, the Bureau Conseil, Belgian "technical assistance" to Katanga's government continued.

The crucial support went to the local army, the Gendarmerie Katangaise. To compensate for the departure of the Belgian troops, Katanga had worked quickly to form its own army under Belgian leadership. At the beginning of October, 231 white men—including 114 officers, 90 noncommissioned officers, and 25 corporals and privates—were involved in overseeing African soldiers. Most had served as officers of the Force Publique. The rest came from the metropolitan forces. This last group had exchanged their Belgian uniforms for Katanga's to outmaneuver the UN. The Brussels ministry of African affairs supervised these men, and the military adviser, Loos, managed their work. Strengthened by the UN resolution of September 20, Hammarskjöld demanded their withdrawal in the beginning of October. Wigny was inclined to concessions, albeit pro forma, but his own diplomats declined. Rothschild declared: "Our officers are an essential and decisive element in maintaining order in Katanga. It is necessary to understand well that within twenty-four hours of their retraction the gendarmerie will fall and soon thereafter the

Tshombe government."[33] Hammarskjöld's order of withdrawal fell on deaf ears. As the backbone of Tshombe's rule, the gendarmerie still caused many Belgian headaches. Disputes among the higher officers about who had command, problems with contracts, tensions among the rank-and-file Africans, and the lack of black officers all bedeviled the force.

After the August invasion by Lumumba's troops was averted, Tshombe was still threatened, not from the outside but from within. The armed uprising of the Baluba in the north expanded. The Belgians ignored its political background and slighted its instigators as looters and bandits, but the gendarmerie was not able to silence the insurrection. While death tolls mounted on both sides, the first Belgian officers lost their lives. On October 17 Tshombe reluctantly agreed to an armistice and the creation of neutral UN territory to seal off the disaffected region, but the agreement was questioned from the get-go because it jeopardized Katanga's sovereignty. The fall of Lumumba had made Katanga's secession look less attractive to the Belgians. The unrest in north Katanga now additionally undermined the legitimacy of an independent Katanga, and enthusiasm for it.[34]

At the same time Katanga's autonomy had one major point in its favor. Tshombe's government could far more easily deal with the incarceration of Lumumba. On October 26 Marlière, still in Leopoldville, asked Brussels to weigh Elisabethville or Jadotville, a city in Katanga with a real prison, as places of detention for the prime minister. "Might either town be considered a reliable vacation spot for Joseph and his friends? Would they be sheltered from all UN intervention?"[35]

All the King's Men

Diverse Belgians encumbered the government in Elisabethville: officials who worked for Katanga and many people who did not; adventurers and idealists; realists and fundamentalists. Major Guy Weber belonged to the last category and drew his faith from his connection with King Baudouin.[36] As the president's military adviser, Weber—always in Belgian uniform—had become Tshombe's shadow. From the time he met the king in Brussels in early August, the major corresponded regularly with Baudouin's chief of staff, René Lefebure. He delivered confidential information to the palace about politics and the military, and about conversations between Tshombe and high UN officers. Weber briefed in no uncertain terms and considered that his letters gave the king a true picture of what was going on, when Baudouin could not trust the Eyskens government, and especially Wigny. Lefebure would never contradict Weber; on the contrary, in the few answers he made, he encouraged the major.[37]

Weber loathed the Belgian politicians, first of all Wigny. As the tensions over Katanga grew, the major was inspired to promote a Machiavellian démarche between Tshombe and Baudouin. On October 6 Weber transmitted to the palace a letter he had typed for the president. Tshombe lambasted the same politicians whom the king detested. They had shown weakness and cowardice in not recognizing Katanga, an "oasis of peace" and a "stronghold against communism," wrote Tshombe, as he declared his own loyalty to the crown:

> One cannot play two cards. . . . My loyalty to your majesty is complete. In the future I see a Belgo-Katangese federation under the patronage of the king. . . . If I took the liberty to express my views to the king, it is because I know that your majesty has followed Katanga's course, and understands and approves it. I also know that the constitution, which holds the king prisoner, in the same way as the democratic culture of Belgium does, will not permit your majesty to respond to me with the manifestation of sympathy that the king would otherwise tender. But I am sure the king will use all his influence to make his ministers understand that my fidelity merits a certain recognition; if Belgium entertains hope of continued influence in Africa, it will be on the basis of Katanga. . . . Katanga has proclaimed its independence, and it has become a reality in all our domains. We protect every Belgian interest, and our mining soil guarantees decades of cooperation.

Tshombe ended his four-page letter with a rhetorical question: "And Belgium would abandon Katanga???"[38] For the time being, Tshombe provoked no reaction from the king. The letter sat on his desk.

On October 26 Lefebure received two mailings from Weber, one dated October 19, the other October 22. In the second letter Weber mentioned Tshombe's desire for an invitation to the king's wedding—a difficulty because Katanga had no diplomatic standing. Weber added: "We've already promised Tshombe many things. Before Rothschild left, there was a suggestion about giving him a decoration—Kasa-Vubu and Lumumba have a Great Ribbon. Then, there was an idea of an autographed picture of the king. Tshombe has received nothing. Now the government has two months to think about inviting him to the wedding."[39]

The first letter of October 19 contained a remarkable report of Mobutu's visit to Elisabethville and his consultation with Tshombe that, as we have noted, occurred on October 16. "An excellent meeting," wrote Weber to Lefebure: "In exchange for some financial support, Mobutu agrees to the recommendations: Status quo until December 31—They see what the lay of the land is—They neutralize completely (and if possible physically . . .) Lumumba" [*On neutralise complétement (et si possible physiquement . . .) Lumumba*]. The three dots tell a story. "Neutralize" in and of itself need not mean murder. Nonetheless "the complete and if possible physical neutralization" of this paragraph does mean murder. Lefebure understood; he put a large question mark in the margin.[40]

On October 26, the day that the two letters came, Lefebure brought them to the king.

The upcoming marriage engrossed Baudouin. He had visited the Flemish and Walloon capitals of Antwerp and Liège with Fabiola, and had introduced the future queen to his people. The fairy-tale wedding was scheduled for December 15, and Baudouin was trying to ignore politics. No one had had an audience with him at the palace for weeks. But Weber's mailings brought the Congo's rough reality back into Baudouin's consciousness and alarmed the sovereign, and Tshombe's letter, which had lain in Baudouin's in-box for about two weeks, had struck all the right chords for the sentimental but principled monarch. His sympathy went out to Katanga. He referred wedding invitations for African politicians to his government—that was his way of answering the issues of Weber's second letter. But without any advice from the government, the king responded to Tshombe's letter on October 28, addressing implicitly the concerns of Weber's first message. Baudouin praised Tshombe's leadership and the example of Katanga. The king encouraged Tshombe to strive for mutual understanding with the leaders in Leo. Then Baudouin added:

> From the time my grand-uncle, King Leopold II, opened civilization to the territory of the old Belgian Congo, the destiny of its people has

Eyskens greets Baudouin and Fabiola. The king, who did not like the Eyskens government, was most proud of his engagement. (© *BelgaImage*)

been, as you know, one of the major cares of the sovereigns who have succeeded to the throne of Belgium. Faithful to this tradition, I have myself followed with the greatest attention, and over the last several months with a growing anxiety, the unfolding events that have agitated the Congo. The drama that has befallen a great part of the land is for me a constant source of distress; an association of 80 years, like that which has united our two peoples, has created affectionate bonds too strong to be dissolved by the politics of a single man.[41]

The king asked Lefebure to send this letter at once. D'Aspremont and Eyskens could be informed; Wigny was not mentioned. The entire government was unaware of the correspondence between Weber and the palace.

Baudouin had just read Weber's letter that recorded the deal between Tshombe and Mobutu. On the one side, Katanga provided cash to Mobutu; on the other, "They neutralize completely (and if possible physically . . .) Lumumba." Two days after reading of the accord, the king sent Tshombe a letter with an implicit sign of approval of murder: "An association of eighty years . . . has created affectionate bonds too strong to be dissolved by the politics of a single man." Before "politics," he had deleted the word "malevolent." Baudouin had relentlessly and successfully pushed Belgium's politicians to more unyielding policies in the Congo. What was he thinking when he read Weber's report and then encouraged Tshombe? This is a serious question for which we have no answer. The day the letter was sent the king traveled to Malines and introduced his fiancée to Archbishop Van Roey, the highest church leader in Belgium. They prepared for the wedding.[42]

On October 26, the day that Baudouin saw Weber's letters, Marlière had asked Brussels if Elisabethville or Jadotville could be considered "a reliable vacation spot for Joseph and his friends? Would they be sheltered from all UN intervention?" Matter-of-factly, Loos replied three days later: "Vacation spots comfortable and secure."[43]

The UN Precipitates Drastic Actions

Belgium and the UN had a more than tense connection. Yet in the late summer, when Hammarskjöld and Cordier had clandestinely subverted the Lumumba government before the opening of the UN General Assembly, the heat had been briefly off Brussels. Then the General Assembly had opened in New York on September 20. Stridently attacked by Khrushchev, Hammarskjöld tried to regain the moral high ground and denounced Belgian colonialism. The Congo now occupied the center of attention, and Belgium was permanently under fire. On October 8 the secretary-general, in accord with the resolution of September 20, requested that Brussels withdraw its military, paramilitary, and civilian personnel from the Congo, and funnel all its assistance, including that to Katanga, through the United Nations. Hammarskjöld used somber words: "The secretary general is convinced that only by implementing these requests will risks be avoided that would make the country a theater of conflict for the entire world and that would be most dangerous for the country itself." In a letter to Tshombe, in which Hammarskjöld conveyed the UN's ultimatum but also sought cooperation, he clarified his notion that only the "containment and elimination of the Belgian factor" would allow the decrease of friction. Ten days later the UN chief again called the Belgian representative on the carpet to express the secretary-general's disapproval over the key role Belgium continued to play in Katanga, even after the dissolution of the technical mission, and over the recruiting of Belgians for positions in Leopoldville courtesy of the efforts of Professor Benoît Verhaegen and his agency. As we have seen, Dayal had explicitly informed Hammarskjöld of these Belgian activities.

The Belgian government considered Hammarskjöld's critique unjustified. "Inadmissible," said Eyskens, at a cabinet meeting. "Offensive," added another minister. And the entire government took the view that Belgium "has not been treated with the deference that ought to be shown to a sovereign state, loyal to the UN since its creation." In its formal reply at the UN, Brussels resorted to legalistic legerdemain, deplored the political intrusion of the secretary-general into the Congo's domestic affairs, emphasized the self-determining right of the Congo to receive bilateral help, and finally pointed to the indispensability of the two thousand civil servants in the Congo in comparison to the two hundred UN technicians.[44]

Shortly thereafter the issue of the military trainees put the Belgians in an awkward position. Notwithstanding the care with which their departure to

Belgium was arranged, the arrival of forty officer candidates from Katanga on October 28 was announced in Belgian newspapers (the trainees
from Leopoldville arrived more secretly). It was a cold shower for Wigny.
The minister of foreign affairs, who on September 6 had asked for control
of affairs in the Congo, knew nothing, and also nothing of the agreement
between Marlière and Mobutu. His position in the UN was undermined
by the comings and goings of the trainees.

At the Belgian cabinet meeting of October 28, there was yet again a
collision between two points of view. D'Aspremont was absent, sick from
jaundice from a trip to Ruanda-Urundi, but his military deputy Loos
had readied an artful memorandum to Eyskens that more or less revealed
d'Aspremont's policy. Wigny opposed the training of the cadets, and
tried to offset the defiance of d'Aspremont—and Gilson. But the minister
of foreign affairs got his comeuppance from Eyskens, who—with the
Loos memo in his hand—appealed for an elastic interpretation of the
UN ban on military assistance.[45] Wigny lamented in his diary:

> I am struck that the cabinet favors the military training. Most of my
> colleagues continue to advocate a politics of force. Don't they under-
> stand that we have to choose between a military policy which can
> only lead to a catastrophe and a policy of civil assistance with spe-
> cific aims? . . . I feel clearly that another policy is being carried out
> behind my back. It's about reconquering the Congo, if not by force,
> at least with military means and counselors. They think that Ka-
> tanga survives because of our military presence and they dream of
> controlling Leopoldville in a similar way.[46]

Hammarskjöld could not let the exposure of Belgian duplicity go by
without broadcasting it. On October 29, he once more took a poke at
Brussels. He condemned Belgium for accepting and training the cadets
from Leopoldville and Elisabethville, a decision that flagrantly violated
the UN resolution of September 20. Soon Cordier and Bunche also be-
rated Belgium in public over its retrograde policy of decolonization.
Then, on November 2, Dayal delivered his devastating report. The UN
representative held back nothing, described the state of the Congo in the
darkest colors, and pointed the finger at Belgium. The Congo crisis was
mainly due to Brussels.[47] Hammarskjöld triumphed one more time at the

tribunal of the General Assembly. The Belgian ministers, who met again on November 4, were indignant. While most of them were belligerent, they also feared that the UN might resuscitate Lumumba. But even with that prospect they continued quarreling among themselves. Wigny criticized d'Aspremont and Gilson, whose "politics of force" consisted of "shoving the UN" and diverged from his own "dexterous" and "careful" approach. But the minister of foreign affairs suffered another defeat when, yet again, Eyskens chose the hard line. The Eyskens ministry decided that it was far-fetched for the UN to equate military education with military support. The training would continue.

Luckily for Wigny, the case against the trainees was lost in the frontal assault by Dayal and Hammarskjöld on all things still Belgian in the Congo, and in his defense of Belgium before the world Wigny would get away with downplaying the military issues. On November 6 he left for New York City for the debate on Dayal's report. The night before, he had set out the standpoint of Brussels in a radio and television speech. For internal consumption, the speech criticized the UN and, not least, Hammarskjöld's presumption. In New York Wigny really did not get the chance to present the Belgian position to the General Assembly. After he was prevented from speaking in a tumultuous sitting, the debate over the Congo was adjourned *sine die* to facilitate the work of a Conciliation Commission for the Congo that had been set up. Wigny resorted to an acrimonious press conference, in which he again bitterly disparaged the UN. He called Dayal's report an indictment and threatened that Belgium would leave the UN.[48]

At the end of October and the beginning of November an extravagant fear that Lumumba would return to power with the help of the United Nations dominated the discussion of the Belgian public and its politicians. Eyskens warned: "In the actual state of things, it is necessary to contemplate the eventual return of Lumumba."[49]

This fear may have inspired another murder attempt. A Greek called "Georges" arrived in Brazzaville, probably in the beginning of November. Belgians in Brussels had hired him to kill Lumumba at his residence. The Belgian parliamentary commission brought the contours of this plot to light. Jo Gérard, a Brussels journalist with the right-wing *Europe Magazine,* who had played a major role in establishing an anticommunist radio station in Brazzaville, served as facilitator. Through Gérard's phone instructions, Marlière's radio operator received a gun and a stack of money in the embassy in Brazzaville from an unidentified person, and handed them to Georges the next day in a bar. Georges was never heard from again. Did he disappear with the money, or was the plot canceled at the last minute?[50] Recalled to Brussels, Marlière got a November 15 telex from Brazzaville with a message from another mystery man, Gabriel: "Urgent for Gérard to suspend operation Gigi. It is necessary to wait for an explanation of the situation."[51] The name Gérard and the enigmatic text likely pointed to the assassination attempt by Georges.

A laconic Ambassador Burden later testified: "The Belgians were sort of toying with the idea of seeing to it that Lumumba was assassinated. I went beyond my instructions and said, well, I didn't think it would be a bad idea either, but I naturally never reported this to Washington—but Lumumba was assassinated. I think it was all to the good."[52] The spooks from Belgium could be every bit as wayward and unsavory as the CIA, and perhaps other security forces also had murder on their minds. But there were more Belgians on the ground, and they were engaged in multiple lethal games.

CHAPTER ELEVEN

Lumumba Imperiled

IN EARLY NOVEMBER, while the Belgians threatened to resign from the United Nations, the United States announced that it would only accept a democratic government if the parliament approved Ileo. That is, the Congo's politicians did not have the right to vote for Lumumba; parliament could open only if it selected someone it did not want. The Congo had precious little in the way of constitutional government. Lumumba alarmed the Americans so much that they had set themselves, in public, against even that. In turn, sequestered in his residence, Lumumba boasted that he would soon be back in office.

A victory for the Americans at the UN blasted the prime minister's dreams. The international organization had admitted the Congo to formal membership on September 20. Overreaching, some of Lumumba's African allies wanted his defenders in the UN seat, rather than a delegation of Kasa-Vubu's. But in the parlous condition in which the Congo found itself, some commentators did not know who should speak for the country in New York. For many, the path of wisdom would leave the seat unfilled. Lumumba's sponsors provoked an intense American reaction. Too late did these sponsors realize that, with US help, Kasa-Vubu might settle his own people in New York.

Both sides engaged in complicated parliamentary and diplomatic tricks. As a measure of its revulsion, the United States pulled out all the stops to defeat the Lumumba deputation. Teaming up with Bomboko, who was at the UN as the commissioners' envoy for foreign affairs, Kasa-Vubu came to New York and addressed the General Assembly on November 8. He would stay in the city until the UN made up its mind. The US Department of State wrote a letter for Kasa-Vubu entreating UN consent to his delegation, and then American diplomats asked the UN's credentials committee to accept the letter.[1] On November 22, with much American arm-twisting, the organization decided for Kasa-Vubu. The series of votes revealed how much the Africans and Asians did *not* want the partnership of Kasa-Vubu and Mobutu. Cold War Americans rejoiced; commentators interested in the West's disengagement from imperialism found the outcome sad and dismal. Kasa-Vubu got an enormous shot in the arm. A few days later he left New York for Leopoldville with international recognition. How could the UN, which had bestowed this legitimacy, forbid Kasa-Vubu the fruits of the vote? Dayal and Hammarskjöld anticipated no change in the UN formula for guarding Lumumba,[2] but the prime minister had to understand the possible consequences. He was holed up in his quarters. Would UN peacekeepers look after him less, and the ANC threaten him more?

Lumumba Breaks Out

On the night of Sunday, November 27, the Leopoldville politicians celebrated the return of Kasa-Vubu from the UN. At 10 P.M., hidden in the back of an automobile, Lumumba left his residence. Neither the Moroccan UN guard, nor the surrounding ring of Mobutu's army, detected him.

Antoine Gizenga, the vice prime minister in the Lumumba cabinet, had relocated in October to Stanleyville. General Lundula and a number of other nationalists flocked around Gizenga, and gave Lumumba a nucleus of disciples. After the UN had decided to recognize the Kasa-Vubu delegation, Gizenga had declared a government, which attracted a part of the ANC. The night of November 27 Lumumba headed for Stanleyville, some twelve hundred miles from Leopoldville. A caravan of three vehicles carried him, his family, and some close colleagues. They went east from the capital out of Leopoldville Province to neighboring Kasai Province, perhaps anticipating a plane at some airport. As soon as Kasa-Vubu and Mobutu—and the Americans and the Belgians—learned of the escape, they had a gloomy foreboding about a Lumumba government.

With the determined assistance of the Belgians and the Americans, the rulers in Leopoldville wanted to capture the prime minister at any cost. The Sûreté under Victor Nendaka swung into action. Devlin and Lahaye pooled resources with Nendaka's security personnel.[3] Frantic, the Belgians made a low-flying reconnaissance plane available. Mobutu's counselor, Marlière, worked with the Africans to erect roadblocks and checkpoints at the ferries necessary to cross various rivers. The Congo had few routes for high-speed automobile trips, and limited airports and planes. The pursuers could be pretty sure that once beyond Leopoldville, Lumumba would head northwest to Stanleyville.

When Dayal and the UN learned of Lumumba's flight, the organization telexed its forces and administrators along the prime minister's likely getaway routes that the peacekeepers should not assist the hunters. However, while the international organization would protect Lumumba in his home, the UN would do nothing for the hunted.[4] Dayal did contemplate a minimal concession. While he did not have Hammarskjöld's approval, Dayal ruminated that "different rules could apply only if individual lives were in danger in specific circumstance but even then . . . [UN] protection could be given solely as a step to restoring peace." In theory the UN men would stay above this battle; in reality they took part in it.

Blockades and rain reduced Lumumba's speed. He traveled slowly because of rudimentary roads and a reasonable desire to stay in friendly territory. Some of the politicians in the convoy got to safety. They might all have made it to Stanleyville had Lumumba simply chosen to get there as quickly as possible. Instead, he stopped along the way to speak to villagers. *Uhuru,* they cried, Swahili for freedom. They wanted to touch him, "our savior." Lumumba could not resist. His eloquence might bring his people to nationhood. The parade of cars progressed less quickly than it could have, and the atmosphere of a joyous campaign journey made Lumumba's trail easy to pick up. His enemies apparently spotted the motorcade from above on November 30.

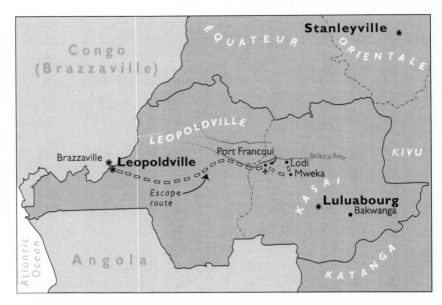

Lumumba breaks out, November 27–December 2, 1960

The next morning, December 1, Lumumba passed through the important junction city of Port Francqui just over the Leopoldville–Kasai provincial border. He then turned south toward Mweka and Luluabourg, the capital of Kasai Province. Everyone assumed that Lumumba was driving to the provincial center. From there he would straightforwardly journey to Stanleyville, maybe by plane. In Luluabourg, however, UN civilian administrators, provincial authorities, and the ANC in the area, acting on their own, agreed that they wanted nothing to do with Lumumba or his pursuers. A visit in Luluabourg would be "inopportune." The officials sent a party to Mweka to persuade Lumumba to modify his travel, and highway closures would turn him from Luluabourg.

At the same time, when members of Leopoldville's Sûreté deplaned in Luluabourg looking for Lumumba, the ANC there would not allow them to leave the airport by car; they had to take again to the air, back to Port Francqui. The Sûreté therefore launched its ground movement against Lumumba from Port Francqui. The UN bureaucrat in Luluabourg wrote that he "agreed with [the local] ANC that they will intercept Lumumba."[5]

In the meantime, at Mweka, instead of continuing south to Lulua-bourg, Lumumba continued north by car—away from Luluabourg. This route would take him and his followers more or less straight to Stanleyville, the second leg of some six hundred miles of an automobile escape instead of a plane flight. Late in the day on December 1, the group arrived in the village of Lodi, north of Mweka on the bank of the Sankuru River. The ferry at Lodi was to take them across the river and to a nearly sure shot at escape. Some forty local ANC soldiers captured him at the river crossing. Under UN orders, troops from Ghana permitted Lumumba's arrest, though at one point these soldiers did prohibit "maltreatment." Again the Sûreté from Leopoldville landed in Luluabourg, now to transport Lumumba to Leopoldville, and again they were seen off, back to Port Francqui. The next day, December 2, the forty soldiers delivered Lumumba from the Lodi-Mweka area to Port Francqui, and a plane carried him from there to the capital. He arrived at 5 P.M.

With Lumumba in custody, the Leopoldville leadership first attempted to ship him to Katanga. On behalf of the Kasa-Vubu regime, from Marlière's office in Brazzaville on December 3, a radio message went out to the headquarters of Katanga's gendarmerie: "Will the Jew accept Satan?" (Will Tshombe accept Lumumba?) Tshombe refused, but Leopoldville insisted. "You know what will happen," Tshombe radioed back in a second message.[6] Mobutu transferred Lumumba to Thysville, south of Leopoldville, where he occupied a cell inside the military compound at Camp Hardy.

Ecce Homo

Again in a tight spot, the UN acted ambiguously and duplicitously. After October 10, the blue helmets had taken no responsibility for Lumumba should he leave his residence. That policy contributed to his arrest. Moreover, the UN functionary on the ground in Luluabourg associated himself with the ANC, which captured Lumumba. Hammarskjöld related that around Port Francqui the UN was "without any possibility" of protecting Lumumba.[7] But this was not true. Hammarskjöld did not exploit the military force he had, and was unwilling finally to cross the Western powers. In any event Mobutu officially complained about Ghana's minimal interference in challenging the mishandling of Lumumba. In addition, Mobutu related that his Sûreté had proposed to kill Lumumba when its attempts to collect him from the local ANC were thwarted. Mobutu said he had ordered his forces not to harm the prime minister.[8]

Mobutu's military still manhandled Lumumba on the flight to Leopoldville, and the battering continued when the ANC offloaded him and other captured politicians to a truck at the airport. Extraordinary newsreel footage showed the ANC roughing up Lumumba in front of a smiling Mobutu. The casual brutality of his soldiers before the world did not bother him. A wide audience witnessed the sadism and saw in it another example of the obscenity of the Congo. The ANC was just as bad as— probably worse than—everyone had said, while the newsreel announced that "a new chapter" had begun "in the dark and tragic history of the Congo." The UN immediately called for humane treatment of the prisoner. The United States joined the outcry and, like the UN, urged a fair trial for Lumumba should the government accuse him of treason. At the same time, Lumumba's molestation had embarrassed the West. Bewailing the fact that the film could not be suppressed, the US Department of State still hoped to minimize Mobutu's smirking presence at Lumumba's return to Leopoldville.[9]

In September the Western powers had struggled to find a judicial raison d'être for making Lumumba go away. They failed with the Kasa-Vubu coup and, as the CIA put it, for a time tried "semi-constitutional means" to shatter Lumumba, when thugs were not trying to murder him.[10] By December, still trying behind the scenes to kill the man, Belgium and the United States publicly set legalities aside in order to immobilize the prime minister. While they attempted to paper over the unseemly, Belgium and the United States moved from constitutional coup-making to the crudest exercise of *force majeure*. The UN did not behave with much greater delicacy. But in trying to moderate the treatment of Lumumba, Dayal infuriated the Leopoldville politicians and their Western advocates. He regarded the Africans as juvenile and immature, and at the same time correctly appraised "the structural situation." This "situation," Dayal wrote, conformed to what the Western missions had worked for: "Mobutu and the ANC are supreme; Kasa-Vubu has been revitalized; the commissioners are unchallenged as a de facto government . . . ;

Lumumba returned to Leopoldville. In a famous picture, Lumumba was at the mercy of Mobutu's soldiers on December 2. (© *BelgaImage*)

Lumumba is under arrest." Still, Dayal concluded in a report to Hammarskjöld, none of this would produce a secure Congo. Dayal stressed the "stark fact" that the ANC governed. He did not mean that Mobutu ran a professional army. Dayal did mean that guns and not discussion ruled Leopoldville, and that for the most part Mobutu commanded the weapons around the city. A normal army, wrote Marlière, had troops that efficiently took orders. Nonetheless, despite his efforts, the ANC "had no organization or command, and did not obey." The value of such soldiers was nil, and they "even constituted a danger to the country."[11]

At Camp Hardy, Lumumba sat out of the glare of the politics of Leopoldville, and the politicians thought he was less intimidating to them. On December 6, Mobutu held a press conference. He produced a medical certificate, signed by two doctors, testifying to Lumumba's satisfactory condition. Mobutu said that the government would try Lumumba for provoking mutiny in the ANC and torturing members of parliament. The colonel did not set a date. He noted that because he had put Lumumba behind bars, an "atmosphere of confidence" needed to grow. Thus, the

College of Commissioners would not yield to the parliament but would stay on after January 1 as a provisional government. The UN in New York had proposed a conciliation commission that would send a number of diplomats to the Congo. They would interview people like Mobutu and Kasa-Vubu and investigate the troubles. The conciliators would set parameters for government by the Congo's elected politicians. In concluding the press conference, Mobutu said he opposed this conciliation commission.[12]

The Politics of the Royal Nuptials

While the Leopoldville politicians worried about what to do with their prisoner, Belgian and American officials negotiated the diplomatic conundrums surrounding the king's marriage. Major Weber wanted Brussels to invite Tshombe to the wedding, set for December 15. But because Katanga had no international status, Tshombe could not wangle an invitation. Instead, he delivered a gift to the royal couple when the king privately received the Katangan president on December 6. Baudouin had anticipated giving Tshombe a decoration, "the same as Lumumba's." The Belgian government first went along but had backed off because of American pressure: a decoration for Tshombe would undermine the Leopoldville moderates. The king greeted Tshombe, but the president retired without a medal. Tshombe, who had looked forward to this honor, threw a fit at the disregard shown him by the Belgian government and threatened to leave immediately: "We will not be treated as children," he said. As this mini-crisis unfolded, Baudouin went to meet his fiancée at the airport, where he argued with Wigny about the medal. That evening d'Aspremont saved the day when he hastily improvised an award ceremony at a dinner for Tshombe. Wigny felt forced to go to demonstrate the unity of the Belgian government. Tshombe loved to wear the Great Ribbon of the Order of the Crown.[13]

Ambassador Burden pestered Washington to have a member of the political elite represent the United States at the wedding. Burden recommended Herbert Hoover Jr., whose father had overseen aid to Belgium during World War I, and also Milton Eisenhower, the president's brother. Then Burden stiffened the conditions—the queen of England might attend—and asked for the "highest possible official." Eisenhower dutifully informed Baudouin that Secretary of State Herter would give the salutations of the United States at the marriage, although before the actual ceremony Herter would go on to other meetings, concluding with a NATO summit in Paris. "May God have Your Majesty in his safe and holy keeping," wrote Eisenhower. He sent a gift of twelve Steuben plates, each bearing the design of a different sign of the zodiac. This "uniquely American" present cost $1,500, with an additional $100 for the box. Eisenhower named Burden as Herter's assistant during the festivities.[14]

When Herter got to Brussels, he received a medal, the Great Ribbon of the Order of Leopold, Belgium's highest award, and higher than the one Tshombe received. At an all-star lunch, Burden treated his guests—including Paul-Henri Spaak—to some of his irreplaceable Château Cheval Blanc, 1947. Then the secretary of state wore a special black silk top hat at an audience with the king, where Herter presented his credentials and Eisenhower's felicitations. Herter wrote to Burden that at his "most elegant" the ambassador had dispelled any doubts about "the warmth of the relations between our two countries."[15]

Spaak had delayed the NATO conference until December 16, so that he could attend the wedding. When he and Herter met up again in Paris at the NATO gathering, Spaak continued to complain about how the United States underestimated Belgium's colonial woes. By this time, however, Lumumba's situation was weak, and the Western powers were united against him. Spaak's grumbles had become only irritating, for he would not publicly deprecate NATO. When he spoke yet another time of his resignation during the December proceedings, the man had become a liability, and others wanted his job. With the British in the lead, the Americans looked for a way to push Spaak gently out of NATO. Eisenhower's reaction had proved excessive, for the Belgian was dispensable.[16]

Soon the celebratory wedding mood turned sour. On November 4 the Eyskens government had introduced a draft spending bill. Cuts and taxes would bring the budget, damaged by the disaster in the Congo, into balance. The Socialist opposition was furious, but waited until after the wedding to protest. The unions started a general strike that paralyzed Belgium's economy for a month, the biggest work stoppage the country had experienced since World War II. Violent sabotage threatened public life. Eyskens again fought to survive. On Friday, January 13, he would win a narrow victory in the Belgian parliament. It approved the spending bill, and the strike died down. For Eyskens, however, this victory was pyrrhic. His government was worn out, and the ministry would resign a month later. From mid-December to mid-January, Lumumba's fate in the distant Congo was not always on the minds of the stressed politicians in Brussels.[17]

The Leopoldville Moderates in Disarray

By the time the soldiers delivered Lumumba to the army camp at Thysville, they had worked him over. As rumors spread of his condition, ripples of anti-regime turbulence went through the Congo. International pressure on the Leopoldville regime increased, and Mobutu allowed the International Red Cross to visit Camp Hardy at the end of December. Lumumba's health had improved, but he was kept in complete isolation.[18] More important, arguments about his custody split Camp Hardy. The quarrels within the ANC testified that even near the capital, Kasa-Vubu and Mobutu had a slack hold on the military. The disturbances afforded Lumumba a little wiggle room, and precipitated more discussion among his enemies about what they should do with him. Although Mobutu had said that Lumumba would go to trial for treason, no one had said where or when such a trial would take place. What would happen if Mobutu made good his intention to continue without the elected parliament after December 31? Camp Hardy could barely hold the man who had every claim to be regarded as the prime minister in the only legitimate government. At least Lumumba had to go to a safer detention.

The Western powers wanted an agreement between Lumumba's opponents in Leopoldville and Elisabethville—now all "moderates"—although Tshombe was most suspicious. At the end of November the African American jazzman Louis Armstrong had toured Africa and performed in Elisabethville. American officials in Leopoldville—both from the CIA and the State Department—took the opportunity to visit with white and black Katangan leaders under the guise of listening to Armstrong.[19] Ambassador Timberlake, who had been regarded as a mediocrity, had matured as a competent expounder of American views. He exhorted Tshombe to work out a modus vivendi with the government of

Kasa-Vubu and Mobutu. Tshombe literally fell to the floor before Timberlake. Did the ambassador want to see Tshombe "in this posture before nonentity Kasa-Vubu, inexperienced Mobutu, or snippet Bomboko"? Tshombe said he preferred death.[20]

Despite Tshombe's preferences, Belgian-assisted attempts to bring Katanga and Leopoldville together occurred in this period. Tshombe and Kasa-Vubu met in Brazzaville to fête Abbé Youlou on the independence of the French Congo in late November. On December 15 they had a real conference in Brazzaville, but it did not succeed. Tshombe was in a difficult position. Despite getting his medal, he was taking a long second look at his connection with Belgium. Katanga established a diplomatic mission in Paris, and Tshombe considered giving the command of Katanga's gendarmerie to a Frenchman.[21]

Military operations by Lumumba's adherents in Stanleyville reinforced all of these concerns. Gizenga had a government and an army. Because of the diplomatic sympathy from the members of the Soviet bloc, he had more legitimacy than Katanga, still a global outcast. At the end of December Stanleyville troops marched south to Kivu Province, adjacent to Katanga. They knocked off the provincial government and set up a new regime under Anicet Kashamura that was a creature of Stanleyville. At the beginning of January 1961, with Belgian help, Mobutu launched a counterattack but failed completely.

Now the danger was clear: Stanleyville threatened both Leopoldville and Elisabethville. Jason Sendwe in Leopoldville was urging the UN again to send him to north Katanga to continue its pacification, and on January 8 Dayal agreed to the visit.[22] The next day Stanleyville forces invaded north Katanga and shrank Tshombe's dominion. Balubakat politicians shaped a separate administration, the Province of Lualaba, another part of the Congo under Stanleyville's wing. Might Sendwe come back, this time in triumph? This was Tshombe's nightmare. On January 12, Tshombe wrote Baudouin asking for help "to save the integrity of Katanga, this anticommunist bulwark, loyal to Belgium, that we wanted to create in central Africa." If Katanga did not get aid, Tshombe warned, he might have to call on France.[23]

Just as Tshombe blackmailed Belgium in asking for help for Katanga, Bomboko did the same for Leopoldville. He had promised to consider

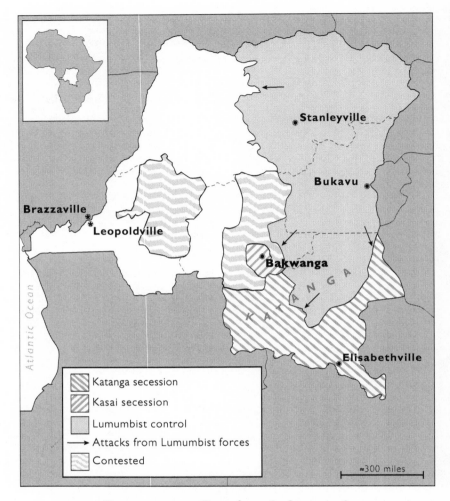

Troop movements, December 1960–January 1961

restoring diplomatic relations in return for Belgian aid to Mobutu for his raid on Kivu. On January 10, Bomboko conferred in Paris with Belgian officials. In the end Bomboko signed an agreement that diplomacy between the two countries would be gradually resumed, in exchange—off the record—for Belgium's equipping a battalion of paratroopers. The next day, still in Paris, Spaak invited Bomboko to an unofficial get-together with NATO ambassadors. Bomboko requested money and matériel to bolster a loyal and efficient army, and received Spaak's strong support.

Wigny had also underscored to Belgium's NATO diplomats the need to remove the "cancer" of Stanleyville "metastasizing" across the Congo. On his return to Leopoldville, Bomboko mentioned Belgian money to the tune of about $2.4 million per month. If that did not work, Burden reported to Washington, the Belgians would try to get Tshombe to lend a hand: he was introducing his own currency, and maybe could be persuaded to turn the old paper money over to Kasa-Vubu to pay the army.[24] The Belgians could only have contemplated credits if everyone received assurances that Lumumba had no future.

While the Americans opposed bilateral aid, they too worried about the progress of the Gizenga nationalists. The State Department still hoped that the UN would step in, while the CIA hoped to work with Belgian spies in the Congo to disrupt the group around Gizenga.[25] As Eisenhower prepared to see Kennedy about the transition, the State Department noted that "no effective counterforce is presently available to block the extension . . . of the Stanleyville regime."[26] Meanwhile, Camp Hardy held Lumumba.

What Will Kennedy Do?

In October and November the policies of the UN and the ANC had restricted Lumumba to his residence, and he had barely appeared to the outside world. Devlin found his assassination plotting temporarily foiled. Then at the end of November Lumumba made his break for Stanleyville, and the first of the CIA's hired killers, WIN, made plans should Lumumba escape the dragnet. More clearly a contract murderer, ROGUE did not turn up in Leopoldville until after the Africans had collared the prime minister and deposited him inside Camp Hardy. Devlin had one "specific recollection" of discussing an "execution squad" with ROGUE, though the work of both hit-men seems to have been confined to talk in their shared hotel in the capital. The formal overseer, Justin O'Donnell, left around the end of the year.[27]

One might argue that the CIA had little need to kill. By December Kasa-Vubu and Mobutu could permanently remove the prime minister from power through a trial or less respectable means. The Americans tell us over and over again that they preferred "a purely African affair" to end the Lumumba presence. Here, they were saying that the savage blacks would exterminate Lumumba, when the whites had moral caveats. In truth, however, no matter what Lumumba's position, Devlin and those around him in the Congo would not rest until someone finished the job. The Africans may have had it in mind, but the Belgians and the Americans fixated on murder. They might say they only wanted the Africans to put Lumumba before a judge. Nonetheless, Devlin and the others had little faith in the efficiency of the Africans, their lust for revenge, or the courage of Leopoldville.

By the autumn, no matter what Lumumba's status, yet another factor entered the calculations of the CIA in Leopoldville. The closely contested presidential campaign in the United States pitted Nixon against Kennedy. The Agency accepted the orientation of Eisenhower, who looked to the English, French, and Belgians even if colonialism disgraced them. The CIA thought Nixon would continue the old policies, but if America voted Kennedy in, he would foolishly consort with Lumumba. Kennedy achieved a slender victory in early November. Had not the president-elect insinuated that the United States had thwarted democracy in the Congo? Now, CIA officials told one another, they had only some ten weeks until Kennedy's inauguration, when policy would change, and politicians would seat Lumumba again in the parliament, to the detriment of the United States.[28]

In early September longtime Democratic diplomat Averell Harriman had been in the Congo as part of a fact-finding mission he was carrying out for presidential candidate Kennedy. Harriman would also inform the State Department, and at the time shared Republican Ambassador Timberlake's concern with Lumumba. Harriman had spoken to Lumumba just after Kasa-Vubu's alteration of the government on September 5, and had reported that Lumumba would cause trouble in power, in jail, or upon release. Harriman briefed Kennedy again after the presidential election in early November. President-elect Kennedy wanted to know if the United States should save Lumumba. Harriman confirmed his earlier observation that rescuing Lumumba held too high a risk for the administration-to-be even if it decided on the wisdom of that policy.[29]

During the campaign Kennedy had received no confidential information about the American government's plans for assassination. Then, on

November 18, Dulles and his second-in-command, Richard Bissell, briefed the president-elect. While Bissell recalled that he did not say anything to Kennedy, he presumed that Dulles did.[30]

In early December, just as Lumumba broke out, Kennedy's youngest brother, Edward, traveled to the Congo at his brother's wish with a delegation from the US Senate. In a press conference in Leopoldville—just after Lumumba's arrest—the younger Kennedy urged the release of all political prisoners, Lumumba included. The president-elect complained that his brother had "his own foreign policy." Kennedy's transition team, however, contemplated plans whereby Lumumba or his deputies would participate in a broad-based coalition. Stories flourished about what would happen after the Democrats took office.[31]

At the UN in New York, Thomas Kanza, a Congo politician sympathetic to Lumumba, used ties to Eleanor Roosevelt, the widow of the former president, and Adlai Stevenson, soon to be Kennedy's ambassador to the UN, to coax American policy toward Lumumba. Ghana's Kwame Nkrumah asked Kennedy to secure Lumumba's freedom. In his autobiography of 1998, Dayal said that the UN had hoped for "a holding operation until the new American president took over, when we might be able to reverse the tide." Dayal even argued that the CIA worked to murder Lumumba to foreclose the chance that Kennedy would sanction a coalition. A study written in the State Department soon after the killing worried about press accounts that were leaked earlier. Gossip about future liberal Kennedy policies, the report said, may have impelled the killers to act.[32]

Whatever Kennedy knew, even the Democratic team did not deviate from Republican objectives regarding Lumumba. The president's famous speeches lifted people's eyes toward the just, but Kennedy barely altered American policy in respect to the Congo. Three weeks before the inauguration, at the end of 1960, a task force of the incoming administration determined that Lumumba should stay in jail until the Congo calmed down. In the first ten days of the administration, the State Department wanted a "back up" scheme that might give a role to his supporters, though not to Lumumba himself. However, the Department of Defense, under the Democrats already an important facet of American policy, fought even this backup plan. The focus shifted to forcing Dayal out, an outcome Brussels also wanted. The Republican administration had previously evinced a desire to have Hammarskjöld's representative move on.[33] The Democrats more forcefully reasoned that because the United States funded the UN, "we are now paying for our own demise" with Dayal in Leopoldville. Since Mobutu's people also hated Dayal, the new Democratic focus on him would satisfy Africans in Leopoldville and remove Lumumba's chief UN defender.[34]

Other ideas may have gone through the heads of Kennedy's "New Frontier" officials, but they barely modified the Eisenhower program in respect to Lumumba. Within weeks of the change of administration, the Democrats went after Dayal as the Republicans had not. When Dayal returned to New York for consultations, Adlai Stevenson at the UN at once made overtures to persuade Dayal to resign on account of his health. Stevenson "really laid it on the line hard." The great progressive performed so ineptly and transparently that Dayal described the new ambassador as "a mountebank," a seller of quack medicines in public places. The CIA did not know all of this, however, and the Democratic victory in November foreshadowed a winter of discontent for Devlin.[35]

Devlin's Fears

While his appraisals of the constant crises in Leopoldville had become repetitious, Devlin's reports around the turn of the year skirted the hysterical. Parts of the army might always move to Lumumba. Mobutu and like-minded politicians vacillated and lacked pull. What if constitutional rule returned? The UN was assembling the conciliation commission that Mobutu had denigrated. These diplomats might demand a position for Lumumba. Devlin tortured himself about the future of the Congo but later wrote that he was distressed when his contacts in Leopoldville dried up and he was left ignorant of events.[36] The distress and ignorance feature as more fiction in Devlin's memoir.

In the fall and winter of 1960–1961, in "keeping the Cold War out of Africa," Devlin had overseen various plans to murder Lumumba. The CIA had paid "the moderates"—at least Mobutu, Ileo, Bomboko, and Nendaka—for their efforts to benefit American goals, and had begged them to wipe out the prime minister. Devlin called the Africans on his payroll by different names, indicating relations that are often blurred or inconsistent—friends, collaborators, agents, contacts, cooperators.[37] As the Senate committee study wrote, these men "had a daily intimate working relationship" with the CIA.[38] According to the committee, Devlin "advised and aided" these men, and urged on them Lumumba's "permanent disposal." In the final act Devlin hoped—in his oft-repeated phrase— "for a purely African affair." On Tuesday morning, January 17, the Leopoldville politicians took Lumumba to Elisabethville. Devlin recollected that "there was a general assumption, once . . . he had been sent to Katanga . . . his goose was cooked."[39] Devlin had learned on January 14 of plans to airlift Lumumba to Kalonji's capital of Bakwanga, a destination even more hostile than Elisabethville. Four contacts reported to him of plans to move Lumumba. Devlin did not tell the Agency about the transfer plan until January 17, when it was too late to do anything.[40] Did he agonize that the supposed concessions of the Kennedy administration might be catching? Did he withhold information out of fear that his overlords would waver in their tenacity?

Devlin's anxieties about a changing of the guard resulted from hyperbolic speculation about the goals of the incoming administration. A more realistic basis existed. On January 5, Eisenhower's CIA policing body, the board of consultants on foreign intelligence activities, had again called for reforms in the CIA and recommended "serious consideration" of firing Dulles if they did not take place. Moreover, in its contest with the CIA, the Department of State in January was throwing up impediments to expanded extra-UN activities to keep Lumumba down and out. Devlin, again, would more than likely not have known any of this, except for the rumor mill calling up images of dramatic policy alteration. Nonetheless, the recalcitrance of the State Department did not amount to much at the end of the outgoing administration. Moreover, Eisenhower did not move on his board's advice and passed the report on to the president-elect. Kennedy did not attend to the counsel until May of 1961, when his humiliation at the Bay of Pigs made him furious at the CIA and resulted in Dulles's dismissal.[41] The Agency's repeated denials of responsibility are a minor matter, and in any event the foolhardy if gruesome activities of the CIA proved ineffectual. But like Shakespeare's Macbeth, Devlin had enough blood on his hands to make "the multitudinous seas incarnadine."

CHAPTER TWELVE

Killing Lumumba

T HREE PROBLEMS beset the Leopoldville politicians. They cringed at the prospects of their military defeat in the Congo itself. They brooded over Kennedy's victory, and they despaired that so many African countries wanted a political place for Lumumba.

On January 2 Kasa-Vubu, under pressure, called a roundtable conference for January 25 and sent off emissaries to Bakwanga and Elisabethville to persuade Kalonji and Tshombe to come. Might Lumumba attend? Pro-Lumumba African and Asian statesmen conferred in Casablanca at the same time and called for his release, and the UN conciliation commission that arrived in Leopoldville on January 4 might do the same. To add to the pressure on the politicians in the capital, Hammarskjöld also reviewed the work of his mission in the Congo from January 4 to January 6, and was briefly back in the country on January 10. Less than a year before, the Belgians had taken Lumumba from a cell so that he might attend the original roundtable in Brussels. There he had prevailed. Were the halfhearted leaders in Leopoldville now apprehensive about a repeat of this scenario? None of them wanted Lumumba at large. They worried that the UN might rescue the prime minister at any moment. Why didn't they kill Lumumba themselves? Too self-doubting and unpopular, they neither commanded their own jails nor trusted their army.

On the early morning of Friday, January 13, discipline in Camp Hardy buckled. The soldiers refused orders unless they were paid; some men wanted Lumumba set free; others thought him an enemy; and still others worried that holding such a dangerous prisoner in an insecure facility would bring disaster. That morning Kasa-Vubu, Mobutu, Bomboko, and Nendaka hurried to Thysville to negotiate with the soldiers. Bomboko, who had just returned from the Paris negotiations with Belgium, promised money to the ANC.[1] The politicians put a lid on the insubordination, yet it showed how Lumumba at the camp troubled Leopoldville to the north. An alarmed populace spread rumors the next day that Lumumba would go free and that his military in Stanleyville would soon descend on Leopoldville. The Stanleyville troops had already taken north Katanga, and even before the Thysville uprising the leaders in Leopoldville had sent their families off to Brussels. On January 13 Devlin cabled Washington that the present government might fall within days, and that Lumumba could be rehabilitated. If the United States did not take "drastic steps" at once, American policy would be defeated.[2] In Brussels, Wigny panicked and called for an immediate meeting with the Western ambassadors. We should meet Bomboko's demand for money and weapons, the minister said, but not without something in return. "That something must be the urgent reconciliation between Kasa-Vubu and Tshombe."[3]

The insurrection at Camp Hardy precipitated a decision to put Lumumba somewhere else. Where could the clique of Kasa-Vubu, Mobutu, and Bomboko relocate him? Katanga was the first option. On January 14, just after noon, from his room in the Belgian embassy in Brazzaville, Lahaye sent a radio message to the headquarters of the gendarmerie in Elisabethville. It was an urgent request from the commissioners in Leopoldville: Might Tshombe accept Lumumba? Ambassador Dupret informed Brussels and urged the Foreign Office to pass the Lahaye message to the Belgian consul general in Elisabethville.[4] Albert Kalonji, perhaps more than anyone, hated Lumumba and wanted to get his hands on him. That same day, the European head of Kalonji's (small) army intercepted the radio message and offered to receive Lumumba in the south Kasai secessionist state.[5] But Kalonji's quirks and unrestrained appetite for revenge in respect to the prime minister were embarrassing. More important,

Ghanaian UN forces at the Bakwanga airport might prevent the landing of a plane, or rescue Lumumba. While Tshombe had not given a green light to bring Lumumba to Elisabethville, Hammarskjöld's pact with Katanga kept international peacekeepers at a distance at Luano airport. The UN supervised the civilian air traffic, but Katanga's military transport had its own area. The UN could not spoil a handover in Elisabethville. Kasa-Vubu and the others prayed for Tshombe's consent to a move more certain of success, but agreed on a transfer to south Kasai. On the morning of Monday, January 16, security chief Nendaka joined Sûreté agent André Lahaye in the office of the Belgian airline, Sabena, at the Leopoldville airport. Lahaye put together an aircraft schedule to take Lumumba to Bakwanga or Elisabethville. The operation would begin that afternoon. Two commissioners, Fernand Kazadi and Jonas Mukamba, were secured to squire Lumumba on his trip.[6]

Lumumba's imprisonment had worried the Belgians from the time Mobutu's troops had surrounded the UN forces at the prime minister's residence in October. When Mobutu's soldiers had captured Lumumba in December, the Belgians again had wanted guarantees that the Africans would keep him out of circulation. When gossip spread that Stanleyville wanted to exchange some of their prisoners for Lumumba, d'Aspremont warned his men in Leopoldville to thwart negotiations at any price. On January 14 d'Aspremont's confidant Loos, upset by the newspaper reports on the Thysville mutiny, advised Marlière to try again to get Lumumba to Tshombe. He sent a message in military code: "Urgently resume Brazza scheme toward Joseph." D'Aspremont wanted an ironclad dungeon. He cabled Tshombe on January 16 to take Lumumba, although the cable arrived late in the afternoon, after Tshombe had made up his mind.[7]

At the last minute Tshombe did go along with the proposal, but Leopoldville clearly originated the negotiations. Tshombe had the least to gain from taking this hot potato. Although he sanctioned the move, he almost immediately backtracked in public. He made up a story that he was presented with a fait accompli when Leopoldville flew Lumumba to him. Tshombe's Belgian advisers had an even more negative attitude. Keener for secessionist independence than their would-be superiors in Belgium, the Europeans in Elisabethville never thought that Lumumba's presence would benefit them. A debilitated Lumumba always on the rim of the consciousness of Brussels would best help Katanga. The Belgians there had little to do with the handover. Brussels and the Belgians in Leopoldville pushed this policy, not those in Elisabethville, although Tshombe and Munongo were in any event putting all the Belgians at arm's length.

What made Tshombe at last say yes? The UN observer in Elisabethville called the choice "an act of suicidal folly."[8] We have some facts but must also conjecture. Albert Delvaux had a role. Serving in Lumumba's cabinet, Delvaux had signed the dismissal of Lumumba in September along with Bomboko. Then Delvaux had been named a member of the Ileo ministry. In the winter, he shuttled back and forth from Leopoldville to Elisabethville, trying to mediate a settlement among Kasa-Vubu, Mobutu, and Tshombe. In Katanga in mid-January, Delvaux continued to press Tshombe. On the morning of Monday, January 16, while Lahaye and Nendaka were coordinating a transfer, Delvaux synchronized a telephone conversation between Kasa-Vubu and Tshombe.[9]

As the press triumphantly reported, the two leaders agreed on a roundtable in Elisabethville, and it is almost impossible that they did not come to terms on the transfer of Lumumba. In mid-January Tshombe's slight base in northern Katanga evaporated when Gizenga's troops marched in and a hostile administration was inaugurated. Its grip strengthened Jason Sendwe. Due back in north Katanga, he would steal the ground from under Tshombe. Sendwe walked freely in Leopoldville. We believe some promise from Kasa-Vubu about Sendwe induced Tshombe to receive Lumumba. But we don't know the exact nature of this promise or when it was to be made good. Leopoldville had offered Lumumba to Tshombe in late November, Tshombe later recalled, and he had exploded: "Lumumba? No! Give me Sendwe instead."[10] After the transfer of Lumumba, Tshombe told a Belgian diplomat in Elisabethville that his assent to the transfer "depended" on the internment of Sendwe; another Belgian official in Leopoldville reported that Tshombe asked Kasa-Vubu for Sendwe "twice, with great insistence."[11] The American consul in Katanga cabled home that "Kasa-Vubu has agreed to arrest Sendwe as quid pro quo for Tshombe taking custody of Lumumba."[12]

Sendwe's incarceration in Leo, even if it could be achieved, might unnecessarily build up Tshombe,[13] and so Leopoldville politicians backed away from their commitment. In early 1961, Sendwe got lucky and survived. But Leopoldville anted up something else. When its bosses had got their hands on Lumumba in early December, they had also rounded up Maurice Mpolo and Joseph Okito, among others. A member of the MNC-Lumumba, the fifty-year-old Okito held the vice presidency of the senate, which had not convened since September 13. If Ileo, the president of the senate, became a genuine prime minister, Okito would take charge of the senate, and could determine what would happen in case Kasa-Vubu's job went vacant. If Lumumba returned as prime minister, Okito might substitute for Kasa-Vubu. Also in the MNC-Lumumba, Maurice Mpolo had presided over the ministry of youth and sports in the Lumumba government, its chief propagandist. He additionally had stood in as commander in chief for Lundula for a time in July, and then argued with Mobutu. In September "General" Mpolo, thirty-two years old, had tried to undercut Mobutu's "neutralization," and was the only serious contender to Mobutu to lead the ANC—perhaps against Tshombe.[14] According to the records, Lumumba, Mpolo, and Okito, along with seven others, occupied individual cells at Camp Hardy.[15]

At the last minute, Kasa-Vubu's detente with Tshombe allowed the government in Leopoldville to dispatch Lumumba not to Bakwanga but to Elisabethville. But Leopoldville at least hesitated on Sendwe but threw in Okito and Mpolo. So we reason.

Transfer to Katanga

On the afternoon of January 16, soon after his deliberations about the airplane schedules, Nendaka traveled to Thysville. He spent the night in a hotel. At about 5:30 the following morning, January 17, Nendaka picked up Lumumba, Okito, and Mpolo from their separate cells. A small convoy with a guard of reliable members of the ANC drove southwest toward the coast, away from Leopoldville, to a minor airstrip near the town of Lukala, forty miles distant, where a small plane had set down. They got there about 8 A.M. The prisoners, Nendaka, and three soldiers made another brief trip, this time by air. They flew 150 miles to Moanda on the coast, a seaside resort once favored on weekends by Belgian colonists, and later by UN officials. Local weather conditions, as well as a desire to stay away from more traveled airports where the UN would have

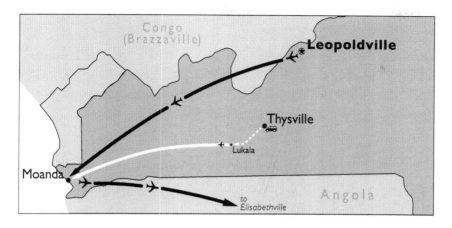

The transfer, January 17, 1961

a presence, or where a military convoy would attract attention, seem to have dictated the exact movements and timing.

While Nendaka and his cargo journeyed to Moanda from Thysville, a DC-4 of Air Congo left Leopoldville for Moanda. Designed for longer trips, this larger plane carried the two commissioners, Kazadi and Mukamba. Both came from south Kasai, and were linked to Kalonji. At the airfield in Moanda the men waited.

Later, like everyone, Nendaka blamed someone else. In respect to this transport, he was obeying Kasa-Vubu's orders and, Nendaka said, Kazadi and Mukamba commandeered the DC-4 for Elisabethville. Yet when Nendaka's small plane touched down in Moanda, the two commissioners may have thought they were ushering Lumumba to Bakwanga. Nendaka ordered them to make for Elisabethville, and the greater length of the flight meant that the DC-4 required extra fuel. After his work at the Leopoldville airport but also after the conversation between Tshombe and Kasa-Vubu, Nendaka had to have been privy to the choice of Elisabethville as the end-of-the-line determined just the day before. In addition to the flight crew, the prisoners boarded with the two commissioners and three soldiers. Nendaka returned to Leopoldville.

The guards were sadistic. They had already mistreated Lumumba, Okito, and Mpolo on the trip from Camp Hardy to Moanda. During the long flight from Moanda to Elisabethville—over eleven hundred miles—it got worse, as the soldiers punched and pounded the nationalists. The pilots fitfully complained, among other things fearing for the safety of their plane. With the commissioners impassive, the crew finally locked the door to the cockpit. Toward 4:30 P.M., now in the southeastern Congo, the DC-4 neared Luano airport outside Elisabethville.[16]

Five Hours on Katanga's Soil

The control tower hastily got in touch with Katanga's politicians for instructions on what to do. While the plane circled the field, airport technicians sought an unavailable Tshombe. At least the time of arrival surprised him. Tshombe was watching a special showing of the film *Freedom,* sponsored by Moral Re-Armament. This worldwide organization, based in the United States, had conservative Christian roots, sought close ties with Western governments, and promoted "the Four Absolutes" of honesty, purity, selflessness, and love. Moral Re-Armament's *Freedom* took up the challenges Christian Africa faced as it moved to independence. That afternoon the movie absorbed Tshombe.[17]

In July 1960, Minister of the Interior Godefroid Munongo had told Lumumba never to set foot in Katanga. Now, in January 1961, Munongo gave permission for the aircraft with Lumumba to descend into the military area, off-limits to the UN. When it touched down about 5 P.M., Munongo was at the airport with an impressive array of force. There were about fifty police and two platoons of the military police of Katanga's army, the Gendarmerie Katangaise, perhaps another sixty men. At a safe distance away in the civilian area, the UN could testify only that Lumumba had come to Elisabethville. A number of Katanga's officials chanced to be at the field. Thus, other African cabinet ministers with some Belgian Francophone advisers also witnessed the landing. The Belgians included the highest echelon of the gendarmerie—a colonel, a lieutenant colonel, and two majors.[18] But Captain Julien Gat, a lower-ranking officer and the Flemish head of the military police, hustled the passengers from the plane to a waiting vehicle. After the in-flight pummeling, Lumumba, Mpolo, and Okito did not debark in good shape, and they suffered more injuries when the MPs loaded them into a military van. As a curious crowd looked on, the truck, a unit in an armed motorcade, quickly whisked away the prisoners.

Over the next two days, Katanga's newspaper, *L'Essor du Katanga,* reported that Kasa-Vubu and Tshombe had spoken on the phone and had seen eye to eye over a roundtable in Elisabethville. An "official communiqué" said that Kasa-Vubu, with the assent of Tshombe, had asked for Lumumba's transfer. *L'Essor* noted that disorder in the Bas-Congo and problems with Lumumba's detention at Camp Hardy prompted Kasa-Vubu. The paper recorded that the other prisoners from Thysville had gone to a jail nearer Leopoldville, and told how, for Lumumba, Elisabethville had replaced Bakwanga.[19] Tshombe's government did not make a secret of the consignment, and the press gave an accurate account. Elisabethville had surely made prearrangements. Now, late on the afternoon of January 17, local security efficiently took over.

Police inspector Frans Verscheure advised a high African law enforcement officer in Katanga. A year before, on January 22, 1960, when colonial authorities sentenced Lumumba in Stanleyville because he had promoted a riot, Verscheure had accompanied the convict to the jail in Jadotville in Katanga. A newspaper photo of Verscheure with Lumumba had given Verscheure a bit of celebrity in Katanga. Belgium had then freed Lumumba, who made his dramatic appearance at the roundtable in Brussels a couple of days afterward. Now a year later, under different circumstances, Verscheure again entered Lumumba's life. About noon on January 17, Munongo told Verscheure that Lumumba might be on his way. Verscheure was to secure a place for detention. His choice fell on farmer Lucien Brouwez. His empty bungalow lay just over two miles down the road from the Luano airport, and Verscheure claimed part of the house for temporary imprisonment. Security men cut the airport's metal fence to furnish a convenient way out. From the point where they breeched the barrier, a car could avoid Luano's main entrance and exit immediately onto the road to Brouwez's. The government meant to get Lumumba speedily away. Verscheure did not go to the airport himself, but that afternoon he was summoned to Tshombe's residence, a quick walk away from the policeman's own office, and told to be at the ready during the evening.[20]

Captain Gat's convoy brought the internees to Brouwez's, and then stood guard to prevent their escape or a UN rescue. The captives

Lumumba and Verscheure. The police inspector escorts Lumumba to prison in
January 1960. (*Photograph by C. N. Thompson, Camera Press London*)

showed up by 5:20 P.M. Munongo and a couple of other officials trailed
Gat to Brouwez's. In all likelihood the politicians if not the soldiers tormented the three men a bit more. But not for long. By this time assistants had interrupted Tshombe at the movies, and he had returned to
his presidential home. He called for a select ministerial conference—a
five-person war cabinet—around 6 P.M. Munongo left the Brouwez farm

almost at once. The president lived some six miles from the place of confinement.

Many considerations suggest that the Elisabethville Africans distanced themselves from the high-level and Francophone Belgians who counseled them. These Europeans did not want Lumumba on their hands. The Africans may have worried that Elisabethville's Belgians would pretend to scruples about Lumumba's treatment. Tshombe and Munongo perhaps wanted to show their self-sufficiency, and their ability to make hard choices. Had not Baudouin intimated to Tshombe that Lumumba was expendable, and had not d'Aspremont asked for his transfer? Belgian policy makers in Katanga seemed to have had little knowledge of the events that were taking place. Moreover, although they all had done everything in their power to endanger Lumumba, these Belgians, like their compatriots in Brussels and Leopoldville and like the Americans, wanted to stay away from a last scene. The Belgians in Katanga may have just sat tight and deliberately absented themselves.

The cabinet group met no more than ninety minutes, approximately from 6:30 to 8:00 P.M. Munongo and Tshombe had probably already fixed on what to do: Lumumba, Mpolo, and Okito must die. Tshombe and Munongo collected the ministers to brief them and involve them in the enterprise. Alcohol is said to have facilitated the formal decision to execute the three adversaries.

Just before 8 P.M. Verscheure received a phone call at his own headquarters. He again walked to the nearby president's mansion. He was to ride with an African official in his new automobile to Brouwez's, stay outside till 8:30, and then remove the prisoners. At 8, too, the ministerial group, including Tshombe, drove to Brouwez's, some for a second visit. They tormented Lumumba for the last time. Jean-Baptiste Kibwe, Katanga's minister of finance, feared and hated Lumumba's nationalism. He called the prime minister a traitor, whose death Katanga would celebrate the next day. The desire to finish off the three cut short the cruelty, and the ministers left. Outside the house, about 8:30 as requested, Verscheure piled Lumumba, Mpolo, and Okito into the backseat of the car. Gat and Verscheure later said that the Africans had divulged to the Flemish officers only that the prisoners were being sent to safer keeping. The motorcade took the road to Jadotville, a distance of eighty miles, where Katanga's penitentiary lay, and, if Gat and Verscheure are to be believed, they thought they were heading there. The two men held subordinate positions in the Belgian command and would simply do what the Africans required.

Someone had selected a spot some thirty miles from Brouwez's where a firing squad would do its duty. Off the highway to Jadotville a dirt track led to the far-off village of Mwadingusha. A little way along this track—a quagmire of red mud because of the rainy season—men had dug out a trench in a secluded area. Local security forces commanded by Munongo's brother-in-law probably took on this job. In this darkness, illuminated by the spotlights of the military trucks, Gat and Verscheure, along with two other lower-grade European servicemen, would issue the fatal orders to African soldiers.

About 9:30 Verscheure and his driver reached the destination with Lumumba, Mpolo, and Okito. Other police and soldiers had mustered. Tshombe, Munongo, Kibwe, and other secessionist officials waited to observe. Verscheure pushed each of the condemned men individually in front of the burial hole. Each prisoner had his own firing squad of four men. Gat gave the order, each time, for the military contingents to pull their triggers. Lumumba came last, and the final group of soldiers sent a second round of bullets into him. One by one the dead were rolled into the pit. Some of the soldiers threw sandy soil over the bodies. The African military and policemen, their Flemish officers, and the Katanga politicians rushed away. They were in such a hurry that an arm remained stuck up through the dirt.

Before long, in his diary, Verscheure wrote: *9.43 L. dead.* In the United States, simultaneously that afternoon, President Eisenhower was practicing his nationwide television speech scheduled for delivery at 8:30 P.M. from Washington. This was his famous farewell address, in which he warned Americans of the undue influence of "the military-industrial complex."

Recollections, some set down decades later, furnish almost our entire knowledge of Lumumba's demise. Like Katanga's ministers, Verscheure and Gat told others what had happened, and the stories circulated for years. Versions of the episode slowly leaked out, beginning with the sketchy but not inaccurate investigation by the United Nations toward the end of 1961. In the late 1980s Gat and Verscheure and some of their accomplices gave interviews, as did Congolese in the early 1990s. Gat and Verscheure told what they remembered, and colleagues recalled what Gat and Verscheure and others had related. Nonetheless, everything had happened a long time ago. The people involved had consciously reflected on what they had previously said, and on what other people had said; perhaps the reflections colored their memories. In 2000, hearings were transcribed in Brussels. The stories changed from the 1960s to the late 1980s to the new century. There are different and often contradictory accounts of how Lumumba faced his end. Almost all of the collaborators, black and white, have themselves died.[21]

A macabre killing of the three politicians took place, but every detailed narrative of the proceedings makes unsubstantiated assumptions; no one has a photographic depiction, however dramatic the occasion. Only Verscheure's diary dates from the time of the murder. This single piece of documentary evidence hardly even counts as a diary but is rather a date book or agenda. The policeman noted engagements that he had scheduled, or perhaps the outcome of some deliberation, or some decision taken. While Verscheure wrote almost all the entries in French, the language he had mastered in the Congo, he set down details pertaining to the murder in his native Flemish. The Verscheure diary—the only primary Flemish source discovered in our inquiries—did not come to light until 2001 during the Belgian parliamentary investigations.

Rest in Peace

Lucas Samalenge, Katanga's minister of information, did not belong to the war cabinet, and may not even have witnessed the events. Late that evening, however, pub crawling through Elisabethville, he drunkenly told everyone that they had bumped off the prime minister. At the start of the next day, January 18, Samalenge's Belgian chief of staff wanted a picture of the captured Lumumba for the press. The minister continued to blab. With a smile he said: "You can't take a photo now; he's dead."[22] Unbelieving, the aide raced over to the president's office for confirmation. When Tshombe learned of Salamenge's indiscretion, the president was distraught; the man turned "gray," said his Western mentor. The secret liquidation at once became public. To prevent further damage for the moment, Tshombe forbade Samalenge to appear at the important ceremony that would occupy the morning. At the Cathedral of Saints Peter and Paul in Elisabethville, the entire unacknowledged government turned up at a Roman Catholic Mass commemorating those who had given their lives in the ongoing fight for the independence of Katanga. At Brouwez's the night before, Jean-Baptiste Kibwe had referred to the coming ritual when he had scorned Lumumba's treachery.

Verscheure had his own difficulties in the early hours of January 18. He began his morning by recounting the events of the night before to his colleague, Gerard Soete, the white counselor to the chief commissioner of Katanga's police. Another Flemish-speaking Belgian, Soete had not been around for the goings-on of the previous evening. Verscheure, exhausted, his eyes bloodshot, described the extraordinary experience. They had forced him to do it, he said, assigned him his task. While Soete sympathized with Verscheure, the killings angered the veteran in the Belgian Congo. Munongo had acted hastily. They were "up shit's creek," said Soete in Flemish. You could not dispatch the prime minister of the Congo when the world, led by the UN, was scrutinizing Elisabethville. Soete appreciated that they were caught in the jaws of history. Might Belgium now pull the plug on Katanga?

The need to attend the memorial Mass for Katanga's heroes interrupted Soete's debriefing of Verscheure. At 11 A.M., black and white together congregated in hushed reverence in the cathedral. Catholic or not, they joined the service honoring the dead who had battled for the separatists. Surrounded by the caskets of the fallen officers, all members of the Belgian military, the European bishop of Katanga, with his several subordinates, conducted the intricate and holy rites. *"Requiem aeternam dona eis, Domine,"* began the army chaplain—"Grant them eternal rest, O Lord. . . . Deliver them, O Lord, from death eternal on that fearful day, when the heavens and the earth shall be moved. . . . Death and nature will marvel, when creatures arise to submit to the Judge. . . . When therefore the Judge will sit, whatever is concealed will appear: nothing will remain unpunished. I tremble . . . till the judgment be upon us."

The services brought together in one room almost the entire cabinet of the government, as well as its Belgian partners and "notable personages" of the self-proclaimed autonomous principality. Minister of Information Samalenge conspicuously absented himself.[23]

After the solemn Mass, the language changed from Latin that no one understood to French when Munongo rallied his security officials at the ministry of the interior. From the neighborhood of the execution he had learned that locals had heard gunfire the night before. They had next stumbled across the grave, catching sight of the arm that still protruded from the earth. Soete vented his irritation with what Katanga had done. He blamed not just those who had carried out their duties but also Munongo, who had expressed a foolish zeal. The discovery of the burial dump was just the beginning. Could Katanga survive the uproar when the deaths were broadcast? Soete disconcerted Munongo. The African told Soete to disinter the bodies and move them somewhere else, far from prying eyes. Munongo did not want the scene to become a shrine where ghouls might procure sacred relics and mementos. Mpolo, Okito, and Lumumba would come out of the earth before the Day of Judgment, whatever the destiny of the men who had died for Katanga.

Gat, Verscheure, and Soete

On the same afternoon of January 18 Soete thus joined another caravan. Its members pulled the three bodies from the shallow hole, some thirty miles outside of Elisabethville. Lumumba, Okito, and Mpolo were wrapped in canvas sheets and thrown in the back of a truck. Soete and a contingent of Africans then drove northeast from Elisabethville. Almost 150 miles away, near the border with Rhodesia, the three were deposited back in the ground, this time more professionally entombed six feet under. Soete and his crew did not return to Elisabethville until the next morning, around 5:30. In his diary Verscheure wrote about Soete's employment in abbreviated Flemish: Lumumba was "Out & away." The next day—January 19—Verscheure wrote about himself: "Sick."

Over the next week Soete warned and disparaged his superiors. The politicians and their lower-level Belgian operatives more clearly realized the enormous consequences that their blood hunger could have. People more important than Soete underscored the imprudence of what they had done. And people other than Minister of Information Samalenge were gossiping.

Munongo oversaw a final solution. The plotters must obliterate all traces of the corpses. Any Lumumba cemetery might be discovered and cause trouble. On January 26 Munongo once more dispatched Soete to excavate the remains a last time, and now to make them disappear. Munongo had asked Verscheure to store two oversize glass containers in his garage. They held sulfuric acid produced by Union Minière that was used in automobile batteries. Soete and an assistant took the acid and a large barrel of acid-resistant metal; they would dissolve the victims. Yet on this second excursion to the Rhodesian border, Soete could at first not find where they had deep-sixed Katanga's enemies, but at last discovered the more extensive resting place.

On the tenth day Lumumba, Mpolo, and Okito rose from the dead a last time. Soete unearthed the cadavers and then used a hacksaw to sever the extremities—arms, legs, heads—from the three decaying carcasses. Soete wore a mask and gloves, and drank a lot. Three upper bodies remained. The lawman repeatedly refilled the barrel with acid. Like the extremities, the torsos were small enough so that the grave robber could throw the chunks of rotting flesh into the vat and have them eaten away. But there was not enough acid, and flesh and bones that had not been obliterated had to be burned, although Soete held on to a few keepsakes like teeth. The butchering took two days and nights, until February 1. "We did things an animal would not do," Soete later recalled.[24] Later, rumors spread in the CIA that Devlin had carried Lumumba's body around in the trunk of a car in Elisabethville; indeed, the rumors became legendary. Was this Devlin bragging? The Agency was just then recruiting agents from the Belgian community in Elisabethville, and the hearsay about the murders usually contained a kernel of truth, if not the entire story.[25] Did Gerard Soete also work for the CIA?

When Leopoldville and Elisabethville publicized the transfer, the UN and the United States, in addition to Belgium, urged that Katanga handle Lumumba in a civilized fashion. The government must give him a fair trial; the Red Cross must check on his well-being and that of his colleagues; no one should harm them; they must receive proper food and medicine as required. The UN, the Americans, and the Belgians had all tried to put an end to Lumumba. They had acted to put him in the power of his enemies. Now the whites exuded anxiety lest any traces take investigators to their doors. Before the Belgian parliament, Foreign Minister Wigny declaimed: "I confirm, in the most solemn way, that we have not been implicated, directly or indirectly, in this transfer."[26]

What did the men in Katanga make of the empathy of the West? Major Weber wrote to Lefebure at the palace: "Look at the politicians. Now they care for Lumumba."[27] Nonetheless, the leaders in Elisabethville fabricated a suitable story. At first they announced that guards kept the prisoners safe and correctly looked after. Then, on January 27, as the chopping and sawing began, Julien Gat and his MPs left Elisabethville in yet another official line of vehicles. Out of uniform, three soldiers sat in the backseat of one of the automobiles. They impersonated Lumumba and his colleagues, whom authorities had already shot, buried, reburied, and were at the very moment dismembering. The party headed northwest from Elisabethville, on a route opposite that of Soete. At various stops witnesses could see the three enemies of Katanga in the rear of the car. The destination was said to be a jail in Kasai, where Kalonji had his little kingdom. Two weeks later, on February 10, Radio Katanga broadcast that the captives had escaped. They had broken through the wall of their jail, seized a car and, when they ran it into a gully, continued on foot. A newspaper photo showed a moping Julien Gat looking over the area where the automobile, a late-model Ford sedan, had supposedly come to grief. Long after, when the truth about the spurious jailbreak came to light, Gat could not escape his contribution to the murders, and feared revenge. He changed his name to Gatry, and rued the picture until he died.

Katanga declared that its gendarmerie was searching for the fugitives, and offered a reward for their arrest. Then, on February 13, Munongo told the world press that villagers in the bush had seized the escapees. The inhabitants had killed the three men. Munongo would not reveal where the deed had taken place, or where the three had been laid to rest, but he did supply death certificates signed by a Belgian doctor serving in Katanga. Munongo professed no sadness about the end of the prime minister. After all, remarked Munongo, Hammarskjöld had accused Lumumba of genocide. Munongo finished confidently: "I am going to speak frankly and bluntly, as I usually do. We shall be accused of having murdered them. My reply is: prove it."[28]

Troubled Minds

Some time after Soete had completed his foul task, Verscheure clumsily reworked his Flemish diary for January 17. We believe he did the rewriting in early February as a minor and almost certainly independent part of the plot.

9.43 L. dood

became

9.43 L. doorgevoerd

Verscheure ineptly overwrote *dood*—dead—on the original entry, changing it to *doorgevoerd*—transferred. Yet he could not resist making a record of the epochal undertakings in which he had a hand. Munongo had invented a fable of Lumumba's end. When Verscheure revised the diary to make it conform to that fiction, he made three new entries. They told, again in abbreviated Flemish, of his friend's travels: Soete goes back (January 25); Soete finds (January 26); Soete finished (February 1).

On February 13, the same day that Munongo publicized the end of Lumumba, Paul-Henri Spaak wrote to the new American president, John Kennedy. The Belgian had been resigning as civilian head of NATO from the time of the August crisis of 1960. Spaak had given formal notice to NATO at the end of January. On February 13 he explained his reasoning to Kennedy. Outside its "geographical limits," NATO had "not been very satisfactory." The Western powers could not be "united in one part of the world and at odds in another." Was the United States, Spaak wrote, "more interested in the UN than NATO?" It appeared that Kennedy would support the "nonaligned" nations and thus "sacrifice the interest or hurt the feelings of the NATO allies." In any event Spaak would no longer head NATO.[29] Kennedy awarded him the Medal of Freedom a week later.

As the ceremony in Washington took place, Dayal in Leopoldville asked Tshombe to send the remains of the murdered men back to the capital. Tshombe refused: "According to our tradition, it is formally forbidden to disinter—be it even for a few seconds—a body which is covered with earth because the deceased would thereby be gravely affected and his soul would haunt those surviving him."[30]

Ambassador Burden had his own tribulations. Within a month of the inauguration, Kennedy dismissed the Republican Burden, who then had to vacate the US embassy in Brussels. But Burden did not leave empty-handed. The Belgians had unsuccessfully lobbied to have him kept on because of the "frank and intimate day-to-day basis" on which he had conducted relations. When he left in February, he got from Baudouin, amid "a blaze of friendly farewells," the same supreme honor of the Great Ribbon of the Order of Leopold that had been awarded to Herter a few months before.[31]

From 1925 to 1961 Dag Hammarskjöld had written poems and reflections in Swedish, collecting them in a personal catalog of contemplations. Then at various points the secretary-general rewrote and edited them. Friends honored his wish to publish the polished meditations after his death as *Markings,* a testament to Hammarskjöld's spiritual journey. The obscure and ambiguous introspections intended to show the author's mental suffering as he lived an unselfish life. W. H. Auden translated these ruminations into English, and noted that *Markings* could make the reader impatient because of its repetition of the single theme of affliction for the sake of humanity. Hammarskjöld made entries on two occasions when Lumumba caught the attention of the world: in early December 1960 when he was captured and knocked about in front of movie cameras; and mid-February 1961, when Munongo announced Lumumba's death and protesters broke into the UN as part of worldwide demonstrations. On both occasions, Hammarskjöld pointed readers to his own afflictions: "The burden remained mine"; "The pain, you shall conceal it"; "I became . . . a reproach. . . . Help me, O Lord my God." The secretary-general wrote American novelist John Steinbeck that Lumumba was a "synthetic martyr."[32]

Frans Verscheure

In 2000 and 2001, the Belgian inquiry deposed many witnesses in a formal setting in Brussels. On two occasions, however, the scholars who
assisted the work of the parliamentary commission interviewed Verscheure casually, the second time at his home near the Belgian seacoast.[33]
The experts hoped to glean a few more details in a final attempt at oral
history. Now seventy-five years old and partially blind, Verscheure used
a video magnifier to illuminate material that he wanted to read. Less intimidating surroundings relaxed and invigorated him. Verscheure wanted
to tell the investigators what had gone on, to get matters at last, it seemed,
off his chest. He appeared mentally on his way to the murder that night
of January 17 just over forty years before.

Munongo wished to do Verscheure a favor by including him in the
execution. As a police officer Verscheure had taken Lumumba to a Katangan prison a year before, and a press photo had publicly exposed
him. "They thought I wanted revenge, but that wasn't true." Waiting
outside the Brouwez house, Verscheure overheard Kibwe's menacing
speech. "I still remember it. It's always stuck in my head." Then Verscheure shepherded the Africans on the bumpy ride to the woods where
they would die. Some native politician drove them all at top speed in "a
brand new Ford." In the backseat Lumumba and his companions were
already at death's door. Someone had hammered wooden splinters under their fingernails, and they were in wretched pain. Mpolo had "shit
his pants," and Verscheure could still smell the reek of the manioc that
Mpolo had eaten. The Belgian police officer took the three men, one at a
time, out of the auto, and led Okito, then Mpolo, and finally Lumumba
in front of the shallow depression.

While they shot Okito, Verscheure—in front of the sedan's open back
door—screened the two others from the finale. "It will soon be over. I
asked them to say their prayers." Then he handed over Mpolo, who
made the sign of the cross and dropped to his knees. Mpolo "began to
say *Het Onze Vader in het Frans . . . Notre Père, qui es aux cieux*. The
shots came in the middle of his prayer . . . in the middle of his prayer."
Verscheure was now screening Lumumba alone: "I told him, 'Please for-
give them, and say your prayers.' . . . But he didn't answer. He *didn't*

answer. He was quiet from the beginning to the end. I didn't see him react at all."

It was 4:00 P.M. on October 2, 2000. Mrs. Verscheure briefly interrupted the interview. She had to give her husband some pills, "important medicine."

Back in early 1961 Verscheure trembles in the dark, feverish, as the shooting brutally breaks the silence of the bush, and the dead men fall into the hastily excavated ditch. He and his chauffeur put down the windows of the Ford as they race back to the president's palace. They tell him to wait in Tshombe's anteroom. "I have some pistachios and a beer—a Jupiler, maybe a Simba." The two commissioners, Kazadi and Mukamba are there. "They keep asking me, as if I am—I don't know— God Almighty. Do I have a hand or an ear for them to take back to Leo? They want to know he's dead. Then Tshombe comes out of his office and has a little talk with me." The president is "shaken by the events; he hadn't expected them." They send Verscheure home.

Verscheure produced for the scholars a shoebox that contained souvenirs of his service in the Congo. There, along with some photographs and other tokens, was the diary—it was the first time historians had seen it. Verscheure had saved only his diary for 1961, and had not availed himself of it after February of that year. The historians at once saw that Verscheure had adjusted the writing for January 17. A police expert later verified this commonsense inference. Verscheure, however, denied any tampering. Nonetheless, he put the diary under his video magnifier, which grotesquely enlarged his crude revision of the facts.

Excerpt from Verscheure agenda. In 2001 the retired police official examined a blown-up image of his diary entry for January 17, 1961. (*Authors' collection*)

Verscheure broke down. He still refused to admit the alteration, ripped open his shirt front, and screamed at his guests now not in Flemish but in what they made out as an African language—Lingala? Swahili?— that they could not understand. The discussions ended abruptly, and the scholars left the apartment. The next day, the family made it known that

Verscheure had had a psychological collapse, and could have no further conversations.

Verscheure arose as a figure out of Joseph Conrad's *Heart of Darkness*. What primal thoughts had gone through his head at various moments of crisis? When, sweating and shivering, he faced a stoic Lumumba and assisted in the murder. When, late that same night, he used Flemish in his diary for the first time to tell what had happened. When, the next morning, he and Soete spoke about these unspeakable acts. When, a few weeks later, he falsified his diary but added particulars about Soete's exploits. When, coming back to Belgium, he decided to save only that diary. When, in 2001, he disintegrated under questioning and relinquished even Flemish for an African language.

What did Verscheure's languages mean to him? As a civil servant obedient to everyday instructions, he employed French, the speech of colonial rule. When these instructions required of him assassination—an act that transcended the common tyrannies of imperialism—he could only talk of his deeds in his mother tongue. And when he faced his own participation, the consequences of his willingness to bend to orders and violate his own compassion, he reverted to a vernacular embedded in the depths of his consciousness. Or in this final and unnerving existential moment did Verscheure try to express a common humanity?

Epilogue

WHO CAUSED this traveling carnival of death? Complex considerations arise in defining responsibility. In 1962 King Baudouin
mulled over clemency for the killer of Prince Rwagasore, recently elected
prime minister of Burundi, a Belgian trusteeship soon to be independent. The king wrote to Foreign Minister Spaak: "On a moral level, we
may question, although the penalties differ, whether the author of an assassination is more culpable than those who conceived the idea and
strove for its implementation by using him as an instrument."[1] In a celebrated Agatha Christie novel, *Murder on the Orient Express,* Hercule
Poirot investigates the demise of the wicked Samuel Ratchett. He has
been stabbed multiple times in his cabin on the train. Poirot has a dozen
suspects, and discovers that all have participated. After drugging Ratchett, they have handed a dagger from one to another, even a little old lady
who has barely broken his skin with a glancing and feeble blow. The accomplices themselves do not know which stroke was lethal. Each is
implicated.[2]

Another aspect of joint accountability turns on the strength of the
common aims, preplanning, and coordination. Many who have examined the Lumumba case have perceived a conspiracy. Unambiguous orders were given at the top and efficiently carried out, and cooperation

occurred internationally. We have found evidence for a conspiracy less compelling, and observe more contingency, confusion, duplication of labor, and bungling. Still, on the ground, Belgian and US security personnel traded information and cooperated. Lumumba drew together a number of committed opponents with more or less the same ideas, and that was enough. Some students focus on some overriding racial or economic or cultural force that governed Lumumba's destiny. Nonetheless, the empirical details of this convoluted tale have a logic that escapes any fatalism.

From mid-July 1960, Belgium tried to emasculate the Lumumba government, and the United States and the UN quickly followed. In September Belgium and the United Nations helped Kasa-Vubu terminate the Lumumba prime ministership. Extreme anticommunists in Belgium prodded those in the United States and, even more fearful of Lumumba out of power, both Brussels and Washington launched wild designs to do him in. Hammarskjöld and Dayal ignored the probability of an assassination, and at least did little to protect the prime minister. Accused by many of being sympathetic to Lumumba, Dayal followed the lead of Hammarskjöld, who persuaded himself he could keep Lumumba down but somehow out of danger. The UN leaders resembled the old lady in *Murder on the Orient Express*. Along with their own attempts to deliver the coup de grâce, US and Belgian officials more and more turned to Lumumba's political opponents in the Congo. The Europeans and Americans goaded the Africans to imprison Lumumba and to secure a capital sentence. The politicians in Leopoldville proved willing to jail him, but were afraid either to bring him to trial or to put him to death. Those in Katanga were not afraid, and the Belgians and Americans and the Leopoldville group knew that. With Western urging, Kasa-Vubu and his cohorts sent Lumumba to Elisabethville and his doom.

The UN collaborated because if Lumumba stayed on, Hammarskjöld believed, the UN would lose stature in the world community. Pressed by an aggrandizing monarchical circle, politicians in Brussels shouldered Lumumba to the abyss but also intended to defend Belgian constitutional democracy. In the long term, American policies shifted power in Africa away from the Europeans to the United States. At the time, Eisenhower wanted Lumumba eradicated to protect the Western alliance. A more vulgar anticommunism guided other US decision makers. All the westerners were motivated to foil the appearance on the world stage of an autonomous African land. Belgium and the United States might have patronized a weak Congo. With the UN, the Europeans and Americans might have contemplated a stronger Congo dependent on the West. But the West could not conceive a stand-alone African state akin to European countries in its economic and political capabilities. Lumumba aspired to a greatness the West would not abide. In part he was exterminated because he was an ambitious black man, but the panic over him was grossly inflated because the prime minister hardly had the resources to create a nation.

Why did the Africans assist the Belgians and Americans? Lumumba frightened many of the blacks; others ached for retribution against him; still others, employed by American and Belgian spies, worried what would happen if they did not do what the whites so evidently wanted.

No government accepted the secessionists in Katanga as legitimate. Even Brussels refused recognition, although it paid the salaries of Elisabethville's European officials, and although they all ultimately swore allegiance to Belgium. It is a nice question whether a regime in Katanga conducted an execution that had on it the fingerprints of Belgium, the United States, and the UN. Or whether Western officialdom simply connived in gangsterism. Ambassador Dupret in Brazzaville relayed to Brussels a remarkable French analysis. For many months the crisis had developed in an atmosphere "half-vaudevillian." By January 1961, however, events had acquired the nature of a merciless conflict. The African traditions of harangue, the drawing of weapons, and retreat had given way to "the most modern methods" of the destruction of a political adversary.[3] With Lumumba's death, the West had given its first postcolonial tutorial. Within a month, six other prominent Lumumba supporters were slaughtered in Kasai, after transfer from Leopoldville. Mobutu followers were killed in Stanleyville.

As these matters go, a clear chain of command exists among those responsible for Lumumba's death, from those running the show to those in the trenches.

The UN chain was: Hammarskjöld, Cordier, and Dayal.
The American chain was: Eisenhower, Gray, Dulles, and Devlin.
From the Belgian metropole: Baudouin, Eyskens, d'Aspremont, and
    Wigny.

In Leopoldville: Lahaye and Marlière; Kasa-Vubu, Mobutu, Bomboko, and Nendaka.
In Elisabethville: Tshombe, Munongo, Gat and Verscheure.

Comparison to *Murder on the Orient Express* should not allow us to
trivialize Lumumba's slaying, but to attend in different ways to a shared
process of murder. The detective story demonstrates that such an offense
can occur without knowing who among a group of assassins delivers the
mortal blow. The story also shows that people who perpetrate a murder
need not be censured. The characters in the novel are deemed innocent
of any crime. People are guilty for things they have done only if we think
their doings bad. Thoughtful readers should reflect on two items in evaluating the liability of those tainted by Lumumba's death. First, the men
who cut down him did not have the same kind of fault as someone who
has killed his neighbor and is declared guilty in a trial. As we have argued, the norms of private life and of a polity regulated by law are only
with difficulty invoked in global politics. At the same time, for example
in World War II, Eisenhower commanded troops that dispatched many
Germans contrary to the rules of battle, yet his oversight of this slaughter
does not evoke the sick feeling as does his role in the Congo. Despite the
fact that all the schemers believed Lumumba worthy of his fortune, this
performance has a stench to it; but how higher politicians are incrimi-
nated constitutes a delicate subject.

Second, we need to ask what position in time has to do with estimates.
In the 1960s the statesmen and their servants embroiled in Lumumba's
death were convinced they had done the right thing, and some men
boasted, truthfully or not, about what they had accomplished. By the
mid-1970s complicity became less attractive. During the US Senate investigations, Robert Johnson, the record taker at the NSC meeting of
August 18, testified that Eisenhower gave the order. The distress in the
United States over the Nixon administration had induced Johnson to
step forward:

> My decision to offer testimony . . . has . . . [made] for me a profound
> personal, moral dilemma. . . . I was privy to a great deal of informa-
> tion that involved . . . confidentiality with high officials. . . . These

responsibilities relate[d] to the very basis of human society . . .
and . . . trust without which no free society can long survive and no
government can operate. I have been forced by recent developments,
however, to weigh against these considerable responsibilities, my
broader responsibilities as a citizen on . . . a major question of public morality, as well as [of] . . . sound policy. . . . I have concluded,
not without a great deal of reluctance, to come . . . with information . . . relating to the assassination.[4]

In 1991, after the Cold War was over, the Congo condemned the homi-
cide. In 2001, Belgium apologized to the Congo in part because Truth
Commissions and ethnic reconciliation made covering over Lumumba's
death ethically unappealing.

Lumumba is visible through the eyes of several other people, among
them Hammarskjöld, Baudouin, Kasa-Vubu, Devlin, Munongo, Verscheure. Very different men, although most acted for their countries.
Unlike the others, Hammarskjöld hardly had a national sense. His Reformed Protestantism ran deeper in him than his Swedishness. However, the humanitarianism that Hammarskjöld mouthed has something
to recommend it, and is indeed the perspective many of the actors used
to make moral judgments on their own behalf and that we have used to
measure the actors. The secretary-general, nonetheless, identified with
his rectitude. Was he more righteous than Lumumba? Of those men
who did have a national identity at their core, who had more compelling
patriotic credentials than Lumumba?

The USSR forced Andrew Cordier to resign from his post as UN
under-secretary in late 1961, after criticizing him for usurping too many
of the responsibilities of the secretary-general. Cordier finished his career as the dean of Columbia University's school of international affairs
and for a time as the university's president. He could not stop telling his
story about early September 1960. Cordier died of cirrhosis of the liver
in 1975, and that year his version of events in the *Public Papers of the
Secretaries-General* had to compete with the US Senate committee's *Alleged Assassination Plots Involving Foreign Leaders*. Allen Dulles, the
spymaster, was also fired in late 1961 for his failure to get rid of Castro.
He died in bed in 1969 when he was seventy-five. Larry Devlin spent
twenty-five years with the CIA. Later appointed station chief in Laos

during the Vietnam War, he was nonetheless famous in the Agency because of the Congo. Like Cordier, Devlin repeated his version of the CIA's efforts in 1960 to his end at the ripe age of eighty-six. After leaving NATO in early 1961, Paul-Henri Spaak served for five years as Belgium's foreign minister, replacing Pierre Wigny. Spaak died replete with honors in 1972. The first building of the European Parliament was named after him. D'Aspremont, Wigny, and Eyskens also received high Belgian decorations before their deaths in 1967, 1986, and 1988 respectively. Frans Verscheure died in 2004. In his final years he proudly wore the medal that Tshombe had personally awarded him in July of 1961 on the first anniversary of Katanga's independence and less than six months after the murder—the Cross of the Commander of the Katangan Order of Merit.

Many chief executives had a hand in the murder. In 1964 Tshombe became prime minister of the Congo after Katanga gave up its bid for independence. President Kasa-Vubu dismissed Tshombe the following year. Then Mobutu deposed Kasa-Vubu, charged Tshombe with treason, and sentenced the Katangan to death in absentia in 1967. That year hijackers took a plane in which Tshombe was traveling to Algeria. He was under house arrest when he died from "heart failure" in 1969, the same year as the death of Kasa-Vubu, who had retired to the Bas-Congo. In 1963 President Kennedy bestowed on Mobutu the Legion of Merit, a military decoration for outstanding conduct. Mobutu ruled the Congo until the mid-1990s. With the help of several presidents in addition to JFK, Mobutu had run his homeland as a kleptocracy—a regime based on vast theft and corruption, not to mention murder.

Toward the end of 1961, in the middle of the UN intervention in the Congo and in the middle of his career, Dag Hammarskjöld died in a suspicious plane crash. He was traveling to Rhodesia to mediate the continuing conflicts between Katanga and the Congo. Western politicians greeted his death with shock and despair. That year he became the only person posthumously awarded the Nobel Peace Prize, and soon achieved the status of a secular saint. After Hammarskjöld, the UN remained a lackluster, preachifying institution. King Baudouin's anxieties about Belgium should the Belgian Congo vanish had a realistic basis. After 1960, without the glue of the Congo, Belgium itself tended toward disintegration. The monarch nonetheless continued to symbolize a national bond, and cherished by his people, Baudouin lived until 1993. His passing contributed to pressures for dividing his country, and some seven years would go by before the Belgian parliamentary commission gestured at his complicity. The adored blue-eyed soldier of democracy Eisenhower departed at age seventy-eight in 1969. Six years elapsed before the Senate committee pointed its finger Eisenhower's way.

Everybody knows what happened to Kennedy in November of 1963. Obscurity cloaks his involvement with Lumumba. Kennedy took over as president on January 20, three days after Lumumba was murdered. We believe the president did not learn of the killing until mid-February, although he may have known about the plans of the CIA and done nothing. Or the CIA may not have told him and not mentioned that it thought Lumumba dead. Which is worse?

It could have been more complicated. David Doyle headed the new CIA post in Elisabethville. While he quickly learned of Lumumba's arrival on January 17, the cable traffic from Katanga made it clear that the CIA had only rumors of what had happened through the first weeks of the Kennedy presidency when Katanga was creating its own version of the death. Doyle reported the rumors and hearsay about the murder until Munongo circulated the official story. At the same time, Doyle wanted to get his hands on Lumumba. On January 19, in a notorious telex, he cabled Devlin: "Thanks for Patrice. If we had known he was coming we would have baked a snake." Doyle soon feared that the jokey cable might get him into trouble because it had reached Allen Dulles. Then, Doyle got a signal that his job was safe. He received a message from Washington that enclosed a cartoon of two men roasting a snake. The CIA called agents engaged in assassination operations "snake eaters." Hardy men, they would crawl on their bellies through jungles, kill the worst reptiles, and eat them.[5]

The CIA may have told Kennedy that it no longer had matters in hand; the blacks were doing god knows what with Lumumba. We do know that the CIA continued to function as a Murder Incorporated, and that Kennedy wanted the Agency to work its black magic on Castro in Cuba.

Lumumba's murder did not solve many problems for all those who shared in its responsibility, yet this particular event illustrates some general truths. Even governments that pride themselves on their democratic transparency inevitably resort to secrecy and deception. Statesmen struggle to justify actions that in the nature of things have little to do with the moral; malice and self-interest are never far from public life. Politics, ambitious to tame the irrational, itself participates in the irrational.

Notes

Essay on Sources

Acknowledgments

Index

Notes

CC   hearings and testimony pertinent to the Senate Select Commit-
tee to Study Governmental Operations with Respect to
Intelligence Activities (the Church Committee), at the National
Archives, College Park, Maryland

CIA   collection of miscellaneous CIA documents, National Archives,
College Park, Maryland

CREST   CIA Records Search Tool, online database available at National
Archives, College Park, Maryland

DDE   Dwight D. Eisenhower Presidential Library, Abilene, Kansas

DOS   U.S. Department of State, records located at National Archives,
College Park, Maryland

FPSFA   Federal Public Service Foreign Affairs, Brussels, Belgium

FRUS   *Foreign Relations of the United States,* various dates

HM   History Matters, compact disc, *The Church Committee Reports*
(testimony and hearings of Senate Select Committee to Study
Governmental Operations with Respect to Intelligence
Activities)

IR   Interim Report of the Senate Select Committee to Study
Governmental Operations with Respect to Intelligence
Activities, *Alleged Assassination Plots Involving Foreign
Leaders* (Washington, DC: Government Printing
Office, 1975)

IRC   International Red Cross Archives, Geneva, Switzerland

JFK   John F. Kennedy Library, Boston, Massachusetts

LCM   Luc De Vos, Emmanuel Gerard, Jules Gérard-Libois, and Philippe Raxhon, *Lumumba: De complotten? De moord* (Leuven: Davidsfonds, 2004)

Minaf   Ministère des affaires africaines, Ministry of African Affairs in Brussels

Mistebel   Mission technique belge, Belgian technical mission in Katanga (Elisabethville)

NA   National Archives, College Park, Maryland

PC   Authors' personal collection

UCL   Université Catholique de Louvain, Louvain-la-Neuve

UN   United Nations Archives, New York City

INTRODUCTION

1. Andrew W. Cordier and Wilder Foote, eds., *Public Papers of the Secretaries-General of the United Nations,* vol. 5, *Dag Hammarskjöld, 1960–1961* (New York: Columbia University Press, 1975), 342; secretary-general's statement, February 15, 1961, box 140, Cordier Papers, Columbia University. Stevenson's speech and the fracas accompanying it can be viewed on YouTube. For reports on the demonstrations see 770G.13, box 1978; and folder 2–1561, box 1960, DOS, RG 59, NA; Brenda Gayle Plummer, *In Search of Power: African Americans in the Era of Decolonization, 1956–1974* (New York: Cambridge University Press, 2013), 116–117; and Roger Lipsey, *Hammarskjöld: A Life* (Ann Arbor: University of Michigan Press, 2013), 478–480.

1. THE CONGO OF THE BELGIANS

1. Robert Rothschild, *Un phénix nommé Europe: Memoires 1945–1995* (Brussels: Racine, 1997), 253.
2. In particular: Adam Hochschild, *King Leopold's Ghost: A Tale of Greed, Terror, and Heroism in Colonial Africa* (New York: Houghton Mifflin, 1998).
3. An excellent case study is Jan Vansina, *Being Colonized: The Kuba Experience in Rural Congo, 1880–1960* (Madison: University of Wisconsin Press, 2010).
4. Guy Vanthemsche, *Belgium and the Congo, 1885–1980* (New York: Cambridge University Press, 2012), 59–64, 78–81.
5. Crawford Young, *Politics in the Congo: Decolonization and Independence* (Princeton, NJ: Princeton University Press 1965), 22, 128–129, 248–249, 266n; René Lemarchand, *Political Awakening in the Belgian Congo* (Berkeley: University of California Press, 1964), 80, 129–130. An exhaustive source for the study of these issues is Bambi Ceuppens, *Congo Made in Flanders? Koloniale Vlaamse Visies op "Blank" en "Zwart" in Belgisch Congo* (Gent: Academia Press, 2003).
6. Marc Depaepe, "Writing Histories of Congolese Colonial Education: A Historiographical View from Belgium," in *Connecting Histories of Education: Transnational*

Exchanges and Cross-Cultural Transfers, ed. Barnita Bagchi, Eckhardt Fuchs, and Kate Rousmaniere (New York: Berghahn Books, 2012), 1–30.

7. See, for example, Ian Scott, *Tumbled House: The Congo at Independence* (London: Oxford University Press, 1979), 47, 53, 64. Scott was the British ambassador to the Congo.

8. William A. M. Burden, *Peggy and I: A Life Too Busy for a Dull Moment* (New York: W. A. M. Burden, 1982), quoting Peggy, 301.

9. An early and outstanding example is Frantz Fanon, *Black Skin, White Masks* (New York: Grove Press, 1952, 1967).

10. Jean Stengers, *Congo: Mythes et réalités* (Brussels: Éditions Racine, 2007), 300.

11. See Basil Davidson's arguments in *The Black Man's Burden: Africa and the Curse of the Nation-State* (New York: Random House, 1992), esp. 50–51, 98–99, 114–116.

12. Yolanda Covington-Ward, "Joseph Kasa-Vubu, ABAKO, and Performances of Kongo Nationalism in the Independence of Congo," *Journal of Black Studies* 43 (2012): 72–94.

13. For a biography, see Jean Omasombo and Benoît Verhaegen, *Patrice Lumumba, jeunesse et apprentissage politique: 1925–1956* (Paris: L'Harmattan, 1998); also their *Acteur politique, de la prison aux portes du pouvoir: Juillet 1956–février 1960* (Paris: L'Harmattan, 2005). For Lumumba and women see Karen Bouwer, *Gender and Decolonization in the Congo: The Legacy of Patrice Lumumba* (New York: Palgrave Macmillan, 2010), 56–68.

14. Lemarchand, *Political Awakening,* 222; Jean Van Lierde, ed., *Lumumba Speaks: The Speeches and Writings of Patrice Lumumba, 1958–1961* (Boston: Little, Brown, 1972), 71, 166.

15. Patrice Lumumba, *Congo, My Country* (New York: Praeger, 1962), 13, 35; Young, *Politics in the Congo,* 145–146, 267–268.

16. See Catherine Hoskyns, *The Congo since Independence, January 1960–December 1961* (London: Oxford University Press, 1965), 21–81; Stengers, *Congo,* 269–293.

17. Vanthemsche, *Belgium,* 217–219.

18. Bunche to Hammarskjöld, June 27 and July 4, 370-12-2, UN.

2. INDEPENDENCE

1. A study of Leopold III during the war: Jan Velaers and Herman Van Goethem, *Leopold III: De koning, het land, de oorlog* (Tielt, Belgium: Lannoo, 1994).

2. See L. J. Cardinal Suenens, *Baudouin, King of the Belgians: The Hidden Life,* trans. Sr. Helen M. Wynne (Brussels: FIAT, 1996).

3. Robin McKown, *Lumumba: A Biography* (New York: Doubleday and Co., 1969), 66.

4. Jean Van Lierde, ed., *Lumumba Speaks: The Speeches and Writings of Patrice Lumumba, 1958–1961* (Boston: Little, Brown, 1972), 272; René Lemarchand, *Political Awakening in the Belgian Congo* (Berkeley: University of California Press, 1964), 152; Herbert F. Weiss, *Political Protest in the Congo: The Parti Solidaire Africain during the Independence Struggle* (Princeton, NJ: Princeton University Press, 1967), 261.

5. The full text of the three speeches is in Jules Gérard-Libois and Benoît Verhaegen, *Congo 1960* (Brussels: CRISP, 1961), 318–330.

6. Robert Murphy, Report, folder 15, box 16, Murphy Papers, Hoover Institution, Stanford University. Bunche to Hammarskjöld, June 27 and July 4, 370-12-2, UN; Ralph

Bunche, Notebook and Notes, Congo, June–July 1960, folder 8, box 283, Bunche Papers, UCLA.

7. Aimé Césaire, *A Season in the Congo,* trans. Gayatri Spivak (New York: Seagull, 2010, 1966), 32.

8. Janssens-Pholien correspondence, December 20, 28, and 30, 1959; and January 9 and 18, 1960, Pholien Papers, Archives of the Royal Palace, Brussels.

9. The most detailed and best documented account of the mutiny is Louis-François Vanderstraeten, *De la Force publique à l'Armée nationale congolaise: Histoire d'une mutinerie, Juillet 1960* (Brussels: Académie Royale de Belgique, 1993). See also Catherine Hoskyns, *The Congo since Independence, January 1960–December 1961* (London: Oxford University Press, 1965).

10. Jitendra Mohan, "Ghana, the Congo, and the United Nations," *Journal of Modern African Studies* 7 (1969): 369–406, esp. 387–393.

11. See Norrie MacQueen, *The United Nations, Peace Operations and the Cold War,* 2nd ed. (Harlow, UK: Pearson Education Ltd., 2011). For the perspective of another nation, see Michael Kennedy and Art Magennis, *Ireland, the United Nations and the Congo: A Military and Diplomatic History, 1960–1* (Dublin, Ireland: Four Courts Press, 2014).

3. THE EMPIRE STRIKES BACK

1. Guy Vanthemsche, *Belgium and the Congo, 1885–1980* (New York: Cambridge University Press, 2012), 101–142.

2. For a biography, see Michel Dumoulin, *Spaak* (Brussels: Éditions Racine, 1999).

3. Gaston Eyskens, *De Memoires* (Tielt, Belgium: Lannoo, 1993), 515–591.

4. Burden Oral History, 23, 28, 33, DDE; William A. M. Burden, *Peggy and I: A Life Too Busy for a Dull Moment* (New York: W. A. M. Burden, 1982), 279–328; Robert Rothschild, *Un phénix nommé Europe: Mémoires 1945–1985* (Brussels: Éditions Racine, 1997), 240–241.

5. Louis-François Vanderstraeten, *De la Force publique à l'Armée nationale congolaise: Histoire d'une mutinerie, Juillet 1960* (Brussels: Académie Royale de Belgique, 1993), 88–96.

6. Jean Van den Bosch, *Pré-Zaïre, le cordon mal coupé: Document* (Brussels: Le Cri, 1986), 42–45; Rothschild, *Phénix nommé Europe,* 245. Van den Bosch was the Belgian ambassador in Leopoldville, Rothschild his deputy.

7. Minutes of the Belgian cabinet, July 12 and 13, National Archives, Brussels (also available on its website, http://extranet.arch.be/lang_pvminister.html); Vanderstraeten, *Mutinerie,* 406–411; *LCM,* 32–39. Gilson communicated the number of Belgian troops to *Le Soir* (Brussels), August 5.

8. Jan De Meyer, Memorandum for the prime minister, July 12, Vandewalle Papers, Royal Museum for Central Africa, Tervuren, Belgium.

9. Kasa-Vubu quoted on July 12 in Vanderstraeten, *Mutinerie,* 397.

10. Burden to Herter, July 22 (303), 7–1760, box 532, DOS, RG 59, NA.

11. Vanderstraeten, *Mutinerie,* 399, 410, 441.

12. Wigny, unpublished Mémoires du Congo, 402, box MC 16, Wigny Papers, UCL, Louvain-la-Neuve.

13. Testimony before the Belgian parliamentary commission in 2001 by Colonel Noël Dedeken, *LCM,* 203–206.

14. Jules Gérard-Libois, *Katanga Secession* (Madison: University of Wisconsin Press, 1966), 320–327; see also Frans Buelens, *Congo 1885–1960: Een financieel-economische geschiedenis* (Berchem, Antwerp: EPO, 2007), 380–392. For the role of Union Minière, see Chambre des représentants de Belgique, *Enquête parlementaire visant à déterminer les circonstances exactes de l'assassinat de Patrice Lumumba et l'implication éventuelle des responsables belges dans celui-ci,* DOC 50 0312/006, November 16, 2001, 516–573.

15. Robiliart (Brussels) to Cousin (Elisabethville), March 23, *LCM,* 83. See also René Brion and Jean-Louis Moreau, *De Generale Maatschappij van België 1822–1997* (Brussels: Mercatorfonds, 1998), 402.

16. Paulus (Paris) to Eyskens, August 6, folder 14, d'Aspremont Lynden Papers, National Archives, Brussels.

17. Union Minière cable of July 12 and notes of the king's chief of staff, *LCM,* 47–48.

18. Full text in Jules Gérard-Libois and Benoît Verhaegen, *Congo 1960* (Brussels: CRISP, 1961), 513–514. See also Burden to Herter, July 23 (314), 7-2160, box 1954, DOS, RG 59, NA. Belgium's shift in policy seen from the perspective of the Belgian diplomats in the Congo: Rothsfild (Elisabethville) to Van den Bosch (Leopoldville), July 21, VIII, 18770, FPSFA.

19. D'Aspremont, "Conversation avec Monsieur Doucy—1er Mars 1960," March 2, Vandewalle Papers. For the framing of Lumumba as a communist, see Anne-Sophie Gijs, "Une ascension politique teintée de rouge: Autorités, Sûreté de l'État et grandes Sociétiés face au 'danger Lumumba' avant l'indépendance du Congo (1956–1960)," *Revue belge d'Histoire contemporaine* 42 (2012): 11–58.

20. D'Aspremont, Memorandum for the prime minister, July 20, folder 6080, Eyskens Papers, State Archives, Louvain, facsimile in *LCM,* 656–659.

21. D'Aspremont (Elisabethville) to Eyskens, August 7, folder 6079, Eyskens Papers,

22. Minutes of Mistebel meeting, July 23, Rothschild Papers, Université Libre de Bruxelles. See also Jean Stengers, "La reconnaissance *de jure* de l'indépendance du Katanga," *Cahiers d'histoire du temps présent* 11 (2003): 177–191.

23. For this section see *LCM,* 58–65. See also Burden to Herter, August 3 (386), 8-160, box 1955, DOS, RG 59, NA; and Memoranda of conversation Herter-Scheyven (Belgian ambassador to the United States), July 28, August 5, *FRUS 1958–1960,* vol. 14, 367–370, 386–390.

24. The minutes of the Crown Council have been published in Chambre des représentants, *Enquête parlementaire,* 614–636.

25. Pirenne Papers, Archives of the Royal Palace, Brussels.

26. For the secretary-general's views see Hammarskjöld to Baudouin, July 31, box M 5, vol. 13, Wigny Papers.

27. Our account of the ministerial crisis is based on primary sources in the Eyskens Papers (folders 6079, 6082, and 6084); the Spaak Papers (folder 180), Fondation P.H. Spaak, Brussels; Van Zeeland Papers (folders 163, 164, 820), UCL, Louvain-la-Neuve; and Wigny Papers (box M 5, vols. 13–15). For an account based on the Spaak Papers, see Dumoulin, *Spaak,* 583–591. In his memoirs (593–600), Eyskens reveals only part

of his meetings with the king. The crisis viewed from the perspective of De Schryver: Godfried Kwanten, *August-Edmond De Schryver 1898–1991: Politieke biografie van een gentleman-staatsman* (Leuven: Leuven University Press, 2001), 565–576.

28. See also Louis Vos, "The Extreme Right in Post-war Belgium: From Nostalgia to Building for the Future," in *Modern Europe after Fascism, 1943–1980s,* ed. Stein Ugelvik Larsen (New York: Columbia University Press, 1998), 344–388.

29. Cleveland (American embassy in Brussels) to Herter, July 29, 7-2860, box 1955, DOS, RG 59, NA.

30. Quoted in Pieter Lagrou, "Een oorlog achter de rug, een oorlog voor de boeg 1944–1965," in *Oost West West Best: België onder de Koude Oorlog (1947–1989),* ed. Mark Van den Wijngaert and Lieve Beullens (Tielt, Belgium: Lannoo, 1997), 131.

31. *De Standaard* (Brussels) and *Le Soir,* August 10.

32. Wigny diary notes, August 10 and 11, M 5, vol. 15, Wigny Papers. For the quote see "Confidential. Department of State. Biographic Information Division. King Baudouin I Belgium," December, 1960, DOS Conference Files, Visit Brussels, box 239, RG 59, NA.

33. Communication of the Belgian government, *Le Soir,* August 2.

34. Rothschild (Mistebel) to Wigny, August 30 (481), VIII, 18770, FPSFA.

35. Eyskens, *Memoires,* 586; Jef Van Bilsen, *Kongo 1945–1965: Het einde van een kolonie* (Leuven: Davidsfonds, 1993), 160.

4. THE COLD WAR COMES TO AFRICA

1. See Steve Weber, *Multilateralism in NATO: Shaping the Postwar Balance of Power, 1945–1961* (Berkeley: University of California Press, 1991), 41–42, 60.

2. *FRUS 1958–1960,* vol. 2, 461n. See also Lawrence S. Kaplan, *NATO and the UN: A Peculiar Relationship* (Columbia: University of Missouri Press, 2010), 49–70.

3. The Congo had a special significance for Americans as exemplifying Africa. See Kelly Enright, *The Maximum of Wilderness: The Jungle in the American Imagination* (Charlottesville: University of Virginia Press, 2012), esp. 44–58, 149.

4. Staff Notes, 802, July 15 (Admin. Conf.), box 51, WH Office, Office of Staff Secretary, Records Subject Series, Alphabetical Series; and Harr to McCone, October 14, Africa, box 1, WH Office, Office of the Special Assistant, National Security Affairs, 1952–1961, OCB Series, Subject Subseries, both in DDE.

5. For an overview, see Larry Grubbs, *Secular Missionaries: Americans and African Development in the 1960s* (Amherst: University of Massachusetts Press, 2009).

6. For official indecision, for example: CIA to Department of State, April 18; CIA Briefing for NSC, July 25, both in *FRUS 1964–1968,* vol. 23, 7–8, 13. For Eisenhower and Herter: Memoranda of conversations, July 13–21, CAH phone calls, 7/1–8/31, box 13, Herter Papers; Record of NSC Actions, NSC 3, 1960 (2) 2246–2314, Ann Whitman, DDE.

7. CIA, NSC Briefing, the Congo, July 14, CREST.

8. Sartre, introduction in *Lumumba Speaks: The Speeches and Writings of Patrice Lumumba, 1958–1961,* ed. Jean Van Lierde (Boston: Little, Brown, 1972).

9. Press Release, July 22, Office International Administration, Congo 1960–1961, file: Congo 1960, box 1, RG 59, NA.

10. Intelligence Note, Cumming to Herter, July 25, 1960, 6–160, box 1831, DOS; Penfield to Herter, June 7, Elections, box 4; CIA Memorandum, August 22, Intelligence, box 5, Congo Working Group; Leopoldville to Secretary of State, August 24, Congo Working Committee, box: Circular Instructions Bureau of Public Affairs, Lot Files 62D370 (11) RG 59, NA; CIA, NSC Briefings, the Congo, July 14, July 21, July 25, July 31, August 11, CREST. See also Alan James, *Britain and the Congo Crisis, 1960–63* (New York: St. Martin's Press, 1996), 61–62.

11. See H. W. Brands, *The Specter of Neutralism: The United States and the Emergence of the Third World, 1947–1960* (New York: Columbia University Press, 1989); and Jason C. Packer, "Small Victory, Missed Chance: The Eisenhower Administration, the Bandung Conference, and the Turning of the Cold War," in *The Eisenhower Administration, the Third World, and the Globalization of the Cold War,* ed. Kathryn Statler and Andrew L. Johns (Lanham, MD: Rowman & Littlefield, 2006), 153–174.

12. Robert Rothschild, *Un Phénix nommé Europe: Mémoires 1945–1995* (Brussels: Éditions Racine, 1997), 244.

13. Peter Grose, *Gentleman Spy: The Life of Allen Dulles* (Boston: Houghton Mifflin, 1994) is exceptional in its revelations. A sketch of Dulles appears in H. W. Brands Jr., *Cold Warriors: Eisenhower's Generation and American Foreign Policy* (New York: Columbia University Press, 1988), which makes the point about moral complacency, 48–67.

14. NSC Meetings, July 15 and July 21, *FRUS 1958–1960,* vol. 14, 309–310, 339 (Gray's notes of the same meeting differ—July 15, Planning Board Notes [NSC] 1960, box 4, White House Office, Office of the Staff Secretary, Records, 1957–1961, National Security Series, DDE).

15. Burden Oral History, 6–55, DDE; William A. M. Burden, *Peggy and I: A Life Too Busy for a Dull Moment* (New York: W. A. M. Burden, 1982), 279–328; Wendy Burden, *Deadend Gene Pool* (New York: Gotham Books, 2010), quote at 233. A biographical sketch of Burden appears in *The Scribner Encylopedia of American Lives,* vol. 1, *1981–1985* (New York: Scribner's, 1998), 115–117.

16. Burden to Department of State, July 19, *FRUS 1958–1960,* vol. 14, 330–332; and Madeleine G. Kalb, *The Congo Cables: The Cold War in Africa—from Eisenhower to Kennedy* (New York: Macmillan Co., 1982), 27–28.

17. Satterthwaite and Kohler to Merchant, February 16, 7–560, box 2601; Brussels to Washington, July 29, 7–2860, box 1955; Burden to Herter, August 4, 123-Burden, box 315, and October 19, 10–160, box 1956, all in DOS, RG 59, NA.

18. See Devlin's early cables to Washington in *FRUS 1964–1968,* vol. 23, 6, 11–12; his memos for March 1960 are in 3–160, box 1831, DOS, RG 59, NA; Sergey Mazov, *A Distant Front in the Cold War: The USSR in West Africa and the Congo, 1956–1964* (Palo Alto, CA: Stanford University Press, 2010), 108; and Larry Devlin, *Chief of Station, Congo: A Memoir of 1960–67* (New York: Perseus Books, 2007), ix, 56.

19. Devlin, *Chief of Station,* 78–79, 106–107, 111; interview with Stephen R. Weissman, October 27, 29, 2010.

20. For one account, see Martin Meredith, *The State of Africa: A History of Fifty Years of Independence* (London: New, 2006), 104–105.

21. See especially Memo of Conversation, July 27, *FRUS 1958–1960,* vol. 14, 359–366.

22. Kevin A. Spooner, *Canada, the Congo Crisis, and UN Peacekeeping, 1960–1964* (Vancouver: UBC Press, 2009), 56–59, and see Robertson Memo, August 1, *Documents on Canadian External Relations,* 1960, vol. 27 (online version, http://www.international .gc.ca/international/index.aspx?lang=eng).

23. NSC Meeting, August 1, 1960, *FRUS 1958–1960,* vol. 14, 372–376.

24. Devlin, *Chief of Station,* 47–48, 54, 260; IR, 14.

25. NSC Meeting, August 1, *FRUS 1958–1960,* vol. 14, 373–375; Memo, August 8, White House Office, Office of the Staff Secretary, Subject Series, 1952–1961, White House Subseries, box 3; Second Draft Record of Actions, August 1, Office of Special Assistant, National Security Affairs, 1952–1961, Special Assistant Series, Presidential Subseries, box 5, DDE.

26. For this notion we are indebted to Stephen R. Weissman and his *American Foreign Policy in the Congo, 1960–1964* (Ithaca, NY: Cornell University Press, 1974), 52–55.

27. Herter to embassy in Brussels, August 2, *FRUS 1958–1960,* vol. 14, 383; and see, for example, Devlin to CIA, August 11; CIA to Devlin, August 12, both in *FRUS 1964–1968,* vol. 23, 14–18.

28. Burden to Herter, July 27 (345), box 1954, July 28 (346), and Freeman (American embassy in Brussels) to Herter, July 30 (369, 370), box 1955, both in DOS, RG 59, NA; Memorandum of conversation, Herter-Scheyven (Belgian ambassador to the United States), July 28, *FRUS 1958–1960,* vol. 14, 367–370.

29. Lodge (USUN) to Herter, August 7 (347), 8-160, box 1955, DOS, RG 59, NA; and in DDE: Synopsis of Intelligence, August 5; Synopsis of State and Intelligence material, August 10 (conversation of August 7), Intelligence Briefing Notes, vol. 11 (5), box 14, White House Office, Office of Staff Secretary, Subject Series, Alphabetical Subseries.

30. Burden to Herter, August 4, 123-Burden, box 315, DOS, RG 59, NA.

31. Conversation with Van Zeeland, August 17, 8-1760; Freeman (American embassy in Brussels) to Herter, August 10, 8-2160, box 1955, both in DOS, RG 59, NA. And see Robert S. Jordan, *Political Leadership in NATO: A Study in Multilateral Diplomacy* (Boulder, CO: Westview Press, 1979), 62, 70–76, 85, 91–94.

32. See, for example, Nolting to Herter, July 5, 740.5612, box 1650, DOS, RG 59, NA; De Staercke (Belgian ambassador to NATO) to Wigny, July 13, doc. 6213, Spaak Papers, Fondation P. H. Spaak, Brussels.

33. Jean Van den Bosch, *Pré-Zaïre, le cordon mal coupé: Document* (Brussels: Le Cri, 1986), 175–177.

34. For the letter, see Spaak to Eisenhower, Paris, August 10, doc. 6221, Spaak Papers; for commentary, Michel Dumoulin, *Spaak* (Brussels: Éditions Racine 1999), 591.

35. Calhoun to Goodpaster, with top-secret enclosure, Wolf to Herter, August 10, Belgium, box 1, White House Office, Office of the Staff Secretary, Records, 1952–1961, International Series, DDE; Paul-Henri Spaak, *The Continuing Battle: Memoirs of a European, 1936–1966* (Boston: Little, Brown, 1971), 358. The issues are discussed in greater generality in "The Evolution of NATO Political Consultation 1949–1962" (May 1963), esp. section 65, footnote 42, NATO Archives, Brussels.

36. Herter to NATO embassy Paris, August 11, Belgium, box 1, White House Office, Office of the Staff Secretary, Records, 1952–1961, International Series, DDE.

37. Burgess (American ambassador to NATO) to Herter, September 10; Washington to USRO, Paris, September 15, JCS 1957–1961, vol. 1 (7), box 103, Norstad Papers, both in DDE.

38. Dillon to Eisenhower, August 19, Belgium, box 1, White House Office, Office of the Staff Secretary, Records, 1952–61, International Series, DDE.

39. Herter-Eisenhower conversation, August 10, *FRUS 1958–1960,* vol. 7, pt. 2, 402–403; Dillon to embassies, August 22, and Conference with Eisenhower, August 16, *FRUS 1958–1960,* vol. 7, pt. 1, 295, 613; IR, 64.

40. Colonel Margot (head of Belgian Military Intelligence), "Situation générale à Berlin," August 2, folder 6097, Eyskens Papers, State Archives, Leuven; Memo, Bohlen to Herter, August 2, *FRUS 1958–1960,* vol. 9, 547ff. Cleveland (American embassy in Brussels) to Herter, July 29, 7–2860, box 1955, DOS, RG 59, NA (quote from General Norstad).

41. NSC Meeting, August 18, *FRUS 1958–1960,* vol. 14, 422–424. See also Kalb, *Congo Cables,* 51–55.

42. Memo, Contingency Planning for the Congo, August 20, 8–1960, box 1955, DOS, RG 59, NA.

5. DAG HAMMARSKJÖLD AND THE UN

1. Speech of October 3, 1960, in Andrew W. Cordier and Wilder Foote, eds., *Public Papers of the Secretaries-General of the United Nations,* vol. 5, *Dag Hammarskjöld, 1960–1961* (New York: Columbia University Press, 1975), 201.

2. Pamphlet printed by Clarendon Press, Oxford, 1961.

3. See Brian Urquhart, *Hammarskjöld* (New York: Knopf, 1972), *A Life in Peace and War* (New York: Harper & Row, 1987), and *Ralph Bunche: An American Life* (New York: Norton, 1993); see also Urquhart, "The Tragedy of Lumumba," review of *The Assassination of Lumumba* by Ludo De Witte, October 4, 2001; "The Tragedy of Lumumba: An Exchange," December 20, 2001; and "Lumumba and the UN" (letter), February 14, 2002, all in *New York Review of Books;* and Urquhart's introduction to Manuel Fröhlich, *Political Ethics and the United Nations: Dag Hammarskjöld as Secretary-General* (London: Routledge, 2008), xi–xii.

4. Conor Cruise O'Brien, *To Katanga and Back, A UN Case History* (New York: Simon & Schuster, 1963), 43.

5. Speech to the Security Council, July 20, in Cordier and Foote, *Public Papers,* vol. 5, *Hammarskjöld,* 43.

6. Thomas G. Weiss, Tatiana Carayannis, Louis Emmerij, and Richard Jolly, *UN Voices: The Struggle for Development and Social Justice* (Bloomington: Indiana University Press, 2005), 162.

7. Bunche to Hammarskjöld, July 16 (80); July 20 (29, 40), 217-1-2, UN.

8. Record of conversation, August 1, box 161, Cordier Papers, Columbia University; Bunche to Hammarskjöld, August 12 (433), 217-1-7, UN.

9. Chronology, August 13, 8–1160, box 1955, DOS, RG 59, NA.

10. Lodge to Herter, July 26, 234, box 1954, DOS, RG 59, NA.

11. The exchanges appear in Rosalyn Higgins, *United Nations Peacekeeping, 1946–1967: Documents and Commentary,* vol. 3, *Africa* (Oxford: Oxford University Press, 1980), 132–136.

12. For the best summary, see Draft Financial Regulations, September 26, 370-3-6, UN.

13. Hammarskjöld to Cordier, August 1 (293); Bunche to Hammarskjöld, August 7 (385); and Hammarskjöld to Cordier, August 14 and 15 (452, 453), 217-1-7, all in UN; Hammarskjöld, Memorandum on Katanga, August 6, box 160; and Report of press conference, August 2 (by Cordier?), box 163, both in Cordier Papers.

14. IR, 14.

15. Sergey Mazov, *A Distant Front in the Cold War: The USSR in West Africa and the Congo, 1956–1964* (Palo Alto, CA: Stanford University Press, 2010), 103, 110–111, 115, 127–129, 160–166.

16. September 1 Press Conference, folder 6, box 98, Ralph Bunche Papers, UCLA, 9–10, 20; and see the discussion in Susan Williams, *Who Killed Hammarskjöld? The UN, the Cold War, and White Supremacy in Africa* (London: C. Hurst, 2011).

17. The best account can be found in a Draft UN History, chap. 18, 304-1-16, UN; and a review in Jean-Claude Willame, *Patrice Lumumba. La crise congolaise revisitée* (Paris: Éditions Karthala, 1990), 187–196.

18. Our view of Soviet policy is based on a reading of Western documents and on two books using Soviet sources: Mazov, *Distant Front,* and particularly the research of Lise A. Namikas, *Battleground Africa: The Cold War in the Congo, 1960–1965* (Stanford, CA: Stanford University Press, 2013), 15, 92–94, 121–124, 223–224.

19. Hammarskjöld to Cordier, August 15 (472), 217-1-7; Draft UN History, chap. 18, 304-1-16, both in UN; Wadsworth memorandum, September 10, *FRUS 1958–1960,* vol. 14, 475, editorial note; Cordier to V. F. Schwalm, August 18, box 55, Cordier Papers.

20. Hammarskjöld to Bunche, August 26 (1278), 217-1-12, UN. See also Alan James, *Britain and the Congo Crisis, 1960–63* (New York: St. Martin's Press, 1996), 64–77.

6. THE GOVERNMENT FALLS

1. Dupret (Davignon and Westhof) to Wigny, August 30 (293, 294), August 31 (303, 304, 308), September 2 (326, "Today I have met Verhaegen who co-ordinates the action of the opposition. Results can be expected before Wednesday September 7"), September 3 (334, 335, 336), September 5 (354, 355, convey messages of Verhaegen), 18.297, FPSFA; Wigny to Dupret (Davignon and Westhof), September 1 (150), box M 7, Wigny Papers, UCL, Louvain-la-Neuve; *LCM,* 116–122. For Verhaegen see also Dupret to Wigny, September 10 (406, "If Kasa-Vubu does not prevail soon, Verhaegen and his friends will be in great danger in Leopoldville"), 18.297, FPSFA.

2. Press Release, Telegrams, Cordier–Dayal, Hammarskjöld–Dayal, Personnel, Da, box 59; Telegram, Dayal–Hammarskjöld, Telegrams, box 162, Cordier Papers, Columbia University; Hammarskjöld to Bunche (1304), 370-12-6, and August 25 (617), 217-1-10, both in UN; and Bunche Pocket Diary 1960, August 27–September 15, folder 11, box 280, Bunche Papers, UCLA. See also Rajeshwar Dayal, *Mission for Hammarskjöld: The Congo Crisis* (New Delhi: Oxford University Press, 1976), 10–13.

3. Dupret (Lahaye) to Wigny and Sûreté, August 29 (276), 18.297, FPSFA. Larry Devlin, *Chief of Station, Congo: A Memoir of 1960–67* (New York: Perseus Books, 2007), 66; Devlin here paraphrases without citation Madeleine G. Kalb, *The Congo Cables: The Cold War in Africa—from Eisenhower to Kennedy* (New York: Macmillan Co., 1982), 67. An account of the conference is in Jean-Claude Willame, *Patrice Lumumba: La crise congolaise revisitée* (Paris: Éditions Karthala, 1990), 358–361.

4. Hammarskjöld to Cordier, September 1 (1437, 1438), 217-1-13, UN.

5. Indar Jit Rikhye, *Military Advisor to the Secretary-General: UN Peacekeeping and the Congo Crisis* (New York: St. Martin's Press, 1993), 88, 91.

6. Cordier–Hammarskjöld teleprinter conversation, September 3, 217-65-9, UN.

7. For example, Memo by Mr. Cordier, Congo, box 160, Cordier Papers (1960).

8. Hammarskjöld to Dayal, Cordier, and Horn, September 5, 217-2-3, UN.

9. Jef Van Bilsen, *Kongo 1945–1965: Het einde van een kolonie* (Leuven: Davidsfonds, 1993), 162–165.

10. The full text in Jules Gérard-Libois and Benoît Verhaegen, *Congo 1960* (Brussels: CRISP, 1961), 818–819.

11. Hammarskjöld to Cordier, September 5 (1553), 375-4-2; Hammarskjöld to Cordier, September 6 (1568, 1581), 217-2-3; Cordier to Hammarskjöld, September 6 (807), 217-2-1; Hammarskjöld to Dayal and Cordier, September 7 (1625), 217-2-3, all in UN; Cook memorandum, September 9, *FRUS 1958–1960*, vol. 14, 467; and see also Rajeshwar Dayal, *A Life of Our Times* (Hyderabad: Orient Longman, 1998), 41.

12. Devlin to CIA, September 5, *FRUS 1964–1968*, vol. 23, 23; Lettres de Lumumba, 751-1-3, UN.

13. Cordier to Hammarskjöld, September 1, 845-1-8; September 5 (797); September 6 (801, 807, 818), 217-2-1, UN.

14. Cordier-Dayal to Hammarskjöld, September 7 (827), 370-8-1; Hammarskjöld to Dayal, September 10 (1717, 1728), 217-2-3, both in UN. The best account of the David plan and the negotiations surrounding it appear in UN draft history, chap. 21, 304-2-1, UN.

15. Cordier to Hammarskjöld, September 5 (794, 797, 799); September 6 (noon) (810); and for the tensions see, for example, Cordier and Dayal to Hammarskjöld, September 6 (midnight) (821), 217-2-1, all in UN.

16. Byrne to Cordier, September 6 (87, 3069); September 8 (90); Hammarskjöld to Byrne, September 8 (40); Berendsen to Cordier, September 8 (92) 736-26-5; Dayal to Byrne, September 8 (856), 217-2-1; Hammarskjöld to Berendsen, September 7 (1605), 217-2-3; September 8 (40, 41), 736-26-5; Byrne to Dayal, September 8 (96); September 9 (98), 736-26-5, all in UN.

17. Stanleyville to ONUC, n.d., 736-1-6, UN; Brian Urquhart, *A Life in Peace and War* (New York: Harper & Row, 1987), 166.

18. Dayal, *Mission for Hammarskjöld*, 28–42; and *Life of Our Times*, 401–406; Rikhye, *Military Advisor*, 92–93 (it is unclear if this book was influenced by Dayal's earlier memoir); and see Brian Urquhart, *Hammarskjöld* (New York: Knopf, 1972), 446; Cordier and Dayal to Hammarskjöld, September 6 (823), 370-8-1, UN.

19. Wadsworth to Herter, November 16, 11–160, box 1957, DOS, RG 59, NA.

20. Cordier to Hammarskjöld, September 6 (808), 370-8-1; (817), 217-2-1; Cordier and Dayal to Hammarskjöld, September 7 (824), 845-1-1; Hammarskjöld to Cordier and Dayal, September 7 (1604), 217-2-3; Draft UN History, chap. 21, 304-2-1, all in UN.

21. Dayal, *Mission for Hammarskjöld*, 46.

22. Examine the following accounts: Memo by Mr. Cordier, Congo, box 160, Cordier Papers (1960); Cordier, Recollections of Dag Hammarskjöld and the United Nations, Columbia University Oral History Collection (1963–1964); Cordier, "Challenge of the Congo," *Think* 31 (July–August 1965): 21–29; and Cordier and Wilder Foote, eds., *Public Papers of the Secretaries-General*, vol. 5, *Hammarskjöld, 1960–1961* (New York: Columbia University Press, 1975), 159–181; and Kalb, *Congo Cables*, 73.

23. Legal Analysis, November 11, 357-20-13, UN.

24. *LCM*, chap. 12; *The Assassination of Patrice Lumumba*, BBC documentary, 2001 (available on YouTube).

25. Van Bilsen, *Kongo*, 162–165.

26. Timberlake to Herter, August 17, 8–1760, box 1955; Timberlake to Herter, September 13, 9–1060, box 1956, both in DOS, RG 59, NA.

27. Jean Van Lierde, ed., *Lumumba Speaks: The Speeches and Writings of Patrice Lumumba, 1958–1961* (Boston: Little, Brown, 1972), 358, 381, quote at 397.

28. Hammarskjöld to Cordier, September 6 (1583), 217-2-3, and see the material, e.g., in 467-65-Congo Constitutional, both in UN; Statement by secretary-general, United Nations Press Release, September 9, box 140, Cordier Papers.

29. Discours prononcé par monsieur Kasa-Vubu, 736-18-6, UN.

30. Unpublished Mémoires du Congo, 513, box MC 16, Wigny Papers; CIA paper prepared for Nixon, September 7, *FRUS 1964–1968*, vol. 23, 26.

31. For the timing, see Thomas Kanza, *Conflict in the Congo: The Rise and Fall of Lumumba* (London: Penguin Books, 1972), 288–292; Van Lierde, *Lumumba Speaks*, 379–405; Urquhart, *Life*, 166–167; and Rikhye, *Military Advisor*, 89–93. And Dayal to Hammarskjöld, September 12 (920), 217-2-2; Hammarskjöld to Dayal, September 12 (1744), 217-2-3, both in UN.

32. Memorandum of conversation with Belgium embassy, September 8, 9–160, box 1956, DOS, RG 59, NA.

33. Memorandum, Bunche, June 9, Civilian Personnel, box 4, Congo Working Group, RG 59, NA.

34. Cook conversation with Hammarskjöld, September 5, *FRUS 1958–1960*, vol. 14, 458–460. See also note on Wallner memorandum of September 7, 461n; and Cook to Department of State, September 7, 467, both ibid.

35. Cook memoranda, September 5 and 9, *FRUS 1958–1960*, vol. 14, 458, 464; Timberlake memoranda, September 7 and 10, 463, 477, ibid.; Harriman memorandum of conversation, September 9, box 406, Zaire, Harriman Papers, Library of Congress.

36. Memoranda, September 5, 7, and 9, *FRUS 1958–1960*, vol. 14, 458, 465–466, 475n. See also Memorandum, August 26, 444, and intelligence estimate, September 13, 485, both ibid. For Wieschoff's statement on an arrest, Van Bilsen Diary notes, folder 6-4-1, Van Bilsen Papers, KADOC Center for Religion, Culture, and Society in Leuven.

37. Statement by secretary-general, United Nations Press Release, September 9, box 140, Cordier Papers; Hammarskjöld to Dayal, September 15 (1861), 217-2-3, and the material, e.g., in 467-65-Congo Constitutional, both in UN.

38. Conor Cruise O'Brien, *Murderous Angels: A Political Tragedy and Comedy in Black and White* (Boston: Little, Brown, 1968); see also O'Brien, *To Katanga and Back, A UN Case History* (New York: Simon & Schuster, 1963). On the silencing, see the material in 370-41-8, UN; and on Korea, for example, August 5, Synopsis of Intelligence and State material reported to the President, box 52, Briefings August 1960, DDE Diary Series, DDE.

7. MOBUTU

1. The text of the radio speech is in Jules Gérard-Libois and Benoît Verhaegen, *Congo 1960* (Brussels: CRISP, 1961), 869. Dayal's appraisal is in his *Mission for Hammarskjöld: The Congo Crisis* (New Delhi: Oxford University Press, 1976), 61–67. A photocopy of the minutes of the College of Commissioners, from September 21 1960, until January 21 1961, is found in folders 01.08.29 and 01.08.30, Jules Gérard-Libois Papers, Royal Museum for Central Africa, Tervuren, Belgium. An analysis of their work by Jean Omasomba Tshonda is in Chambre des représentants de Belgique, *Enquête parlementaire visant à déterminer les circonstances exactes de l'assassinat de Patrice Lumumba et l'implication éventuelle des responsables belges dans celui-ci,* DOC 50 0312/006, November 16, 2001, 939–969.

2. Louis-François Vanderstraeten, *De la Force publique à l'Armée nationale congolaise: Histoire d'une mutinerie, Juillet 1960* (Brussels: Académie Royale de Belgique, 1993), 241.

3. "Séance du conseil des ministres du lundi 5 septembre 1960," VII/BV/RDC/Lumumba/007/01, Verhaegen Papers, Royal Museum for Central Africa, Tervuren, Belgium. Cordier to Hammarskjöld, September 6 (800), Dayal to Hammarskjöld, September 9 (863), 217-2-1, both in UN.

4. See John Waterbury, *The Commander of the Faithful: The Moroccan Political Elite; A Study in Segmented Politics* (New York: Columbia University Press, 1970), 287–289; Dwight L. Ling, *Morocco and Tunisia: A Comparative History* (Washington, DC: University Press of America, 1979), 36–37, 121. For an outstanding examination of Morocco's politics at this time, Douglas E. Ashford, *Political Change in Morocco* (Princeton, NJ: Princeton University Press, 1961).

5. Van Bilsen to Brasseur, October 7, box 17, Brasseur Papers, State Archives, Arlon, Belgium; Timberlake to Herter, September 26, *FRUS 1958–1960,* vol. 14, 505.

6. Cordier to Hammarskjöld, September 5 (795, 799), September 6 (800, 822), 217-2-1, UN.

7. Timberlake to Herter, September 9, *FRUS 1958–1960,* vol. 14, 471–472.

8. Quoted from Catherine Hoskyns, *The Congo since Independence: January 1960–December 1961* (London: Oxford University Press, 1965), 222.

9. Timberlake to Herter, September 18, September 26, *FRUS 1958–1960,* vol. 14, 494, 505.

10. Timberlake to Herter, September 13, 9–1060, box 956, DOS; Memo, Mobutu, September 11, Political Activities, box 4, Congo Working Group; Memo Mobutu, Bureau of

African Affairs, Research Relating to the Congo and Congo Coordinating Committee, 1960–1964, box 4, RG 59, all in NA; Dupret to Wigny, September 15 (463, 473), 18.297, FPSFA.

11. Dayal, *Mission for Hammarskjöld,,* 57, 86–88; and see the cables from Dayal to Hammarskjöld in mid-September, 217-2-2, UN; and Contra-projet, September 17, Cables, 1960–1961, box 160, Cordier Papers, Columbia University.

12. Timberlake to Herter, October 27, 10–2060, box 1957, DOS, RG 59, NA.

13. The role of the CIA was first discussed by Hoskyns, in *Congo since Independence,* 215–216; and becomes a central element in Stephen R. Weissman, *American Foreign Policy in the Congo, 1960–1964* (Ithaca, NY: Cornell University Press, 1974), 95–99; Madeleine G. Kalb, *The Congo Cables: The Cold War in Africa—from Eisenhower to Kennedy* (New York: Macmillan Co., 1982), 89–101; and Richard D. Mahoney, *JFK: Ordeal in Africa* (New York: Oxford University Press, 1983).

14. Devlin's most elaborate account is found in *Chief of Station, Congo: A Memoir of 1960–67* (New York: Perseus Books, 2007), 72, 79–84. The story is incoherent, and his dates do not make sense.

15. Devlin to CIA, September 13, 21, 28, October 2, 11, 29–30, 37, 39, 40–41, 43; and CIA NSC Briefing, September 15, 32, both in *FRUS 1964–1968,* vol. 23.

16. Dayal to Hammarskjöld, September 10 (878), 217-2-1, September 12 (913), 217-2-2, UN.

17. Dupret to Wigny, August 26 (253), 18.297, FPSFA.

18. See Devlin's memos for March 1960 in 3–160, box 1831, DOS, RG 59, NA; and Devlin, *Chief of Station,* 71–79, 97–98, 183, 209, and see quote in picture section of the book.

19. Memorandum of conversation Herter–Lord Home, September 18, 9–1060, box 1956, DOS, RG 59, NA; see the Dayal-Hammarskjöld cables for September in 217-2-2-4, UN; Minutes of commissioners' meetings, October 1960, Gérard-Libois Papers; Dupret to Wigny, September 23 (540), September 24 (545, 549, 551 quote), September 26 (553 quote), September 27 (559), 18.297, FPSFA; and Timberlake to Herter, September 26, *FRUS 1958–1960,* vol. 14, 505. Kettani was recalled to Morocco at the end of September, and the recall may account for the increasing influence of Devlin and Marlière on Mobutu.

20. Quoted from Kalb, *Congo Cables,* 112.

21. Lumumba's Legal Position, October 14, Loi Fondamentale, box 1, Congo Working Group, RG 59, NA; Herter-Hammarskjöld conversation, September 26, *FRUS 1958–1960,* vol. 14, 506–507; Timberlake-Dayal conversation, October 11, 518, ibid.

22. Wadsworth-Hammarskjöld conversations, October 11, October 15, *FRUS 1958–1960,* vol. 14, 524, 529–531; Bohlen-Hammarskjöld conversation, October 22, 546–549, ibid.

23. Wadsworth-Hammarskjöld conversations, October 15, 531; Bohlen-Hammarskjöld conversation, October 22, 549, 552; Wadsworth-Hammarskjöld conversations, October 29, 559, all in *FRUS 1958–1960,* vol. 14.

24. Wadsworth-Dayal conversation, November 7, Records of the Foreign Service, US Mission to the UN, Central Subject File, 1946–1961, Congo, folder 9–12/60, box 78, RG 84, NA.

25. ONUC 538, October 10, 736-4-11; Dayal to Hammarskjöld, October 13 (1240), 736-5-4, both in UN; Marlière to Loos, October 1, October 21, AF/1/56 (P1332), FPSFA.

26. ONUC 538, October 10, 736-4-11; ONUC 548, 735-15-03; Dayal to Hammarskjöld, October 13 (1240), 736-5-4, all in UN.

27. Nicholls (British ambassador to Belgium) to Wigny, October 24, box M 7, Wigny Papers, UCL, Louvain-la-Neuve.
28. Dayal to Hammarskjöld, September 15 (984), 217-2-2, UN.
29. Dayal to Hammarskjöld, September 14 (955), 217-2-2, UN.

8. AFRICANS AGAINST LUMUMBA

1. Benoît Verhaegen and Charles Tshimanga, *L'ABAKO et l'indépendance du Congo belge: Dix ans de nationalisme kongo (1950–1960)* (Paris: L'Harmattan, 2003).
2. Thomas Kanza, *Conflict in the Congo: The Rise and Fall of Lumumba* (London: Penguin Books, 1972); Cléophas Kamitatu, *La grande mystification du Congo-Kinshasa: Les crimes de Mobutu* (Paris: F. Maspero, 1971).
3. These issues are broached in the collection of essays edited by Bruce Berman, Dickson Eyoh, and Will Kymlicka, *Ethnicity and Democracy in Africa* (Oxford: James Curry, 2004); in Crawford Young, "Nation, Ethnicity, and Citizenship: Dilemmas of Democracy and Civil Order in Africa," in *Making Nations, Creating Strangers: States and Citizenship in Africa*, ed. Sara Dorman, Daniel Hammett, and Paul Nugent (Leiden: Brill, 2007), 241–264; and in Ngũgĩ Thiong'o, "The Myth of *Tribe* in African Politics," *Transition* 101 (2009): 16–23.
4. Patrice Lumumba, *Congo, My Country* (New York: Praeger, 1962), 173.
5. For readers interested in the details of Katanga's rivalries, see Kabuya Lumuna Sando, *Nord-Katanga 1960–64, de la sécession à la guerre civile: Le meurtre des chefs* (Paris: L'Harmattan, 1992).
6. Catherine Hoskyns, *The Congo since Independence, January 1960–December 1961* (London: Oxford University Press, 1965), 280.
7. Memo, Sendwe, October 16, 1962, Jason Sendwe, box 4, Congo Working Group, RG 59, NA; Clare Timberlake, "First Year of Independence in the Congo: Events and Issues" (MA thesis, George Washington University, 1963), 75.
8. See the helpful reports of the American consul in Elisabethville, William Canup, e.g., Electoral Campaign in Katanga, May 19, 5–160, box 1831, DOS, RG 59, NA.
9. Dibwe dia Mwembu, "Popular Memories of Patrice Lumumba," in *A Congo Chronicle: Patrice Lumumba in Urban Art*, by Bogumil Jewsiewicki (New York: Museum of African Art, 1999), 62.
10. Weber to king's chief of staff, October 19, *LCM*, 519. See also Canup to Herter, November 25, 11–1760; Burden to Herter, December 1, 12–160, box 1957; Cleveland to Department of State, December 6, 12–1160, box 1958, all in DOS, RG 59, NA.
11. Van den Bloock (Belgian consulate general in Elisabethville) to Rothschild (Brussels), October 29, Rothschild Papers, Université Libre de Bruxelles.
12. See the memos and telegrams of Timberlake and Canup in 11–160, box 1957, DOS, RG 59, NA.

9. THE CENTRAL INTELLIGENCE AGENCY

1. Chronology of Lumumba testimony, box 55, 07-M-133, CC.
2. IR, 51–62, 65–70.

3. "Address before the 15th General Assembly of the United Nations, New York City. September 22, 1960," *Public Papers of the Presidents of the United States: Dwight D. Eisenhower, 1960–61* (Washington, DC: Government Printing Office, 1961), 708–710, 712, 718–719.

4. Max Weber's essay "Politics as a Vocation" is available online; see also Hans Morgenthau, *Politics among Nations: The Struggle for Power and Peace* (New York: Knopf, 1948). For up-to-date academic discussion, see C. A. J. Coady, *Messy Morality: The Challenge of Politics* (New York: Oxford University Press, 2008); Janos Kis, *Politics as a Moral Problem* (New York: Central European University Press, 2008); and John J. Mearsheimer, *Why Leaders Lie: The Truth about Lying in International Politics* (New York: Oxford University Press, 2011).

5. Bissell Testimony, 9/10/1975, 32, HM.

6. Bissell Testimony, 6/11/75, 55–56, HM.

7. See the affidavits in 07-M-06, box 48; 07-M-51 and 07-M-53, box 52; and 07-M-83, box 53, CC.

8. Helms Testimony, 6/13/75, 153, 154, HM.

9. On subvention, see Charles G. Cogan, "Avoiding the Breakup: The US-UN Intervention in the Congo, 1960–1965," Kennedy School of Government Case Program CR14-99-1549.0 (1999), 41, 42, 43. Cogan was a former CIA officer. For rendition, see Devlin in Stephen R. Weissman, "'An Extraordinary Rendition,'" *Intelligence and National Security* 25 (2010): 202.

10. Agatha Christie, *The Murder of Roger Ackroyd* (New York: Dodd, Mead, 1926), 165.

11. IR, 55–60.

12. For the running battle, see White House Office, Special Assistant National Security Affairs, 1952–1961, NSC Series, Subject Subseries, box 8; Special Assistant Series, Presidential Subseries, box 5; and White House Office, Office of the Staff Secretary, 1952–1961, Subject Series, White House Subseries, box 3, all in DDE; and Patrick Coyne's report to John Kennedy, May 9, 1961, Covert Operations, Foreign Intelligence Advisory Board Briefing Material, box 94, Presidents Office Files, JFK. For Eisenhower's frustration, Tim Weiner, *Legacy of Ashes: The History of the CIA* (New York: Doubleday, 2007), 166–167; and *FRUS 1961–1963*, vol. 25, Documents 78–87. Kenneth Michael Absher, Michael C. Desch, Roman Popadiuk, et al., *Privileged and Confidential: The Secret History of the President's Intelligence Advisory Board* (Lexington: University of Kentucky Press, 2012), mainly a compendium of primary sources, is a devastating chronicle of the CIA under Dulles. See esp. pp. 31, 35–36, 44.

13. Memo on Congo Contingency Planning, August 23, 8–1960, box 1955, DOS, RG 59, NA.

14. IR, 15; John Prados, *Safe for Democracy: The Secret Wars of the CIA* (Chicago: Ivan R. Dee, 2006), 275–276; Sean Kelly, *America's Tyrant: The CIA and Mobutu of Zaire* (Washington, DC: American University Press, 1993), 57.

15. IR, 60; Chronology of Lumumba testimonies, 07-M-133, box 55, CC.

16. IR, 15–16; Larry Devlin, *Chief of Station, Congo: A Memoir of 1960–67* (New York: Perseus Books, 2007), 56–57.

17. Weissman, "'Rendition,'" 203.

18. IR, 17, 62; Devlin, *Chief of Station,* 63–64, 67, 70; NSC Meeting, September 7, *FRUS 1958–1960,* vol. 14, 460–462.

19. NSC Meeting, September 21, *FRUS 1958–1960,* vol. 14, 496–497; IR, 62.

20. IR, 17–18.

21. IR, 22–23. Interview and Meeting Summary with Devlin, August 20, 1975, 07-M-53, box 53, CC. For Devlin's recollections see, for example, the BBC documentary *The Assassination of Patrice Lumumba,* 2001 (available on YouTube). For the nickname: Joseph J. Trento, *The Secret History of the CIA* (Roseville, CA: Prima Publishing, 2001), 193–197.

22. Burden-Dillon conversation, September 16, box 15, Telcon September 1960, Dillon Papers, JFK; Eisenhower to Baudouin, September 19, International, box 3, Belgium (1), Ann Whitman, DDE.

23. Jonathan Kwitny, *Endless Enemies: The Making of an Unfriendly World* (New York: St. Martin's Press, 1984), 57 (italics in text omitted).

24. Here we rely on two different stories that appear in Devlin, *Chief of Station,* 52, 86.

25. IR, 60, 64; Summary of interview with Gray, July 5, 1975, 07-M-06, box 48, CC; Affidavit, July 10, 1975, box 2, Church Committee (3), Gray Papers, DDE.

26. IR, 54, but compare 59.

27. For Castro, see Lars Schoultz, *That Infernal Little Cuban Republic: The United States and the Cuban Revolution* (Chapel Hill: University of North Carolina Press, 2009), 126, 128, 192–993; and Weiner, *Legacy of Ashes,* 73–179. The anti-Castro view, which makes clear the fears he inspired, appears in Frank R. Villafaña, *Cold War in the Congo: The Confrontation of Cuban Military Forces, 1960–1967* (New Brunswick, NJ: Transaction Publishers, 2009), 3–29; on the other side, Morris H. Morley, *Imperial State and Revolution: The United States and Cuba, 1952–1985* (New York: Cambridge University Press, 1987), 72–130.

28. Dulles and Tweedy to Devlin, September 24; CIA to Department of State, January 14, 1961, both in *FRUS 1964–1968,* vol. 23, 39, 74; and Weissman, "'Rendition,'" 204–206.

29. For Devlin in 1960, see Devlin to CIA, November 3, *FRUS 1964–1968,* vol. 23, 55; for his later accounts see IR, 26; Devlin (alias Victor Hedgeman), Testimony, 8/21/75, 112–13, HM; Devlin interview with Terry Gross, *Fresh Air,* March 13, 2007; interview for the BBC *Assassination of Patrice Lumumba*; and Devlin, *Chief of Station,* 96. For Gottlieb, see Lennzer to Hart, October 14, 1975, 07-M-77, box 52, CC.

30. IR, 23, 25, 27, 32.

31. Memorandum of conversation Wigny-Burden, September 9, M 7, vol. 20bis, Wigny Papers, UCL, Louvain-la-Neuve; *Europe Magazine,* October 19, 1960, 29–32.

32. Memo, August 19, with annotations, WH Central, OF, Pt. 2, box 853, 162 (2); Dillon to Eisenhower, August 19, Belgium, with proposed toast enclosed, White House Office, Office of the Staff Secretary, box 1, International Series, Records, 1952–61, both in DDE.

33. IR, 25, 27.

34. For the identities of Devlin's assistants, see Devlin, *Chief of Station,* 66, 90, 96, 139; and Testimony: Richard Bissell, 9/10/75, 80, and Bronson Tweedy, 10/9/75 (afternoon), 12–14, and 10/10/75 (morning), 36–47, HM; IR, 28–29.

35. IR, 25, 31–32, 37; Dayal to Hammarskjöld, October 10 (1218), 217-2-6, UN; Prados, *Safe for Democracy,* 275–276; David W. Doyle, *True Men and Traitors: From the OSS to the CIA, My Life in the Shadows* (New York: John Wiley, 2001), 129–130, 145. Doyle recalled that Devlin refused a rifle because of his high moral notions.

36. IR, 18–19, 32, 37–43; Interview and Meeting Summary, Devlin, August 20, 1975, 07-M-83, box 53, CC.

37. IR, 23, 45–46; and see the Chronology of Lumumba testimonies in 07-M-133, box 55; Interview and Meeting Summary, Devlin, August 20, 1975, 07-M-83; Memorandum, WIROGUE Section of Report, November 25, 1975, 07-M-87, box 53, all in CC; and Memorandum, WIROGUE, December 1960, CIA-Miscellaneous, box 6, F-1, CIA.

38. His identity has long been a mystery, although researchers have argued for Mozes Maschkivitzan. See Richard D. Mahoney, *Sons and Brothers: The Days of Jack and Bobby Kennedy* (New York: Arcade, 1999), 91–95.

39. IR, 43–44.

40. For example, see Alan James, *Britain and the Congo Crisis, 1960–63* (New York: St. Martin's Press, 1996), 63; and Calder Walton, *Empire of Secrets: British Intelligence, the Cold War, and the Twilight of Empire* (London: Harper Press, 2013).

10. THE RETURN OF THE BELGIANS

1. Gaston Eyskens, *De Memoires* (Tielt, Belgium: Lannoo, 1993), 587.

2. Dupret to Wigny, September 6 (358 quote, 365), 18.297, FPSFA.

3. Van Bilsen diary notes, and letters to Kasa-Vubu, September–October, folder 6-4-1, Van Bilsen Papers, KADOC Center for Religion, Culture, and Society, Leuven; Van Bilsen quoted in Dayal to Hammarskjöld, October 6 (1188, 1189), 217-2-6, UN. For Kasa-Vubu's anti-Belgian resentment: Burden to Herter, July 21 (295–296), box 1954, DOS, RG 59, NA.

4. Dupret to Wigny, September 17 (491), conveying a personal message of Georges Denis, September 16, 18.297, FPSFA. Full text in *LCM*, 161–163.

5. Annick Van Ostade, "Le manifeste de 'Conscience africaine': Les origines et les implications immédiates," in *Recueil d'études Congo 1955–1960* (Brussels: Académie royale des Sciences d'Outre-Mer, 1992), 525–555. On the support of the Christian trade union for Ileo, see Timberlake to Herter, August 8 (359), box 1955, 8–160, RG 59, NA.

6. Zana Aziza Etambala, *Congo '55–'65. Van koning Boudewijn tot president Mobutu* (Tielt, Belgium: Lannoo, 1999), 221–229.

7. Walter Pluym and Olivier Boehme, *De Nationale Bank van België 1939–1971. III: Van de golden sixties tot de val van Bretton Woods* (Brussels: National Bank of Belgium, 2005), 373–470, esp. 400–407.

8. Dupret to Wigny, September 21 (520), September 22 (534), October 4 (606), October 13 (655), October 20 (700), October 21 (702), October 26 (729), November 28 (865), 18.297, FPSFA.

9. Dayal to Hammarskjöld, September 24 (1068), October 5 (1181), October 6 (1189), and October 18 (1268), 217-2-6, UN. Luc Gillon was rector of Lovanium from 1954. His memoirs treat this episode briefly: Gillon, *Servir: En actes et en vérité* (Paris-Gembloux: Éditions Duculot, 1988), 148–171. On Lovanium University, see Ruben Mantels, *Geleerd in de tropen: Leuven, Congo & de wetenschap, 1885–1960* (Leuven: Leuven University Press, 2007).

10. "Compte rendu de l'entretien de M. Christian Herter, Secrétaire d'État avec M. Pierre Wigny, Ministre des Affaires Étrangères," September 26, doc. 6223, Spaak Papers,

Fondation P.H. Spaak, Brussels; Memorandum of conversation Herter-Wigny, September 26, Conference Files, box 235, RG 59, NA.

11. Wigny to Dupret, September 6 (163, 164 and 165), box M 7, vol. 20bis, Wigny Papers, UCL, Louvain-la-Neuve.

12. Dupret to Wigny, September 17 (491), conveying a personal message of Georges Denis, September 16, 18.297, FPSFA. Rom was subsequently arrested by Lumumba's partisans. See Memorandum of Rom's interrogation, September 14, by minister of justice Rémy Mwamba in VII-BV/RDC/Lumumba, Verhaegen Papers, Royal Museum for Central Africa, Tervuren, Belgium.

13. Wigny memorandum, September 11, facsimile in *LCM,* 664–666; Dupret to Wigny, September 16 (486), conveying a message of Étienne Davignon, 18.297, FPSFA.

14. Memorandum of conversation Dillon-Wigny, October 11, *FRUS 1958–1960,* vol. 14, 521–524.

15. D'Aspremont to Dupret, September 27 (Minaf 61327), conveying a message of Wigny to d'Aspremont, September 26, AF/1/56 (P1332), FPSFA. Full text in *LCM,* 171.

16. D'Aspremont to Tshombe, September 28, folder 106, d'Aspremont Lynden Papers, National Archives, Brussels. Full text in *LCM,* 155–156.

17. Draft signed d'Aspremont and dated October 5, AF/1/56 (P1332), FPSFA; message received in Elisabethville and dated October 6 (Minaf 65706) in Rothschild Papers, Université Libre de Bruxelles; and Vandewalle Papers, Royal Museum for Central Africa, Tervuren, Belgium. First published in Frédéric Vandewalle, *Mille et quatre jours. Contes du Zaïre et du Shaba* (Brussels: F. Vandewalle, 1974–1975), document 65. Ludo De Witte raised an ongoing controversy with his book *De moord op Lumumba* (Leuven: Van Halewyck, 1999), but only presented the full text of the message in the French translation (*L'assassinat de Lumumba,* Paris: Éditions Karthala, 2000, facsimile on 387).

18. Quote in Dupret to Wigny, October 4 (606) conveying a message of Benoît Verhaegen; and also Dupret to Wigny, September 12 (431), October 17 (678), and October 18 (680), all in 18.297, FPSFA.

19. Minutes of the Belgian cabinet; see also Wigny's unpublished Mémoires du Congo, 487–489, box MC 16, Wigny Papers. There was no standing Congo committee after September 3 as De Witte, *De moord op Lumumba,* 99–109, claimed.

20. De Witte, *De moord op Lumumba,* 109–116, was the first to draw attention to Loos's activity.

21. *LCM,* 133–134, 662–663 (facsimile of memorandum entitled "Opération-L.").

22. Dupret to Wigny, September 12 (424, 428), September 13 (438); Marlière (Brazzaville) to Loos (Minaf), September 12, all in 18.297, FPSPA; Dayal to Hammarskjöld, September 14 (955, 967), 217-2-6, UN.

23. Lahaye to Paul Woot de Trixhe (director Sûreté), August 10, *LCM,* 178–179 (from Archives of State Security).

24. Marlière's actions are discussed in *LCM,* 183–188.

25. The Pilaet mission is discussed in *LCM,* 189–199. His mission reports are to be found in the Pilaet Papers, CEGESOMA Center for Historical Research on War and Contemporary Society, Brussels.

26. *LCM,* 474–498, quote 489.

27. To escape criticism from the UN Marlière became, shortly thereafter, the official counselor of Ferdinand Kazadi, the commissioner of defense.

28. Marlière to Loos, October 3 and 5, and Minaf to Marlière, October 5, AF/1/56 (P1332), FPSFA.

29. Wigny to Dupret, September 6, Wigny to Rothschild (Mistebel), September 7 (215), box M 7, vol. 20, Wigny Papers; Rothschild (Mistebel) to Wigny and d'Aspremont, September 6 (569), September 8 (623), 18.290; and d'Aspremont (in Usumbura) to Minaf, October 12 and 14, AF/1/56 (P1332), FPSFA.

30. Rothschild (Mistebel) to Wigny and d'Aspremont, October 7 (1108), 18.290, FPSFA; Tshombe to Eyskens, October 8, 10, and 12, folder 6079, Eyskens Papers, State Archives, Leuven.

31. Dayal to Hammarskjöld, October 17 (1258, 1259) 217, UN.

32. Olivier Boehme, "The Involvement of the Belgian Central Bank in the Katanga Secession, 1960–1963," *African Economic History* 33 (2005): 1–29.

33. Rothschild (Mistebel) to Wigny and d'Aspremont, October 11 (1208); figures in Van den Bloock (Mistebel) to Wigny and d'Aspremont, October 8 (1134, 1135), Rothschild (Mistebel) to Wigny and d'Aspremont, October 14 (1251), all in 18.290, FPSFA; Dayal to Hammarskjöld, October 18 (1268, 1269, 1270), 217, UN.

34. A still valuable account on the Baluba rebellion is Jules Gérard-Libois, *Katanga Secession* (Madison: University of Wisconsin Press, 1966); Rothschild (Mistebel) to Wigny and d'Aspremont, October 6 (1083), October 11 (1209), Crener/Bloock (Belgian consulate general in Elisabethville) to Wigny, October 20 (1349), 18.290, FPSFA; Dayal to Hammarskjöld, October 17 (1258,1259), 217-2-2, UN; and correspondence of René Smal (Mistebel) to Loos, September–October 1960, Loos Papers, Royal Museum for Central Africa, Tervuren, Belgium.

35. Marlière to Loos, October 26, AF/1/56 (P1332), FPSFA.

36. See his memoirs, Guy Weber, *Le Katanga de Moïse Tshombe ou le drame de la loyauté* (Brussels: Éditions Louis Musin, 1983).

37. The discussion in the following pages is based on *LCM,* 516–541.

38. Tshombe to Baudouin, October 6, Rothschild Papers. The original has not been filed in the Archives of the Royal Palace. Weber typed the letter and showed the unsigned document to Ambassador Rothschild (Mistebel), who took a photocopy, which has been kept in his papers.

39. Rothschild (Mistebel) proposes a photograph: Rothschild to Van den Bosch, October 14, Rothschild Papers; Rothschild to Wigny and d'Aspremont, October 14 (1264, 1269), both in 18.290, FPSFA.

40. Facsimile in *LCM,* 673–674.

41. Full text of the letter dated October 28 in Vandewalle, *Mille et quatre jours,* vol. 3, document 79; see also *LCM,* 516–523.

42. The visit, intended to be incognito, was reported in the press. See *La Libre Belgique* (Brussels), October 29.

43. Loos to Marlière, October 29 (75329), AF/1/56, FPSFA.

44. See S-0845-0003-08-00001: Secretary-General's correspondence with Belgium, UN Online Archives (pdf-file, 74–75). See also "Évolution de la crise congolaise de septembre 1960 à avril 1961," *Chronique de politique étrangère* 14, nos. 5–6 (septembre-

novembre 1961) (Brussels: Institut royal des relations internationales): 786–792; and Minutes of the Belgian cabinet, October 21.

45. Minutes of the Belgian cabinet, October 28; Loos memorandum, October 28, folder 6073, Eyskens Papers.

46. Diary notes (Wigny), October 27 and 28, PC. Wigny memorandum, October 31, folder 6073, Eyskens Papers.

47. Second Dayal report, November 2, S/4557; Reply of the Belgian government, December 7, A/4629, S-0845-0003-08-00001: Secretary-General's correspondence with Belgium, UN Online Archives (pdf-file, 22–32). See also "Évolution de la crise congolaise," 758–785.

48. Verbatim record in "The Press Conference of Mr. Wigny, Minister of Foreign Affairs of Belgium. November 14," S-0845-0003-08-00001: Secretary-General's correspondence with Belgium, UN Online Archives (pdf-file, 55–70). See also Jules Gérard-Libois, *Le rôle de la Belgique dans l'opération des Nations Unies au Congo (1960–1961)* (Brussels: CRISP, 1965).

49. Minutes of the Belgian cabinet, November 4.

50. Testimony of Paul Heureux, Marlière's radio operator, before the Belgian parliamentary commission in September 2001. Written text in *LCM,* 233–234.

51. Dupret to d'Aspremont, November 15, conveying a message from "Gabriel" to Marlière, Loos Papers.

52. Burden, Oral History, 42, DDE.

11. LUMUMBA IMPERILED

1. Herter to Wadsworth, November 7, and Editorial Note, November 8, *FRUS 1958–1960,* vol. 2, 437, 442–443.

2. Dayal to Hammarskjöld, November 23 (1502), 217-3-6; Hammarskjöld to Dayal, November 23 (3709), 217-3-9, both in UN.

3. Rothschild (Brazzaville) to Wigny, December 1 (880), conveying a message of agent 070a (i.e., Lahaye), 18.297, FPSFA. Full text in *LCM,* 260–261. The most complete account of the breakout is in G. Heinz and H. Donnay, *Lumumba: The Last Fifty Days* (New York: Grove Press, 1969).

4. For this narrative see the UN reports in 735-15-3, especially Veillet-Lavallee to Dayal, December 3. Our narrative should be compared to Ludo De Witte, *Assassination of Lumumba* (New York: Verso, 2001), 52–56.

5. Dayal to Hammarskjöld, December 1 (1561), 217-3-7, UN.

6. Testimony of Paul Heureux, Marlière's radio operator at the Belgian consulate general in Brazzaville, before the Belgian parliamentary commission in September 2001. See *LCM,* 232–235. The "Satan-Jew" exchange has been wrongly situated on January 14 in Jacques Brassinne and Jean Kestergat, *Qui a tué Patrice Lumumba?* (Paris: Éditions Duculot, 1991), 107–113; and De Witte, *Assassination,* 199–200.

7. Hammarskjöld statement, February 15, 1961, SG/1008, box 140, Cordier Papers, Columbia University.

8. See the exceptionally useful report, Dayal to Hammarskjöld, December 4 (1595), 735-15-3, UN.

9. Timberlake to Herter, December 3, 12–160, box 1957, DOS, RG 59, NA.

10. CIA to Devlin, September 13, *FRUS 1964–1968,* vol. 23, 31.

11. Dayal to Hammarskjöld, December 5 (1604), and December 7 (1618), 217-3-7, UN; Dupret to Wigny, January 16 (58), conveying a message of Marlière, 18.297, FPSFA.

12. Dayal to Hammarskjöld, December 5 (1605), 217-3-7; December 6 (1617), 735-15-03, both in UN.

13. *LCM,* 523–529; Cleveland (American embassy in Brussels) to Herter, December 9 (529), December 16 (546, 547); Memorandum of conversation Burden-d'Aspremont, December 3, 12–168, box 1957; Memorandum of conversation Cleveland-Rothschild, December 6; Memorandum of conversation Freeman-Van den Bosch, December 7, 12–160, box 1958, all in RG 59, NA. See also Guy Weber, *Le Katanga de Moïse Tshombe ou le drame de la loyauté* (Brussels: Éditions Louis Musin, 1983), 156–157.

14. Burden memos, October 12, 14, 16 (2), WH Central, OF, Pt. 2, box 853; Eisenhower to Baudouin, December 2, Belgium (1), 3, International, Ann Whitman; Chron File, all in DDE; December 1960 (2), box 9, Herter Papers, DDE. Also Burden to Herter, October 19, 611.55/10–1960 (microfilm); Visit to Brussels, box 239; and Note, December 2, 123-Burden, box 315, all in DOS, RG 59, NA.

15. See the material in DOS Conference Files, box 239, RG 59, NA.

16. US delegation to NATO capitals, December 16, 396.1-PA, box 736; Memo of conversation, Norway, United Kingdom, US representatives, December 18, box 240; Memorandum: British antipathy to Spaak, December 18, box 239, all in DOS Conference Files, RG 59, NA.

17. Jean Neuville and Jacques Yerna, *Le choc de l'hiver '60–'61: Les grèves contre la loi unique* (Brussels: CRISP, 1990).

18. Comité International de la Croix-Rouge (CICR) Note no. 415, "Rapport technique sur la visite aux détenus politiques du camp militaire Hardy, à Thysville, effectuée le 27 décembre 1960," December 28; CICR Note no. 419, "Remarques complémentaires au rapport technique sur le visite aux détenus politiques du Camp militaire Hardy, à Thysville," December 30; Thudichum to Bomboko, January 16; CICR Note no. 479, "Concerne déténus politiques," January 17, all in B AG 225 229 (001–007), IRC.

19. For an innovative study of this Cold War issue see Penny M. Van Eschen, *Satchmo Blows Up the World: Jazz Ambassadors Play the Cold War* (Cambridge, MA: Harvard University Press, 2004), esp. 59–91.

20. Canup to Herter, November 25, 11–1760, box 1957, DOS, RG 59, NA.

21. Tshombe Papers (Royal Museum for Central Africa, Tervuren, Belgium), box 6 (Trinquier) and box 12 (diplomatic mission in Paris).

22. McIlvaine to Herter, December 2, 12–160, box 1957; Timberlake to Herter, January 9, 1–161; Canup to Herter, January 20, 1–1361, box 1958, all in DOS, RG 59, NA. Dayal to Abbas, January 8, 217-4-2, UN.

23. Tshombe to Baudouin, January 12, full text in *LCM,* 533–534.

24. *LCM,* 273–280; Wigny's instructions for Ambassador Rothschild (quote), January 9, 1961, box M 10, vol. 30, Wigny Papers, UCL, Louvain-la-Neuve; Burden to Herter, January 13, 1–1361, box 1958, DOS Memorandum for Herter, January 13, box 1954, DOS, RG 59, NA.

25. Herter to UN, Elisabethville, and Leopoldville, January 11, 1–161, box 1958, DOS, RG 59, NA; CIA to Devlin, December 31, *FRUS 1964–1968,* vol. 23, 71–72.

26. Satterthwaite to Herter, January 17, Bureau of African Affairs, Records relating to the Congo and Congo Working Group, 1960–1964, box 5, RG 59, NA.

27. IR, 18–19, 23, 43–48; Interview and Meeting Summary, Devlin, August 20, 1975, 07-M-83, box 53, CC.

28. See especially Devlin to CIA, January 26, 1961, *FRUS 1964–1968,* vol. 23, 83–85.

29. Larry Devlin, *Chief of Station, Congo: A Memoir of 1960–67* (New York, Perseus Books, 2007), 124; Madeleine G. Kalb, *The Congo Cables: The Cold War in Africa—from Eisenhower to Kennedy* (New York: Macmillan Co., 1982), 79–80; Richard D. Mahoney, *JFK: Ordeal in Africa* (New York: Oxford University Press, 1983), 31, 48; Harriman to Secretary of State, September 13, *FRUS 1958–1960,* vol. 14, 486–487; and Lise A. Namikas, *Battleground Africa: The Cold War in the Congo, 1960–1965* (Stanford, CA: Stanford University Press, 2013).

30. James Srodes, *Allen Dulles: Master of Spies* (Washington, DC: Henry Regnery and Co., 1999), 508, 510; IR, 120–121; Allen Dulles memorandum, June 1, 1961, *FRUS 1961–1963,* Microfiche Supplement to vols. 10–12, no. 265. But see also Peter Grose, *Gentleman Spy: The Life of Allen Dulles* (Boston: Houghton Mifflin, 1994), 512.

31. Kalb, *Congo Cables,* 194–195.

32. Thomas Kanza, *Conflict in the Congo: The Rise and Fall of Lumumba* (London: Penguin Books, 1972), 320; Mahoney, *JFK,* 63–64; Rajeshwar Dayal, *A Life of Our Times* (Hyderabad: Orient Longman, 1998), 441, 446–447; Analytic Chronology, Supplement, March 9, 1961, 3–5, box 27, NSF Files, JFK.

33. Timberlake to Herter, October 25, 10–2060, box 1957; Bohlen to Herter, December 6, 12–160, box 533; and Herter to Brussels, Leopoldville, and Elisabethville, January 19, 1–1361, box 1958, all in DOS, RG 59, NA.

34. See the discussions in *FRUS 1961–1963,* vol. 20, 24–49; African Report, December 31, 1960, 40–41, Pre Presidential Papers, box 1073, JFK. Also Nitze to Cleveland, January 31, 1961, 611.70G (microfilm); Conversation with Belgian Ambassador, February 2, 1961, 1–461, box 518, both in DOS; "Talking Paper circulated to Congo Task Force, March 1," Congo Working Committee, 1961, box: Circular Instructions Bureau of Public Affairs, Lot Files 62D370 (11), RG 59, NA.

35. Dayal, *Life,* 455; Stevenson quoted from Memorandum: Dayal, March 20, Civilian Personnel, box 4, Congo Working Group, RG 59, NA; Mahoney, *JFK,* 62–69; Kalb, *Congo Cables,* 175; Sean Kelly, *America's Tyrant: The CIA and Mobutu of Zaire* (Washington, DC: American University Press, 1993), 70.

36. IR, 49; Devlin, *Chief of Station,* 127–129.

37. Devlin, *Chief of Station,* e.g. 57–58, 67, 88, 111, 145, 149–150, 154, 160.

38. Stephen R. Weissman, "'An Extraordinary Rendition,'" *Intelligence and National Security* 25 (2010): quoted at 209; IR, 17.

39. IR, 49–50.

40. Devlin to CIA, January 17, 1961, *FRUS 1964–1968,* vol. 23, 79; Devlin (alias Victor Hedgeman), Testimony, 8/21/75, 112–113, HM; Devlin, *Chief of Station,* 96; Weissman, "'Rendition,'" 218–222.

41. Patrick Coyne, Summary of Recommendations, January 4, 1961, Foreign Intelligence Advisory Board Briefing Material, box 94, Presidents Office Files, JFK.

12. KILLING LUMUMBA

1. Dupret to Wigny, January 13 (46, 49), January 14 (51), 15 (57), January 17 (61, 65), all conveying messages of Lahaye and his assistant, 18.297, FPSFA.
2. IR, 49.
3. "Compte rendu de l'entretien [January 13] de M. le Ministre des Affaires étrangères avec MM. les ambassadeurs des États-Unis et de France, ainsi qu'avec le conseiller de l'ambassade de Grande-Bretagne," January 14, box M 10, vol. 30, Wigny Papers, UCL, Louvain-la-Neuve.
4. Dupret to Wigny, January 14 (53), 18.297, FPSFA. As a result of the weekend, Dupret's cable wasn't transmitted to Elisabethville until Monday, January 16. The Belgian military in Brazzaville had radio communication with their colleagues in Elisabethville, while the Belgian diplomats in Africa could only communicate through the Brussels ministry of foreign affairs. Facsimile of Lahaye's radio message to the gendarmerie in Jacques Brassinne, *Enquête sur la mort de Patrice Lumumba* (unpublished PhD diss., Université Libre de Bruxelles, 1990), vol. 3, annexes (9.1 and 9.2).
5. G. Heinz and H. Donnay, *Lumumba: The Last Fifty Days* (New York: Grove Press, 1969), 97.
6. Transfer scheme in Lahaye's handwriting: first published in the report of the Sovereign National Conference of the Congo, 1991. The original was confiscated with some other documents at Nendaka's residence in Brussels in 2001 by the Belgian parliamentary commission and published in its report. See facsimile in *LCM*, 679.
7. Minaf to Marlière and Lahaye, January 10, FPSFA; Loos to Marlière, January 14, Loos Papers, Royal Museum for Central Africa, Tervuren, Belgium; d'Aspremont to Crener (Belgian consul general in Elisabethville), with personal message for Tshombe, January 16 (Minaf 06416), FPSFA, facsimile of the handwritten draft and of the printed message in *LCM*, 681–683; and see *LCM*, chap. 11. The January 16 cable was not written before 5:10 P.M. in Brussels and did not arrive before 6:10 in Elisabethville (see technical discussion in *LCM*, 309–316).
8. Dayal to Hammarskjöld, January 18, 217-4-2, UN.
9. "La mission de M. Delvaux au Katanga. Léo et Katanga se retrouvent. Accord réciproque pour la Table Ronde. Le téléphone refonctionne entre MM. Kasa-Vubu et Tshombe," *Le Courrier d'Afrique*, January 17.
10. Quoted from an interview with Tshombe in *Pourquoi Pas?*, January 31, 1964. This issue of the magazine was seized by the Belgian government; a copy is to be found in B AG 225 229 (001–007), IRC. See also Jacques Brassinne and Jean Kestergat, *Qui a tué Patrice Lumumba?* (Paris: Éditions Duculot, 1991), 115–117.
11. Dupret to Wigny, January 28 (140), conveying a message of Denis, 18.297, FPSFA; Bloock (Belgian consulate general in Elisabethville) to Wigny, February 13 (133), 18.290, FPSFA.
12. Canup to Herter, January 20, 1–1361, box 1958, DOS, RG 59, NA.

13. Dupret to Wigny, January 28 (140), conveying a message of Denis, 18.297, FPSFA.

14. Jules Gérard-Libois, *Katanga Secession* (Madison: University of Wisconsin Press, 1966), 143; Francis Monheim, *Mobutu, l'homme seul* (Brussels: Éditions Actuelles, 1962), 104–106, 109; Jean Van den Bosch, *Pré-Zaïre. Le cordon mal coupé. Document* (Brussels: Le Cri, 1986), 104, 123, 185, 193.

15. Comité International de la Croix-Rouge Note no. 415, "Rapport technique sur la visite aux détenus politiques du camp militaire Hardy, à Thysville, effectuée le 27 décembre 1960," December 28, B AG 225 229 (001–007), IRC.

16. Brassinne and Kestergat, *Qui a tué Lumumba?*, 132–135.

17. Daniel Sack, *Moral Re-Armament: The Reinvention of an American Religious Movement* (New York: Palgrave Macmillan, 2009), 149–150, 158.

18. Some happened to be at the airport by chance. The Belgian commander of the gendarmerie, his adviser Colonel Frédéric Van de Walle, and the Belgian chief of staff of the Katangan secretary of defense had just returned with their plane from a two-day inspection visit to northern Katanga. Van de Walle does not seem to have played a role in the preparation of the transfer, as Ludo De Witte, *De moord op Lumumba* (Leuven: Van Halewyck, 1999), 214, argued.

19. *L'Essor du Katanga,* January 18, 19, and 20.

20. For the last hours of Lumumba, Okito, and Mpolo, see Brassinne and Kestergat, *Qui a tué Lumumba?*; De Witte, *De moord;* and *LCM*.

21. See Brassinne, *Enquête,* vol. 4: Témoignages, esp. the interviews with Julien Gat (May 20, 1987), Gerard Soete (August 28, 1987, and June 8, 1988), and Frans Verscheure (April 18, 1988); and Chambre des représentants de Belgique, *Enquête parlementaire visant à déterminer les circonstances exactes de l'assassinat de Patrice Lumumba et l'implication éventuelle des responsables belges dans celui-ci,* DOC 50 0312/006, November 16, 2001, 682–827.

22. Interview with Etienne Ugeux (June 15, 1987), in Brassinne, *Enquête,* vol. 4: Témoignages. *LCM,* 423–429.

23. *L'Essor du Katanga,* January 19; the paper reported the absence of another minister.

24. BBC documentary, *The Assassination of Patrice Lumumba,* 2001 (available on YouTube). Gerard Soete recounted this scene in his autobiographic novel, *Het einde van de grijshemden: Onze koloniale politie* (Zedelgem, Belgium: Uitgeverij Flandria Nostra, 1993), 90–106.

25. See John Stockwell, *In Search of Enemies: A CIA Story* (New York: Norton, 1978), 105; Kevin C. Dunn, *Imagining the Congo: The International Relations of Identity* (New York: Palgrave Macmillan, 2003), 96; John Prados, *Safe for Democracy: The Secret Wars of the CIA* (Chicago: Ivan R. Dee, 2006), 278; and David W. Doyle, *True Men and Traitors: From the OSS to the CIA; My Life in the Shadows* (New York: John Wiley, 2001), 145.

26. Proceedings of the Belgian Senate, Session 1960–1961, January 24, 182.

27. Weber to Lefebure, February 17, *LCM,* 531.

28. Munongo Press Conference, February 13, box 142, Cordier Papers, Columbia University.

29. Paul-Henri Spaak, *The Continuing Battle: Memoirs of a European, 1936–1966* (Boston: Little, Brown, 1971), 344–353.

30. Quoted from Heinz and Donnay, *Lumumba,* 188.
31. Paris to Secretary of State, January 15; Brussels to Washington, March 2, 123-Burden, box 315, both in DOS, RG 59, NA; Burden Oral History, 35, DDE.
32. Hammarskjöld, *Markings,* trans. W. H. Auden, with a foreword (New York: Knopf, 1964), xviii–xix, 200–205; Carl F. Hovde, "The Dag Hammarskjöld–John Steinbeck Correspondence," *Development Dialogue* 1–2 (1997): 124. Roger Lipsey, in *Hammarskjöld: A Life* (Ann Arbor: University of Michigan Press, 2013), 458, 467–468, 484, has a doubtful reading.
33. Verbatim record of the October 2, 2000, interview, in folder 01.13.77, Jules Gérard-Libois Papers, Royal Museum for Central Africa, Tervuren, Belgium. For the second meeting, June 19, 2001, see a reference in Sven Augustijnen, *Spectres* (Brussels: ASA Publishers, 2011), 128.

EPILOGUE

1. Baudouin to Spaak, June 1, 1962, doc. 6488, Spaak Papers, Fondation P.H.Spaak, Brussels.
2. Agatha Christie, *Murder on the Orient Express: A Hercule Poirot Mystery* (Collins: London, 1934).
3. Dupret to Wigny, January 24 (110), 18.297, FPSFA.
4. IR, 55n.
5. David Doyle, *True Men and Traitors: From the OSS to the CIA, My Life in the Shadows* (New York: John Wiley, 2001), 148; John Prados, *Safe for Democracy: The Secret Wars of the CIA* (Chicago: Ivan R. Dee, 2006), 277–278; IR, 51; Transcript of testimony by Devlin (under pseudonym of Hedgeman) to Senate Intelligence Committee, 8/21/75, p. 70, HM; Loch K. Johnson, *Bombs, Bugs, Drugs, and Thugs: Intelligence and America's Quest for Security* (New York: NYU Press, 2000), 102.

Essay on Sources

HISTORIOGRAPHY

Detailed accounts of the circumstances leading to the death of Lumumba have been available for almost fifty years. New research has incrementally enlarged the information we have, but the accepted and powerful interpretation of the Lumumba assassination has remained constant for many years. This interpretation, mostly an English-language phenomenon, has several elements, some mutually allied, some competing. A first element highlights the American CIA and its promotion of the military leader Joseph Mobutu, who indeed gained full power in the Congo in 1965 and ruled repressively into the 1990s. This view is elaborated in several excellent monographs that appeared in the aftermath of the Vietnam War and the Watergate scandals when American foreign policy was frequently regarded as both malign and incompetent: Stephen R. Weissman, *American Foreign Policy in the Congo 1960–1964* (Ithaca, NY: Cornell University Press, 1974); Madeleine G. Kalb, *The Congo Cables: The Cold War in Africa—from Eisenhower to Kennedy* (New York: Macmillan Co., 1982); and Richard D. Mahoney, *JFK: Ordeal in Africa* (New York: Oxford University Press, 1983). More recently these views have been supplemented by Lise Namikas, *Battleground Africa: The Cold War in the Congo, 1960–1965* (Stanford, CA: Stanford University Press, 2013). Through its outstanding use of Russian sources, *Battleground Africa* brings to the forefront what had to be less explicit in the earlier writing— the role of the USSR in the Cold War standoff in the Congo. An excellent summary of these notions is Robert B. Rakove, *Kennedy, Johnson, and the Nonaligned World* (New York: Cambridge University Press, 2013), 20–21.

Another element in the accepted interpretation asserts that the security services of the colonial powers, and in particular elements of the Belgian government, perpetrated the murder to maintain imperial prerogatives. This approach received compelling confirmation in a book by Ludo De Witte, *The Assassination of Lumumba* (New York: Verso, 2001), which was translated into English from a French rendering of the original Dutch, *De Moord op Lumumba* (Leuven: Van Halewyck, 1999).

A third element, contributed by scholars in Africana studies, finds the vicious policies of Belgium and the United States typical of Western interest in the continent. These scholars look to the past to explain the plight of Africa today, and suggest that if Lumumba had not been killed, the Congo's subsequent history would have been dramatically changed.

Our own understanding of the Congo in 1960 and 1961 has absorbed this scheme of interpretation. Nonetheless, we believe that it has reduced the murder to the expression of a crude global American anticommunism and deliberate and conspiratorial planning by the US and the Belgian security services. The received story is a morality play about the failed Cold War ideals of the West in respect to colonial peoples.

Instead, we shift the perspective, partly as a result of the exploitation of novel archival material, partly as a result of reevaluating material. The Soviet-US contest in the Cold War certainly established the context in which the events in the Congo played themselves out, but the two superpowers had a limited role in circumstances on the ground. The Soviets engaged in angry rhetoric about neocolonialism but in 1960 were circumspect in the actions they took. The Americans also refused to intervene in a crucial way. Their murderous clandestine doings were limited to two operatives and two hired killers of the CIA, and we downplay the organization's autonomous impact.

Rather, in understanding the Cold War context of policy, we emphasize the commitment of the United States to NATO, headed at the time by a Belgian secretary-general, Paul-Henri Spaak. This commitment looked to defend Western Europe from the Soviet Union, and decisively shaped the response of the Eisenhower administration to Lumumba.

In addition to the NATO concern of the Americans, we examine three other groups involved in the assassination, and show that their roles differ from what earlier studies have alleged. The UN and its intervention are described in detail. The organization wanted to establish its bona fides as a new force in world affairs and, unlike the Soviet Union or the United States, put a large bureaucracy in the Congo and controlled an international army there. Readers are invited to examine our view of the UN and Dag Hammarskjöld in contrast to a sunny and more conventional view most recently presented in Roger Lipsey, in *Hammarskjöld: A Life* (Ann Arbor: University of Michigan Press, 2013). We also give independent responsibility to the anti-Lumumba Africans. They acted on their own and had a far better sense of their country than the intervening forces. We explore the varying motivations and anxieties of these men, and the complications of their politics. We refuse to see them only as Western stooges and refrain from making a hero of Lumumba, though we recognize his singular abilities. Finally, we illuminate the Belgian response, dominated by its experienced colonial bureaucracy of many thousands of men. They were still in the Congo in early July, and began to return in early September. Their expertise in the country far exceeded that of America or the USSR.

The positions of the participants are uniquely interwoven. Eisenhower responded to a danger to NATO, as the UN tried to vault into a new worldly position. Frustrated by Belgium's seeming capitulation to the United States and the United Nations, King Baudouin compromised his constitutional monarchy to keep Belgium in the Congo. The Congo's own leading politicians, such as Joseph Kasa-Vubu, Joseph Mobutu, and Jason Sendwe, confounded all the Western entities in pursuing their own goals.

THE COLD WAR

The best study of diplomacy during the period is Marc Trachtenberg, *A Constructed Peace* (Princeton, NJ: Princeton University Press, 1999). A thought-provoking comprehensive treatment is Odd Arne Westad, *The Global Cold War: Third World Interventions and the Making of Our Times* (New York: Cambridge University Press, 2005). A more recent overview with an outstanding bibliography is Campbell Craig and Fredrik Logevall, *America's Cold War: The Politics of Insecurity* (Cambridge, MA: Harvard University Press, 2009).

In stressing politics, this book implicitly sets aside economic interpretations, one type of which, for example, can be found in David N. Gibbs, *The Political Economy of Third World Intervention* (Chicago: University of Chicago Press, 1991) and John Kent, *America, the UN and Decolonisation: Cold War Conflict in the Congo* (London: Routledge, 2010). We have also largely stepped out of disputes about a cultural construal of the Lumumba murder. Nonetheless, just as we do not want to diminish an economic treatment, we do not mean to diminish the cultural outlook exemplified by Kevin C. Dunn, *Imagining the Congo: The International Relations of Identity* (New York: Palgrave Macmillan, 2003); Bambi Ceuppens, *Congo Made in Flanders? Koloniale Vlaamse Visies op "Blank" en "Zwart" in Belgisch Congo* (Gent: Academia Press, 2003); and Lieve Spaas, *How Belgium Colonized the Mind of the Congo: Seeking the Memory of an African People* (Lewiston, NY: Edwin Mellen Press, 2007).

COMPARATIVE ANALYSIS OF CULTURE

International Cold War history that links up with decolonization touches on the concerns of Africanists and the comparative analysis of culture found in subaltern studies. We are aware of the linguistic minefields that must be traversed even in briefly mentioning some of these issues. Helpful to us in framing our own ideas have been Henrietta L. Moore and Todd Sanders, "Anthropology and Epistemology," in *Anthropology in Theory: Issues in Epistemology,* ed. Moore and Sanders (Oxford: Blackwell, 2006), 1–21; essays by Frederick Cooper: "Conflict and Connection: Rethinking Colonial African History," *American Historical Review* 99 (1994): 1516–1545; "Between Metropole and Colony: Rethinking a Research Agenda" (with Ann Laura Stoler), in *Tensions of Empire: Colonial Cultures in a Bourgeois World,* ed. Cooper and Stoler (Berkeley: University of California Press, 1997), 1–56; and "Possibility and Constraint: African Independence in Historical Perspective," *Journal of African History* 49 (2008): 167–196.

Also the following: Basil Davidson, *The Black Man's Burden: Africa and the Curse of the Nation-State* (New York: Random House, 1992); two essays in volume 50 (1994) of the *Journal of Anthropological Research:* Christian Krohn-Hansen, "The Anthropology of Violent Interaction,"

367–381, and Andrea L. Smith, "Colonialism and the Poisoning of Europe: Towards an Anthropology of Colonists," 383–393; Wyatt Mac-Gaffey, "Changing Representations in Central African History," *Journal of African History* 46 (2005): 189–207; the introduction and essays 1 and 7 in James Ferguson, *Global Shadows: Africa in the Neoliberal World Order* (Durham, NC: Duke University Press, 2006); Gareth Austin, "Reciprocal Comparison and African History: Tackling Conceptual Eurocentrism in the Study of Africa's Economic Past," *African Studies Review* 50 (2007): 1–28; Benjamin Rubbers, "The Story of a Tragedy: How People in Haut-Katanga Interpret the Post-Colonial History of Congo," *Journal of Modern African Studies* 47 (2009): 267–289; and the introduction in Elleke Boehmer and Sarah De Mul, eds., *The Postcolonial Low Countries: Literature, Colonialism, and Multiculturalism* (Lanham, MD: Lexington Books, 2012), 1–22.

HISTORY OF THE CONGO

Surveys include Martin Meredith, *The State of Africa: A History of Fifty Years of Independence* (London: Free, 2006); Isodore Ndaywel è Nziem, *Histoire générale du Congo: De l'héritage ancien à la République Démocratique* (Paris: De Boeck and Larcier, 1998); Georges Nzongola-Ntalaja, *The Congo from Leopold to Kabila: A People's History* (New York: Zed Books, 2002); and David Van Reybrouck, *Congo: The Epic History of a People* (New York: HarperCollins, 2014). Adam Hochschild's *King Leopold's Ghost: A Tale of Greed, Terror, and Heroism in Colonial Africa* (New York: Houghton Mifflin, 1998) should be supplemented with Daniel Van Groenweghe, *Rood Rubber. Leopold II en zijn Kongo* (Leuven: Van Halewyck, 1985, rev. 2010). An excellent historiographical study is Guy Vanthemsche, "The Historiography of Belgian Colonialism in the Congo," in *Europe and the World in European Historiography*, ed. Csaba Lévai (Pisa, Italy: University of Pisa Press, 2006), 89–119. The most recent survey is his *Belgium and the Congo, 1885–1980* (New York: Cambridge University Press, 2012). See also Jean Stengers, *Congo: Mythes et réalités* (Brussels: Éditions Racine, 2007), and I. Goddeeris and S. Kiangu, "Congomania in Academia: Recent Historical Research on the Belgian Colonial Past," *BMGN-LCHR (Low Countries Historical Review)*, 2011: 54–74.

INDEPENDENCE

Details about events in the Congo from the late 1950s to independence can be found in a number of estimable and empirically rich older histories. They include René Lemarchand, *Political Awakening in the Belgian Congo* (Berkeley: University of California Press, 1964); Catherine Hoskyns, *The Congo since Independence, January 1960–December 1961* (London: Oxford University Press, 1965); Crawford Young, *Politics in the Congo: Decolonization and Independence* (Princeton, NJ: Princeton University Press, 1965); Herbert F. Weiss, *Political Protest in the Congo: The Parti Solidaire Africain during the Independence Struggle* (Princeton, NJ: Princeton University Press, 1967). Two important revisions of the Congo crisis, based on new material, are Jean-Claude Willame, *Patrice Lumumba: La crise congolaise revisitée* (Paris: Éditions Karthala, 1990); and Ludo De Witte, *Krisis in Kongo: De rol van de Verenigde Naties, de regering-Eyskens en het koningshuis in de omverwerping van Lumumba en de opkomst van Mobutu* (Leuven: Van Halewyck, 1996). More recent studies include Zana Etambala, *Congo 55/65: Van koning Boudewijn tot president Mobutu* (Tielt: Lannoo, 1999), and *De teloorgang van een modelkolonie: Belgisch Congo 1958–1960* (Leuven: Acco, 2008).

THE CONGO'S POLITICIANS

Notes to the individual chapters indicate the material we have used in portraying Lumumba. We recommend two opposed biographies of Mobutu: a critical Sean Kelly, *America's Tyrant: The CIA and Mobutu of Zaire* (Washington, DC: American University Press, 1993); and a sympathetic Francis Monheim, *Mobutu, l'homme seul* (Brussels: Éditions Actuelles, 1962). A. B. Assensoh and Yvette M. Alex-Assensoh, *African Military History and Politics: Coups and Ideological Incursions, 1900–Present* (New York: Palgrave Macmillan, 2001), suggests the wrong way Mobutu has been interpreted. The outstanding book on Katanga and its politicians is Jules Gérard-Libois, *Katanga Secession* (Madison: University of Wisconsin Press, 1966). On Jason Sendwe, see Kabuya Lumuna Sando, *Nord-Katanga 1960–64: De la sécession à la guerre civile. Le meurtre des chefs* (Paris: L'Harmattan, 1992). Wyatt MacGaffey, *Kongo Political Cul-*

ture: The Conceptual Challenge of the Particular (Bloomington: Indiana University Press, 2000), alludes to many aspects of politicking in the Congo, including "the palaver." In *United Nations: Sacred Drama,* by Conor Cruise O'Brien and Felix Topolski (New York: Simon & Schuster, 1968), O'Brien includes an outstanding contemporary essay on palavering as westerners understood it: David Brokensha, "The Leopard-Skin Priest," 301–308. Still useful is Pierre Artigue, *Qui sont les leaders Congolais?* (Brussels: Éditions Europe-Afrique, 1961).

BELGIAN POLICY

No comprehensive monograph exists on the Belgian position in the unfolding Congo crisis. Belgian policy in the summer of 1960 has been dealt with in the memoirs of some important players: Jean Van den Bosch (the Belgian ambassador in Leopoldville), *Pré-Zaïre, le cordon mal coupé: Document* (Brussels: Le Cri, 1986) was an eye-opener, more than Gaston Eyskens (the prime minister), *De Memoires* (Tielt, Belgium: Lannoo, 1993). An outstanding source for the mutiny and the Belgian military intervention is Louis-François Vanderstraeten, *De la Force publique à l'Armée nationale congolaise: Histoire d'une mutinerie, Juillet 1960* (Brussels: Académie Royale de Belgique, 1993). See also the biography of the last minister of colonies: Godfried Kwanten, *August-Edmond De Schryver 1898–1991: Politieke biografie van een gentleman-staatsman* (Leuven: Leuven University Press, 2001).

The role of the Belgians in Katanga has been dealt with in Gérard-Libois, *Katanga Secession,* and extensively illustrated in Frédéric Vandewalle, *Mille et quatre jours. Contes du Zaïre et du Shaba* (Brussels: F. Vandewalle, 1974–1975). In this not widely known book the author (a Belgian colonel, the former chief of the Belgo-Congolese Sûreté, and adviser to Katanga's gendarmerie) used the archives of Jacques Bartelous (chief of staff of Tshombe) and Henri Crener (the Belgian consul general in Elisabethville), which he managed to preserve after their expulsion from Katanga.

AMERICAN POLICY

For the foreign policy of Eisenhower and Kennedy see the aforementioned books by Weissman, *American Foreign Policy in the Congo;* Kalb,

Congo Cables; Mahoney, *JFK: Ordeal in Africa;* and Namikas, *Battle-ground Africa.* Peter Schraeder, "Sapphire Anniversary Reflections on the Study of United States Foreign Policy towards Africa," *Journal of Modern African Studies* 41 (2003): 139–152, reviews some forty-five books and gives a comprehensive sense of scholarship in the field at the turn of century. On decolonization there are David Ryan and Victor Pungong, eds., *The United States and Decolonization: Power and Freedom* (New York: St. Martin's Press, 2000); Kathryn Statler and Andrew L. Johns, eds., *The Eisenhower Administration, the Third World, and the Global-ization of the Cold War* (Lanham, MD: Rowman & Littlefield, 2006); Philip E. Muehlenbeck, *Betting on the Africans: John F. Kennedy's Courting of African Nationalist Leaders* (New York: Oxford University Press, 2012); and Robert J. McMahon, ed., *The Cold War in the Third World* (New York: Oxford University Press, 2013). On the UN, Caroline Pruden, *Conditional Partners: Eisenhower, the United Nations, and the Search for a Permanent Peace* (Baton Rouge: LSU Press, 1998).

The State Department's official series *Foreign Relations of the United States* (Washington, DC: Government Printing Office), with various ti-tles and dates of publication, is an invaluable resource. We have cited this crucial set of published documents, with editorial comment, as *FRUS,* identifying the document and date, volume number, and pages.

THE UNITED NATIONS

A recent history is Stanley Meisler, *United Nations: A History,* rev. ed. (New York: Grove Press, 2011). Readers might also examine Evan Lu-ard, *A History of the United Nations,* vol. 2 (New York: St. Martin's Press, 1989), 198–316. The most recent literature looks more at words than acts: Mark Mazower, *No Enchanted Palace: The End of Imperial-ism and the Ideological Origins of the United Nations* (Princeton, NJ: Princeton University Press, 2009); and Samuel Mohn, *The Last Utopia: Human Rights in History* (Cambridge, MA: Harvard University Press, 2010). A first-rate introduction to peacekeeping is Norrie MacQueen, *The United Nations, Peace Operations and the Cold War,* 2nd ed. (Har-low, UK: Pearson Education Limited, 2011). On the Congo operation (ONUC) see Lyman M. Tondel Jr., ed., *The Legal Aspects of the United Nations Action in the Congo: Background Papers and Proceedings of the*

Second Hammarskjöld Forum (Dobbs Ferry, NY: Oceana Publications, 1963); Georges Abi-Saab, *The United Nations Operation in the Congo, 1960–1964* (Oxford: Oxford University Press, 1978); and Rosalyn Higgins, *United Nations Peacekeeping, 1946–1967: Documents and Commentary*, vol. 3, *Africa* (Oxford: Oxford University Press, 1980). A reliable guide to material about Hammarskjöld is Manuel Fröhlich, *Political Ethics and the United Nations: Dag Hammarskjöld as Secretary-General* (London: Routledge, 2008). Our treatment of Hammarskjöld, integrating belief and action, should be compared to Jodok Troy, "Dag Hammarskjöld: An International Civil Servant Uniting Mystics and Realistic Diplomatic Engagement," *Diplomacy & Statecraft* 21(2010): 434–450; and Lipsey, *Hammarskjöld*, 367–497. On Ralph Bunche, especially to be recommended are Pearl T. Robinson, "Ralph Bunche and African Studies: Reflections on the Politics of Knowledge," *African Studies Review* 51 (2008): 1–16, and the essays in Robert A. Hill and Edmond J.Keller, eds., *Trustee for the Human Community: Ralph J. Bunche, the United Nations, and the Decolonization of Africa* (Athens: Ohio University Press, 2010).

SOVIET POLICY

While we have interpreted Russian moves from Western sources, we have not ourselves examined the available USSR archives. For this material we are mainly indebted to two existing English-language studies: Sergey Mazov, *A Distant Front in the Cold War: The USSR in West Africa and the Congo, 1956–1964* (Palo Alto, CA: Stanford University Press, 2010), and Namikas, *Battleground Africa*. These works note the lack of material on the Congo in 1960, and argue on the basis of what is available that—as we believe—Soviet aims were limited. Interested readers are also urged to explore our differences with Mazov, especially over non-Russian materials. Readers should also examine Aleksandr Fursenko and Timothy Naftali, *Khrushchev's Cold War: The Inside Story of an American Adversary* (New York: Norton, 2006), 292–322, which compellingly joins Castro and Lumumba. Of less pertinence to us is Ilya V. Gaiduk, *Divided Together: The United States and the Soviet Union in the United Nations, 1945–1965* (Stanford, CA: Stanford University Press, 2012).

Mazov has also contributed to the publication of the documentation of Soviet activities in Africa: Sergey V. Mazov, *Politika SSSR v Zapadnoi Afrike, 1956–1964: Neizvestnye stranitsy istorii kholodnoi voiny* [The policy of the USSR in West Africa, 1956–1964: Unknown pages of Cold War history] (Moscow: Nauka, 2008); and a document collection: *Rossia i Afrika. Dokumenty i materialy. XVIII v.–1960. T. II. 1917–1960* [Russia and Africa. Documents and materials. 18th century–1960. Vol. 2, 1917–1960], ed. Apollon B. Davidson and Sergey V. Mazov.

<h2 style="text-align:center">THE CIA</h2>

Essential material pertaining to the CIA is published in the US Senate report on assassinations prepared by the committee headed by Frank Church: Interim Report of the Senate Select Committee, *Alleged Assassination Plots Involving Foreign Leaders* (Washington, DC: Government Printing Office, 1975) (cited as IR), 13–70. Supplementing this report is *FRUS 1964–1968*, vol. 23, *Congo, 1960–1968* (Washington, DC: Government Printing Offce, 2013), a unique volume released to compensate for the deficiencies and omissions of *FRUS 1958–1960*, vol. 14, *Africa, 1958–1960;* and *FRUS 1961–1963*, vol. 20, *Congo Crisis.* However, *FRUS 1964–1968*, vol. 23, is still incomplete, and in part censored.

An adjunct to IR and *FRUS 1964–1968*, vol. 23, is the history of the CIA prepared by committee staff member Anne Karalekas, published in *The Central Intelligence Agency: History and Documents*, ed. William M. Leary (Tuscaloosa: University of Alabama Press, 1984), esp. 54–75. The best study of the CIA is Tim Weiner, *Legacy of Ashes: The History of the CIA* (New York: Doubleday, 2007). On the politics of the CIA an excellent recent survey is Joshua Rovner, *Fixing the Facts: National Security and the Politics of Intelligence* (Ithaca, NY: Cornell University Press, 2011).

Available at the National Archives in College Park, Maryland, is the CIA-sponsored five-volume biography of Allen Dulles, *Allen Welsh Dulles as Director of Central Intelligence: 26 February, 1953–29 November, 1961*, by Wayne G. Jackson, although we have not found such sponsored work to be of much help. Kenneth Michael Absher, Michael C. Desch, Roman Popadiuk, et al., *Privileged and Confidential: The Secret History of the President's Intelligence Advisory Board* (Lexington: University of Kentucky Press, 2012) comprehensively treats the complaints about Dulles, 14–74. Evan Thomas's *Ike's Bluff: President Eisenhower's Secret Battle to Save the World* (New York: Little Brown, 2012), 302–307, has an outstanding section on Allen Dulles; and Stephen Kinzer's *The Brothers: John Foster Dulles, Allen Dulles, and Their Secret World War* (New York: Henry Holt, 2013) is excellent in its treatment of Allen Dulles's personality and his stewardship of the CIA, although his case study of Lumumba cannot be relied on.

As we have noted, the dominant interpretation in the American literature on Lumumba gives great weight to the CIA and particularly to its influence on Joseph Mobutu in September 1960. Here two examples are relevant. The interested reader should examine the treatment by Weissman in *American Foreign Policy in the Congo*, 96–97; his "Opening the Secret Files on Lumumba's Murder," *Washington Post*, July 21, 2002; his "'An Extraordinary Rendition,'" *Intelligence and National Security* 25 (2010): 198–222; and his "What Really Happened in Congo," *Foreign Affairs* 93, no. 4 (July/August 2014): 14–24. Like Weissman, Kalb's *Congo Cables*, 89–97, made declarations of CIA influence on Mobutu. Our own text downplays the memories of CIA employees that have been used to construct the interpretation. Most important is the memoir of Larry Devlin, *Chief of Station, Congo: A Memoir of 1960–67* (New York: Perseus Books, 2007), which brought together his many prior recollections. *Chief of Station* was written when Devlin was in his mid-eighties and was based on Kalb's book. Devlin copied parts of it without attribution and contributed a commentary. See, for example, *Chief of Station*, 34ff, and *Congo Cables*, 5ff. Devlin, moreover, told stories that are contradicted by the contemporary evidence, or were contradicted by other stories that he told. *FRUS 1964–1968*, vol. 23, 29–30, has more on Devlin's accounts.

We do not reject the growing role of the CIA in bolstering Mobutu after September 14, 1960, but see no convincing evidence for the CIA's decisive intervention on September 14, or for clear anti-Lumumba policies on the part of Mobutu in September 1960. We believe that in the memories of CIA sources events that took place over a series of months were melded.

In our view the circumstances of the Lumumba murder were confused. In its immediate aftermath the CIA took credit for it, despite the

Agency's inept administration and execution of covert operations. Then, when the assassination became problematic in the 1970s, the CIA disavowed its former avowals. All of this makes it more than difficult if one is out to establish the truth. Our notes have more on these issues. Readers must judge for themselves if our use of recollections of CIA functionaries is justified.

THE MURDER

The story of Lumumba's jailing in December and murder in January has been subject to much debate, and the historiography is discussed in Luc De Vos, Emmanuel Gerard, Jules Gérard-Libois, and Philippe Raxhon, *Lumumba: De complotten? De moord* (Leuven, 2004) (cited as *LCM*).

Three important works, however, need to be mentioned separately: G. Heinz (alias for Jules Gérard-Libois) and H. Donnay (alias for Jacques Brassinne), *Lumumba: The Last Fifty Days* (New York: Grove Press, 1969, original in French, 1965); Jacques Brassinne, *Enquête sur la mort de Patrice Lumumba,* unpublished PhD diss., Université Libre de Bruxelles, 1990, published as Jacques Brassinne and Jean Kestergat, *Qui a tué Patrice Lumumba?* (Paris: Éditions Duculot, 1991); and Ludo De Witte's compelling *The Assassination of Lumumba.* De Witte based his account to some extent on Vandewalle, *Mille et quatre jours,* but added new material, especially for the Brazzaville scene, from material in the Belgium Foreign Office. De Witte presented his book as opposed to Brassinne's, although he also used much of the original material (and especially the interviews) released in Brassinne's PhD dissertation. As a Belgian civil servant, Brassinne was present in Katanga in January 1961.

UNPUBLISHED PRIMARY SOURCES

The United Nations Archives in New York City has extraordinarily large, rich, and minimally organized collections on its operations in the Congo. Spending some time with various hard-copy finding aids is the best way to prepare for research. In our own citations, we have identified documents and then cited the collection number followed by the box number and a final reference to a specific folder within a box—for example, Hammarskjöld to Cordier, October 6, 745-4-6, UN. An adjunct to the United Nations Archives are the papers of Ralph Bunche at UCLA and, especially, of Andrew Cordier at Columbia University in New York City. We were unable to find at the UN records of meetings; many such memoranda exist in the Cordier Papers.

The Eisenhower Presidential Library in Abilene, Kansas (DDE) holds the papers of the president and those of various officials in his administration. Less useful were similar materials at the Kennedy Presidential Library in Boston (JFK).

The United States Department of State (DOS) generated voluminous sets of documents about the Congo in this period, and they are at the National Archives in College Park, Maryland (NA). Other governmental entities, often only vaguely described but usually with some association with the State Department, also have their records cached at NA. An excellent guide to collections that we accessed is presented in Carl Ashley, "Research Resources for Diplomatic History," *Perspectives on History: Magazine of the American Historical Association,* May 2011, 55–56.

The Church Committee's work in IR and *FRUS 1964–1968,* vol. 23, constitutes the main body of evidence for investigating the Central Intelligence Agency in 1960. Some of the hearings of the committee and the testimony of officials are available for researchers, with much other material, at the NA (cited as CC). History Matters has produced a CD-ROM with the released testimony, otherwise only available at CC. We have cited this material from the CD-ROM as HM. A small collection of miscellaneous CIA documents (CIA) at NA is connected to the Church Committee materials. In addition, CIA operational cables from the period, again almost all extracted by the Church Committee, are on the CIA's website. Finally, the CREST system at NA allows researchers to access one of four computers with search engines that will call up all the intelligence documents declassified by the CIA's own procedures. In our case, we obtained a number of CIA National Security Council briefings for the Congo (CREST). Many other documents that we have used at the NA are still partially censored, including those we have successfully requested under the Freedom of Information Act.

Other collections in the United States did not prove helpful. For example, the following Princeton University materials were disappointing: the papers of UN ambassador Adlai Stevenson; those of Hammarskjöld's

assistant Henry Labouisse; and those of Under Secretary of State Livingston Merchant. Other material could not be found—for example, the
papers of Ambassador William Burden. The Averell Harriman Papers
are at the Library of Congress; those of Dean Acheson (of some interest
for 1960) at Yale University; of Robert Murphy (also of some worth for
that year) at the Hoover Institution. Also at the Hoover Institution are
the papers of individual scholars of Africa and the Congo. These collections are uncataloged and of varying value: Herbert Weiss; René Lemarchand; and Ernest Lefever. George Washington University houses
the National Security Archives, a significant collection of documents. The
Woodrow Wilson International Center convened a "critical oral history"
conference on the Congo crisis on September 23–24, 2004, under the auspices of the Cold War International History Project. The transcript of the
conference and a collection of documents are available on the center's
website.

Formal decisions of the Belgian government and a verbatim report of
some of their internal discussions can be found in the minutes of the cabinet meetings, a copy of which is kept in the National Archives in Brussels
(also available on its website, http://extranet.arch.be/lang_pvminister.
html). The Federal Public Service Foreign Affairs in Brussels (FPSFA)
holds the most important records of the Belgian government pertaining
to the independence of the Congo (diplomatic archives, African archives). In addition to these government collections there are important
individual collections available, located at various institutions. Of central importance are the papers of Prime Minister Gaston Eyskens (State
Archives in Leuven), of Minister of Foreign Affairs Pierre Wigny (Archives of the UCL Université Catholique de Louvain in Louvain-la-
Neuve), and of the Ministers of African Affairs August De Schryver
(KADOC Center for Religion, Culture, and Society in Leuven) and Harold d'Aspremont Lynden (National Archives in Brussels). The Wigny
Papers contain a complete collection of the daily memoranda of the minister; the d'Aspremont Papers hold the records of the Congo crisis desk
of the Belgian government in the summer of 1960, and the books of its
secret funds. The papers of these cabinet ministers should be comple-
mented by the papers of two key diplomats: Ambassador Jean Van den
Bosch (CEGESOMA Center for Historical Research on War and Con-

temporary Society in Brussels) and Robert Rothschild (Université Libre de Bruxelles); by the papers of a crucial civil servant, Jules Loos, adviser to the Ministry of African Affairs; and by the papers of a high-ranking army officer, Frédéric Vandewalle (Royal Museum for Central Africa in Tervuren, Belgium). The papers of Paul-Henri Spaak, minister of state and secretary-general of NATO, are kept in the Fondation P.H. Spaak in Brussels. We consulted a digital copy in the Archives of the UCL Université Catholique de Louvain. That university also holds the papers of Paul Van Zeeland, minister of state. The Archives of the Royal Palace hold the papers of Jacques Pirenne, adviser to the king; and of Joseph Pholien, chairman of the senate committee for African affairs. The State Archives in Arlon contain the papers of Maurice Brasseur, vice president of the senate. The papers of Jef Van Bilsen, Belgian adviser to President Kasa-Vubu, can be found at KADOC, and the papers of Edouard Pilaet, secret agent acting for private companies, at CEGESOMA.

Some of the collections of the Belgian government pertaining to the independence of the Congo remain closed, although they were opened to the experts on the parliamentary commission of 2000. The most important are the Baudouin Cabinet Papers at the Archives of the Royal Palace, and the State Security Archives in Brussels. Relevant material from these archives, as well as from other sources, was published in the records of the parliamentary inquiry: Chambre des représentants de Belgique, *Enquête parlementaire visant à déterminer les circonstances exactes de l'assassinat de Patrice Lumumba et l'implication éventuelle des responsables belges dans celui-ci*, DOC 50 0312/006, November 16, 2001, also available online. We have cited from the Dutch version of the jointly authored book on the experts' report, Luc De Vos, Emmanuel Gerard, Jules Gérard-Libois, and Philippe Raxhon, *Lumumba: De complotten? De moord* (Leuven: Davidsfonds, 2004) *(LCM)*. There is also a French version (*Les secrets de l'affaire Lumumba*, Brussels: Racine, 2005).

Congolese sources are scarce. Some are kept in the Royal Museum for Central Africa (Tervuren, Belgium): the Moïse Tshombe Papers are uncataloged; the Benoît Verhaegen Papers contain numerous documents written by various Congolese politicians; the Jules Gérard-Libois Papers have copies of the minutes of the College of Commissioners (as does the chaotic Herbert Weiss collection at the Hoover

Institution). Victor Nendaka had a small collection of papers seized by the Belgian parliamentary commission, and important documents are published in Jules Gérard-Libois and Benoît Verhaegen, *Congo 1960* (Brussels: CRISP, 1961). The Congolese press is also an important source of information (*Le Courrier d'Afrique,* Leopoldville; *L'Essor du Congo, L'Essor du Katanga*, Elisabethville), as is the Belgian.

The NATO archives are located at the NATO headquarters in Brussels. Some documents can be accessed on the NATO website. There are pertinent files on the Congo's political prisoners in the archives of the International Red Cross at their offices in Geneva (IRC).

Acknowledgments

For critical readings of the book at various stages we would like to thank the anonymous readers for Harvard University Press, and Richard Beeman, Elizabeth Block, Richard Freeland, Idesbald Godderis, David Hollinger, Edward Mannino, Stephanie McCurry, Leo Ribuffo, Charles Rosenberg, Susan Schulten, Marc Trachtenberg, Sarah Van Beurden, Louis Vos, Zana Aziza Etambala, and most of all Stephen Weissman.

For various forms of assistance we would like to thank Klaas Keirse, who did the research in the International Red Cross headquarters in Geneva Switzerland, and Niels Matheve.

Both Elizabeth Block and Greet Castermans created an environment that made the writing, in two countries, possible. And so too did Deborah Broadnax and Carine De Greef.

All translations of Dutch and French into English are our own, but for assistance with translations we are indebted to Pieter Brandwijk and, especially, Antonia Tripp. For help with the Russian we would like to thank Benjamin Nathans.

We gratefully acknowledge the support of KU Leuven–University of Leuven, the Mellon Foundation, and the University of Pennsylvania. We are beholden to the archivists of the many manuscript depositories we have used, and to our editor, Kathleen McDermott, and the staff at Harvard University Press; and to our agent, Richard Balkin.

Our six original maps were created for the book by Rosemarie D'Alba Art and Design, and we are more than appreciative of the work of Rosemarie D'Alba herself. Information on the map "UN soldiers" comes from Congo Intelligence Situation Report, October 4, 1960, White House Office, Office of the Staff

Secretary, Records 1952–1961, International Series, box 3, Eisenhower Library; information on the map "Troop movements" is from the Jules Loos Papers, February 10, 1961; and information on the maps "Lumumba breaks out" and "The transfer" is from Luc De Vos, Emmanuel Gerard, Jules Gérard-Libois, and Philippe Raxhon, *Lumumba: De complotten? De moord* (Leuven: Davids-fonds, 2004), 696–699.

Index